COLIN FARRELL
LIVING DANGEROUSLY

COLIN FARRELL
LIVING DANGEROUSLY

JANE KELLY

JOHN BLAKE

Published by John Blake Publishing Ltd,
3, Bramber Court, 2 Bramber Road,
London W14 9PB, England

www.blake.co.uk

First published in hardback in 2005

ISBN 1 84454 171 1

British Library Cataloguing-in-Publication Data:

A catalogue record for this book is available from the British Library.

Design by www.envydesign.co.uk

Printed in Great Britain by Creative Print and Design Group, Wales

1 3 5 7 9 10 8 6 4 2

Papers used by John Blake Publishing are natural, recyclable products made
from wood grown in sustainable forests. The manufacturing processes
conform to the environmental regulations of the country of origin.

Every attempt has been made to contact the relevant copyright-holders,
but some were unobtainable. We would be grateful if the appropriate
people could contact us.

For Brian Eastty

ACKNOWLEDGEMENTS

For their help, support and offering invaluable information in the writing of this book, I would like to thank: The BBC Loans Dept at White City; Kathleen Dickson at the British Film Institute Archive; the patient assistants in the BFI reading room; generous journalists Robert Barrett, Julian Champkin, John McEntee, Sue Reid, Richard Pendlebury, and John Thaxter in London; Danno Hanks and Mary Pickering in LA; Annette Witheridge in New York; writer Kieran Prendiville; producer Alexander Bodman at the Performance Space in Sydney; Mary Carr, Peter Barry and Tony Jordan in Dublin; Katy Daborn and Adrian Green in London; and numerous taxi drivers in London, Dublin and Derry for their sound opinions and advice.

CONTENTS

INTRODUCTION

I t's called 'a new style of gentlemen's cabaret', but it's as old as the hills.

Girls, mostly naked except for spiked high heels and a shining sheath of body oil, teeter and slither around the room serving not canapés and cocktails but their own smooth flesh.

As speakers blast out 'Funkytown', by Lipps, Inc, men – many with big, fat cigars between their teeth – recline on red-leather sofas, watching, clocking, assessing, paying.

As if responding to an invisible signal, or perhaps just impatient to get started, the females ooze forward, leaning over the men, craning their necks down to lick their own nipples, pushing breasts, some as hard and round as footballs, into damp male faces, spreading their legs by raising one painted foot on to a stool or glass-topped table.

Among the viewers, one dark young man stands out, more animated and louder than any of the others. While some like to do these things quietly and discreetly, not really wanting to be noticed, he can't help shouting out his delight. 'Lovely fucking tits!' … 'Great peachy arse!' … as if there is almost too much of what he wants on show and he just can't take it all in.

He has a girl with him, a blonde he picked up at Heathrow Airport. But, sadly for her, he can't take his eyes off some naked young dancers cavorting around poles, peeling off slinky gowns and G-strings as they gyrate.

Suddenly, he dashes out to his chauffeur waiting among the stretch limos idling outside, telling him to scram because it's going to be a good night… yet another one.

New girls are brought before him as he settles in a corner with a pint of Guinness in his hand and a bottle of whisky beside him. He views the line-up – brown, pink, ochre, all shimmying above him. Among them, Veronika – large, blonde and busty, with a touch of Erik the Viking; Evelyn, the thinnest, brownest thing you'd ever see outside a box of Twiglets; teak-coloured Tia; Tiffany with slanting green eyes; Leora… Jessie… Dawn… they all seem to have chosen their names from a quaint romantic novel, or a range of hair-care products.

There's something for everyone's taste and, as he has almost everyone's tastes in one brain, he takes two – Norse maiden and Creole.

He pays a girl to dance for the abandoned blonde, hands his friends £2,000 in club vouchers to keep them supplied with Cristal champagne and their favourite Kettle One vodka shots, and orders more champagne bottles for himself. He disappears with the two beauties through a locked door, down a darkened corridor, into a smoked-glass-mirrored private room where the sofas are soft and black, the club's secret, candlelit chamber to enjoy the girls dancing in comfort. When he eventually returns, he rounds up his pals and takes them all out for breakfast.

Is this some Saudi Prince out on a spree in the decadent West, or some Eastern Sultan who can command girls to line up and dance for him at a snap of his fingers? No, it's Colin Farrell, the new emperor of Hollywood, and we are in a strip club on New York's rundown East 60th Street, between 1st and 2nd Avenue, with traffic roaring overhead. But we could be with him in any bar or any city in the western world, on any night that he goes out.

'We offered to do a double-act for him, but he laughed and said he was happy with us separately,' Veronika from Budapest revealed after her private audience with him. 'He kept complimenting us on our breasts and bottoms... he chatted about his next film, and just kept saying that he couldn't believe his luck, that he was a boy from Dublin who had suddenly become a big Hollywood actor.'

He is not the only one to be surprised; although he has great talent, his luck has been astonishing.

It took Alexander the Great just over six years to leave his homeland, cross the Euphrates, conquer the Persians and make himself ruler of the known world. It took Colin Farrell roughly five years to get from *Ballykissangel* to Hollywood. With meteoric speed, he rocketed from a genteel background – without even the kudos of being working class, jobbing aimlessly for a while on the fringes of his profession – to sudden A-list celebrity, commanding upwards of $8 million a picture, heralded as 'the new James Dean' and 'the new Brad Pitt'.

It seems that the gods have granted him every one of his boyhood wishes. His story reverberates with the echoes of ancient legend. Equipped with good looks, self-confidence and a sharp and calculating mind – he came, he saw, he bought drinks and went to bed with almost everyone... and no one stopped him.

And, whatever you think about his constant swearing, drinking and serial shagging, like the heroes of the past, he is brave.

He told Robin Lane Fox, the historical adviser on the film *Alexander*, 'I don't give a fuck for fear, it's a waste of time,' and, as the US press watches, genuinely shocked and bewildered at his beer-guzzling, chain-smoking, womanising ways, he has taken on the full force of American Puritanism and has, apparently, won.

Hollywood is usually only interested in attractive men who can be sure to return them big bucks. Bad boy behaviour such as Colin's – divorce, drinking, swearing, drugs, tattoos, a driving ban and, above all, smoking – usually have a negative effect on a career. Mickey Rourke and Robert Downey, Jr are prime examples.

But here they are paying Colin, a hell-raiser, always propping up bars, often half-jarred, a scruffy-looking lucky chancer, millions of dollars to be just who he is, a contradiction of all the good, clean values that America professes to live by.

To make matters worse, he has measured out his success by stealing away Hollywood's precious female icons, wrapping himself around Britney Spears, Demi Moore, Maeve Quinlan, Angelina Jolie, Robin Wright Penn, Salma Hayek and a legion of Californian actresses, models and waitresses. No doubt he'd get around to Dame Julie Andrews, Lauren Bacall and even Dame Judi Dench if they were available.

There is something essentially epic about young Colin and, if we are to understand the scale of his achievements so far, it is worth looking in intimate detail at the path he has taken from his childhood in provincial Ireland to Hollywood stardom. Then, maybe, we might be able to answer the question, just how did he conquer Hollywood and become so rich and successful so fast, and just who is he – the man behind that oh-so-pretty face?

CHAPTER ONE

A GURRIER IS BORN

Colin Andrew Farrell was born prematurely on 31 May 1976, in Dublin's Coombe Hospital, which specialises in difficult pregnancies. 'We called him Colin because it was such a beautiful boy's name,' says his father Eamon, beaming with fondness and joy at the memory.

Weighing only 1 pound 8 ounces at birth, he was so premature that he only just made it. Fragile and the youngest of four children, it is possible to imagine the special, overwhelming love and protectiveness that his parents, particularly his mother Rita, must have felt for him as they took him back to the family home.

But he never needed any encouragement about loving the life he'd only just scraped into and, from birth, Colin was always made to feel special. 'I was the youngest,' he says, 'and my mum let me get away with murder.'

According to friends, he was quite simply adored by his mother, a devotion he always unashamedly repaid, kissing her in public even if it meant other boys calling him a sissy.

1

If you ask Eamon Farrell anything about his son, he will just spread his arms wide in a gesture that looks like acceptance and resignation and say, 'Ask his mother. Ask her, don't ask me. She knows everything about him, I don't.'

Rita remains at the core of his life. He still calls himself her 'little fella' and, like the great Alexander, the character he was to emulate on screen, her 'strong hands', as he calls them, are always there supporting him, no matter what he does.

A few years before Colin was born, his parents and their three young children moved to the affluent suburb of Castleknock, Dublin 8, the best address in the city.

Through the Castleknock Gate of Phoenix Park, one of its nine ornamental gateways, take a hairpin to the right and you are in Park View, a quiet estate lined with cherry trees, where Eamon bought a red-brick, five-bedroom, detached house with an imposing, red-tiled driveway.

The Farrell children grew up in these tranquil tree-lined avenues where you could be 50 miles from the city rather than just three. The area is entirely protected by its position, forming an enclosed dell, nestling up against Phoenix Park, the biggest green space in Europe, nearly 2,000 acres of gardens and lakes surrounded by seven miles of wall.

The ancient park, with its 300 deer, is a huge green thumbprint, a mark of distinction for those who live near it; on one side of the wall are the people in the town who are still striving, while on the other side live people like the Farrells and their neighbours who have made it.

For Eamon and his neighbours, such as the Portuguese–Irish Mantero family, who had done well in commodity trading in London, and the Gilsons, who had political connections, this area was the place to be and they wanted houses built there.

Until the 1960s, the 'Barony of Castleknock' was almost entirely rural. The poet William Wordsworth, who visited in

1829, commented on its 'peculiarly striking wildness'. In 1900, a Dublin historian noted the area's 'high degree of beauty', and called it 'one of the most healthy and delightful places in Ireland'. But Colin's birth coincided with the building of the new Dublin suburbs, with turf ripped out and replaced by concrete, and hedgerow by smart houses.

Tony Jordan, 56, who works in a government finance department and became Colin's football coach, moved to the area in 1980. 'Like a lot of people, I came up from a slightly less well-to-do area,' he says. 'We went there because we wanted our children to be brought up in the best environment you can find. Castleknock is very middle class, there is a lot of money around there, and Phoenix Park is a fantastic facility for anyone with children.'

The offspring of the well-to-do have been taken to the park for daily walks since it was first opened to the public by the Earl of Chesterfield in 1745. Sir Winston Churchill was taken there as a small boy in the 1880s, when his parents lived in the Viceroy's Palace in the centre of the park. One day, when Winston was out riding a small donkey, led by his nanny Miss Everest, she saw some strange men coming towards them. Thinking they were dangerous Irish Nationalists, she ran away as fast as she could, pulling the donkey and Winston behind her. He fell off his mount and cut his head open. He later said this was his first, painful introduction to Irish politics.

Another reason to take children to the park is that it has a very good zoo. Now 30 acres, it is one of the oldest zoos in the world and, coincidentally, provided Hollywood's first Castleknock film star. In 1928, Dublin Zoo produced Leo, who grew up to become the roaring trademark lion for MGM Films. There have been no other film stars from the area since then... until Colin.

For Eamon, moving to Dublin 8 was the sign that he had

really arrived, but he had to work hard to maintain such a lifestyle. Colin, who likes to pose as a foul-mouthed bad lad – a 'gurrier', as they say in Dublin – is always keen to point out that his family come from working-class Dublin stock.

Rita's father, James Monaghan, was a van driver who, according to Colin, later rose to driving 'nice Bentleys and Jags' for the small number of wealthy people in the city at the time. Her mother Elizabeth, the daughter of a boot-maker, was a tailor. Colin remembers hearing how his grandmother would make all her children's school uniforms herself in the front parlour.

Rita became a secretary. She was a beautiful girl with dark eyes and toffee-coloured hair and she made an excellent catch when she met Eamon. He was a 'Jackeen', a working-class chap, the son of a builder's labourer from the north side of Dublin, but he was also famous in Ireland as a semi-professional footballer, a star of the Shamrock Rovers, then Ireland's leading team, the Manchester United of their day. In 1961, a crowd of over 30,000 watched them defeat Red Star Belgrade.

Colin still has his boyish admiration for his father's early fame. 'I've been into pubs in certain parts of Dublin where there are people who saw my dad play in front of a crowd of 40,000,' he says. 'I still have a great big scrapbook of his newspaper clippings and his jersey with three shamrocks on the back.'

Dublin civil servant Brendan Duffy has followed the fortunes of the team for 40 years, and he was always thrilled to see Eamon Farrell on the pitch, along with his younger brother Tommy.

'Eamon – known as "Mo" – was a fine-looking fella,' he says. 'Five-foot-eight, well built, a great player, tenacious, attacking, very brave. Tommy was a solid centre-half.'

Brendan's eyes glaze over as he recalls how Eamon won

four caps at inter-league level and played in the 1962 cup final, Shamrocks against Shelbourne from Ringsend, Dublin. Shelbourne were the favourites but the Shamrocks won 4–1. The memory of it still makes him glow with contentment.

Local football was always taken very seriously in Dublin. 'In those days, the small teams were very significant,' he says, 'and Shamrock Rovers were the most famous team. They won more cups and leagues than any other team in Ireland and the Farrell brothers were famous in Dublin.

'Football was a working-class movement but it was supported at all levels of society... the club ground at Glenmalure Park was always jam-packed. In those days, 20,000 men would turn up to a match, with people taking two bus rides to get there.'

In the late 1960s, at the beginning of the Troubles in Northern Ireland, there was an attempt to get teams from the north and south together. Eamon had played in the north and went to these peace-making contests, but the Catholic players' buses were often stoned and the matches had to be abandoned.

Tony Jordan, a close neighbour of the Farrells', also admired Eamon. 'He was always a gentleman,' says Tony, 'very gentle, he never got excited, always philosophical, logical and controlled. He is not an emotional man and he could never really understand the emotionalism around football. I once saw him badly fouled at a game in Northern Ireland. Wilbur Cush, one of their leading players, made an aggressive tackle on him, but he never retaliated, he just walked away.'

Eamon, originally Edward John Farrell, and Rita Margaret Monaghan married on 30 January 1967, in the Mourne Road Church, in Rita's home parish of Drimnagh, Dublin. They were a very glamorous couple, and he was a good catch as a husband because he was not only a local celebrity, but also he was ambitious and hard working outside the game. As they say with great emphasis in Ireland, he was 'a good provider'.

Described on his marriage certificate as a 'salesman', Eamon wouldn't stay in that position for long.

'Eventually, my father did very well,' says Colin, 'but he didn't start out like that.'

'He was a working-class man who started out with little and ended up with a lot,' says Tony. 'A very good businessman.'

In common with many Irish lads who are good at sport, Eamon and Tommy, who eventually owned his own printing company, used the sporting world to make connections and get ahead in business. Eamon owned a newsagent's and ran a few shops in the north of Dublin, in the Finglas area, the roughest part of town, which was made famous in Alan Parker's film *The Commitments*.

Until about ten years ago, an address in Finglas debarred a man from most jobs and all credit. Things are more flexible today, but it is still a solidly working-class area with a significant crime problem, where ATM machines and security vans are regularly raided by local gangs. But, despite the down-at-heel nature of the area, where all deals had to be done in cash, Eamon enjoyed owning shops and loved dealing with the public.

When his first child, Eamon Martin, was born in December 1968, he was described on the child's certificate as a 'caterer'. But he soon moved into the restaurant business and also became a major supplier of tinned foods for Dunne's Stores, which are scattered throughout Ireland.

Catherine Mary was born in October 1970, named after Eamon's mother, and Claudine Ann followed in 1972. By the time Colin arrived, when Rita was 33 and he was 34, he owned a successful restaurant on Baggot Street in the commercial centre of the city.

'We are a very simple family. We work hard, like a drink and a good time,' says Colin, emphasising their practical side. 'I don't come from stock that sits around and analyses life too much.'

For years, Eamon didn't have any time for drinking or thinking. His work meant travelling five days a week all over Ireland on very poor roads and, at weekends, he was outside coaching Colin, hoping that his son might become the third footballing Farrell, perhaps becoming even more famous as a player than he had been.

'Apart from work,' says Tony, 'football was my whole life, and it was his, too. 'He was totally self-employed. Time was money for Eamon, but he was prepared to put all his spare time at weekends into coaching Colin and the boys.'

Tony saw football as a way into Castleknock society. 'I arrived when the new housing estates were still going up,' he says, 'and I thought starting a football club would be a good idea; it would help me get to know people and it was something we needed. I also had a son who wanted to play.'

Gimlet-eyed and very determined, a tough, no-nonsense man, in 1987 he started an adult team, then, two years later, when Colin was 11, he founded the Laurel Lodge Team, which expanded and became Castleknock Celtic. This took in one schoolboy team, a senior team, and also a team of boys from nearby Castleknock College.

He first met Colin at this time. 'He came up to me with some of his friends and told me his dad had played for the Shamrock Rovers and he'd get him to help me run the team. He introduced me to his father. I put the team together and became secretary of the club while Eamon managed it. I trained the boys during the week, and he would take over at weekends. He gave them lots of coaching, he had ideas about formations and the best positions for players, he favoured rather old-fashioned tactics. He was very keen for Colin to play and we both put in a lot of time.'

Peter Barry, 30, first met Colin at the age of five, at St Bridget's National School in the village of Castleknock. He says, 'Colin was a slight little fella, very cheerful and cheeky and we became friends. His father invested a lot in Colin's talent as a footballer,' he recalls. 'He thought that Colin would grow up to be like him, perhaps become what he had wanted to be – a really great player.'

'Everything was done very seriously,' says Tony. 'Notes were written after a game, then we'd have a team talk... it was all very advanced and thorough.'

A 1989 video taken on the football pitch shows that Colin was a small but wiry lad, with floppy black curls and a very cheeky, elfin face. His position was left-half, with number six on his jersey just like his dad. But, according to Tony, he could play in any position, and he was a great goalkeeper and striker.

A North Dublin Junior Leagues magazine at the time called Colin 'a valuable member of the team, with an incredible turn of speed'.

He was the golden boy of the team in those days and Tony is particularly fond of a bit of video film taken when Colin was 12, showing the boy 'getting the ball under', as he puts it proudly, threading it through and making an incisive pass. 'He was faster than his father but, like him, he was a very brave player,' he says, 'and he would put his head where you'd hesitate to put your boot. I thought he had the makings. He should have played for Arsenal.' Despite his footballing prowess, Tony says that Colin did not really come under much pressure from his father and they were happy times all round.

Inside their beautiful home, the Farrells seemed to most of their neighbours a good sound, happy family. There is a statue of the Virgin Mary in the hall, holding the infant Jesus in her arms, and Rita acted the role of perfect Irish Catholic wife and mother. She went regularly to church with the children, which Colin later called 'horrible', and he was confirmed at 12, alongside Peter, at the local church, Our Lady Mother of the Church.

'Mrs Farrell was a full-time mother to the kids,' says Tony, 'and she was happy if they were happy.' She willingly gave hospitality to all Colin's friends in the young Castleknock Celtic team. 'Eamon would invite us all back,' says Tony. 'It was a very big house, at least five bedrooms and a big sitting room. Fourteen boys could sit in there comfortably watching football videos. Some of the boys would stay with Colin... there were regular sleepovers, as they are now called.

'Colin's birthday parties were great,' remembers Peter, who now owns a successful business recruitment firm in Dublin. 'Everything was laid on for the kids, with home-made cakes. His mother was a very nice lady, and his sisters were lovely.'

But he also can't help admitting that he thought his friend was a bit of a show-off. 'He liked pretending to be Simon Le Bon,' he says, as if confiding a terrible secret. 'At one of his birthday parties, we had a karaoke and he pretended to be Le Bon to entertain his family. He loved Duran Duran and he was a real show-off. He used to show off at football, too, and later rugby – why go out and play a straightforward game if you can do things in a really flashy way and make yourself look wonderful? He always liked to be the one that stood out, and his mother paid a lot of attention to him. You could see how they adored each other.'

Rita tried to see that all her children were happy in their different ways, and Eamon insists that, although he was strict, he was a very fair father. 'I didn't favour any of my children,' he declares. 'I think they are all wonderfully talented.'

They were all attractive and talented. 'Mrs Farrell was a

very nice-looking woman and very gentle,' says Tony. 'The girls were real beauties, too.'

Eamon junior, despite looking like his father in build and height, had no interest in football. He was sent to an Irish dancing class, and Colin was obliged by his mother to go with him.

From an early age, Catherine wanted to be an actress, so she was sent to drama classes. Aged 12, Colin was impressed and excited to see her play Puck in a production of *A Midsummer Night's Dream*, at Mount Sackville, her exclusive girls' school.

Despite all the football, Colin, like Catherine, was also attracted to drama. At St Bridget's, their class teacher, Brendan McNamee, was very keen on getting his pupils involved in acting. 'Brendan was a great man for the plays,' says Peter. 'We had to perform new ones every couple of weeks, all in Irish, so that we could hear the language being used. No one was much good at Irish... Colin wasn't special at it, but we all had to learn it.

'Then, when he was about 11, Colin decided he wanted to produce and appear in a play in English about Colditz, the German World War II prison.'

They were too young to have seen the BBC series, starring David McCallum, but his idea came from a popular board game of the time called 'Escape from Colditz'.

'Colin was interested in the action,' he says, 'but not the words so much. We didn't write enough... there wasn't enough script. There were four of us in it... we had to perform it in class and it lasted for about two minutes with a lot of ad-libbing. It was a mess but that was the first inkling I got that Colin really liked drama.'

Not coming from the professional classes, neither Rita nor Eamon were quite certain about academic achievement. It wasn't a high priority, but they wanted the best for their children and assumed that they would do well in whatever field they chose.

When it came to choosing Colin's secondary education, they didn't have to look far, as a school considered one of the very best in Ireland was right on their shining, terracotta doorstep.

CHAPTER TWO

TROUBLED TEENS

Castleknock College is a very traditional place; in fact, there is something about it that closely resembles Hogwart's School in *Harry Potter*. The teachers still glide about unsmilingly in academic gowns, and have no wish to discuss Colin Farrell, no matter how famous he is. After all, he was a pupil who never quite got the hang of things there.

It was founded in 1835 by four wealthy Dublin students who wanted to become priests and were determined to spread strict orthodox Catholicism to the urban poor. Having borrowed money from their parents and some rich French Catholic immigrants, they bought 40 acres of land and established their school.

The college now owns over 100 acres, plus farms, including some fascinating places for boys to explore. While some boys have to make do with playing fields and bike sheds, the pupils at Castleknock have historic mounds to play on.

One is reputed to be the burial place of the father of Finn McCoohal, the legendary 'Irish King Arthur'. Another, known as Windmill Hill, was the site of the royal palace of

King Cnucha in Viking times. Later in its history, it was supposedly visited by St Patrick, the Patron Saint of Ireland, who came to preach a sermon to a local prince who was going astray. The prince dozed off during the sermon and was apparently condemned by Patrick to sleep inside the hill until the Day of Judgement.

Local legend says he is still there, beneath an 80-foot tower, built by the Normans, and which became a large fortified castle in the Middle Ages. It was eventually blown apart by General Monk during the Civil War in the 17th century and is now a picturesque ruin.

As if all this wasn't enough to stimulate the imagination of young boys, there are two ghosts on the school premises. In the 12th century, a beautiful young girl called Eileen was abducted by Roger Tyrell, the local baron, who imprisoned her in the Norman tower, where she committed suicide rather than submit to his evil wiles.

Now known as 'the White Lady of Castleknock', she has been seen gliding mournfully around the ruins at night and it is sad that she didn't meet Colin when he was there, as he would surely have put her out of her lonely virgin misery.

St Bridget, sometimes known as 'the Bride of Ireland', who died in 525 AD, is also said to visit the school grounds once every seven years. She might also have been a good friend to Colin if they'd coincided, as one of her reputed miracles was turning her bathwater into beer to satisfy the thirst of unexpected visitors.

Within these historic, grandly Gothic surroundings, the aim of the school was to create not high flying witches and warlocks, but a 'nursery of saints'. Following the teaching of St Vincent de Paul, boys and staff were supposed to live together 'in the manner of dear friends', and encouraged to be 'kind and perfect gentlemen'. This worked very well... at least, until the 1980s, when Colin arrived.

Over the years, the college has produced a high proportion of bishops who have been sent to all corners of the world. Former old boys also include Lt Col Reynolds, VC, the hero of Rorke's Drift in 1879, and several Irish heads of state, including Liam Cosgrave. But, above all, the school has provided the nation with 26 international rugby players.

For working-class people like the Farrells, to get a son into such an elitist institution was a huge achievement and showed to the world that they were now part of a new aspiring, moneyed class. It was one of the most expensive schools in the land at £2,000 a year, but it offered every aspect of a fine traditional education, as well as more spooks and saints than you could shake a terrified stick at.

Colin arrived in September 1988, as unhappy and insignificant as Harry Potter on his first day, to begin his training as a 'gentleman' and a 'saint'.

His mother dropped him off on the long, winding drive up to the school, and waved goodbye to her youngest son, who stood waving back, looking forlorn in his grey trousers, sky-blue shirt and navy jumper emblazoned with the Latin motto 'NOS AUTEM IN NOMINE DOMINI', meaning 'We, however, trust in the name of the Lord'.

He was luckier than the boys of previous generations. In earlier times, boys only had a small playground and were taken on very long walks through the grounds, plus occasional excursions by jaunting car, a horse-drawn carriage, to the Vale of Avoca, where Colin would one day work on the *Ballykissangel* series.

In those days, the CC boys were fed mainly on bread and beer and quite a few of them died off during each term from afflictions such as cholera, TB and 'fits', when they would be hastily buried in the school grounds with not too many questions asked.

In Colin's time, the school was less like a boot camp with

Latin thrown in, and there was good pastoral care, although boys probably had to find their own beer.

By the 1980s, the school was able to offer its 580 boys an up-to-date gymnasium, and the chance to play rugby, golf, tennis, squash, badminton, javelin, cycling, athletics and show-jumping. There was also, of course, football, both Gaelic and English. In fact, there is no escape from sport at the school.

The Farrells were giving their youngest son the best start in life that they could, but, although he was good at sport, enjoying football, basketball and riding, from the start he found things at the great school rather difficult.

Peter, who went on to Castleknock with Colin, remembers him at St Bridget's, their first school, as 'very intelligent, good at English and Maths... Popular, good fun and quite cheeky'. But at secondary school, he was not the same boy.

He had 'adjustment' problems. He now had to mix with not just children like himself from the professional classes, but the sons of farmers who were sent there as boarders, tough lads who didn't like 'Jackeens', spoiled townies and wimps.

Somewhat contrary to the teachings of St Vincent, there was a strange tradition in the school that boarders picked on the day-boys and would bully them at the slightest excuse. According to Peter, a lot of boys left because of the bullying.

'Colin had a problem because of the rugby,' he says. Those 26 international rugby caps hung over every boy in the school. 'We were all supposed to play... it was at the heart of the school. Its ethos was Catholicism and rugby. But some people said Colin didn't want to play because he was worried about damaging his pretty face. He could give as good as he got, but he did look quite delicate... he had a touch of asthma, and he was quickly seen as effeminate.'

Indeed, Colin was not like other teenage boys; he had his

own way of doing things, regardless of what other people thought. 'What made this worse was his relationship with his mother,' says Peter. 'He would never hold back with the affection he felt for her. She would drop him off in the car each morning and he would kiss her goodbye quite openly. Everyone would see, and that kind of thing just wasn't done. At that age, being teenagers, a lot of boys were ashamed of being seen with their mothers. They certainly didn't kiss them goodbye so openly. They thought he was a sissy, but he didn't seem to care about it, so he got picked on.

'We really formed two groups in the school as we grew up – the boys who were very good at rugby, who were also often the bullies. They thought we were soft and we thought they were just thick. They were wrong and we were right. I went to a reunion recently and there they all were, just the same, not changed much at all, still stuck in all their old ways of thinking.'

Peter still seems rather embittered by these experiences he and Colin had at the school, and he is possibly right about the way things turned out after they had all left. After all, he and Colin are doing very well, while their former tormentors haven't got much to say for themselves.

Richie Molloy, now runs a BMW dealership in Finglas. When questioned about what went on at school, he said with a twinkle, 'Colin was quite good at soccer, but, sure, everyone took the mick out of everyone else at that place.'

Molloy is surprised by Colin's reputation as a bad boy. 'He certainly never got into any trouble at Castleknock,' he says indignantly. 'He might portray himself now as this Irish rebel, but there was nothing rebellious about him when he was in school. He was just an ordinary school kid like the rest of us. He pretends he's from a tough, working-class part of Dublin, but he's not. He comes from a very respectable, upper-class part of the city. He wants people to think he's this hard-drinking rebel, but all he's really doing is following a long line of Irish storytellers.'

As Colin's personality and temperament developed throughout his teenage years, it became more and more obvious that Castleknock College was not the right sort of environment in which he was going to shine. There was little drama or creative work going on; the school was academic, a place that produced statesmen, lawyers and sportsmen, not actors and artists.

But his problems weren't only at school. From his early teens onwards, his parents' marriage started to disintegrate. Outwardly, he came from a happy, prosperous home, but, within its walls, Rita and Eamon were increasingly strangers and he was beginning to resent his father. As a boy, he had adored his dad, the famous footballer. He was the envy of his mates and was determined to follow his father as a sportsman. 'Because of my father, I thought I wanted to be a footballer, and at one time I had delusions of grandeur,' he says. 'I was all right, I suppose, but I just wasn't good enough.'

As he got older, he came to dislike the older man who was the traditional breadwinner and authority figure and, as he lost his respect for his father, he lost interest in the game.

While his mother let him 'get away with murder', he says his father was too domineering at home. Years later, on the set of *Alexander*, he told writer Robin Lane Fox how family holidays became a nightmare as his father took charge and 'presided' over everything. 'He was too much of a disciplinarian,' he says. 'I got away lighter because I was the baby of the four, but he wasn't nice to my brother and sisters.'

His mother was at the opposite extreme, a liberal parent influenced by the mores of the 1960s rather than traditional ideas. 'She was a firm believer in doing whatever makes you happy,' says Colin. 'She instilled into us all the notion that we could be whatever we wanted to be if we did it for the right reason, out of love or complete hunger for that thing.

'She'd say she wanted me to be a lawyer but, at the end of the day, you've got to live with yourself. It doesn't matter if you've got a big fucking car and you are getting invited to all the fucking charity balls in the world if you're not happy.'

His father was more firm in his wish to see his children behave well and succeed in the world, as he had done. With a doting mother who didn't impose any boundaries, and a distant, unemotional father who was slightly disappointed in him, Colin naturally became confused and resentful. While his mother is always 'just great', he is very ambivalent about his father.

Eamon Farrell is a man of great charm, now large, white-haired and amiable. By choice, he has carried on doing what he knows best; interacting with the public. He owns and runs a small shop, the Down to Earth Health Food Shop on George Street in Dublin. The window promises 'natural health solutions', allergy testing and mini facials, as well as vitamin pills and rice crackers.

'Do you think I'm well co-ordinated?' he says striking a slightly camp pose and laughing, when I comment on his beautiful clothes – a stylish pea-green shirt, grey sweater and slacks. 'I'm really happy with this place,' he says, beaming and climbing a ladder to reach for some special muesli for a customer. 'I don't talk about what happened in the past... I only think about the future.'

The fact that Colin has become more famous than he could ever have imagined rather puts the past and his old ambitions for his son into perspective, and he says he is not worrying about it now. 'It's a wonderful thing he has done, he's marvellous, a cracker, but it's his life. I don't know much about it. He's a great guy, he has a huge heart and I don't worry about him or the life he leads now in Hollywood because I know that he was well brought up, and he knows right from wrong.'

Then he goes on bustling about the shop as if it really has nothing to do with him, his world and Colin's forever quite separate.

Tony Jordan says he never noticed anything wrong at the Farrells' home during Colin's teenage years, but Peter takes a different view. 'I was at parties at his house there over several years and I never saw his father there,' he says. 'I rarely saw his parents together. It seemed to me that he stayed upstairs while she stayed down.'

'They were in the same feckin' house,' says Colin, 'but they weren't exactly tripping the light fantastic. I don't know whether they should have stayed together.'

'The dad was away a lot working, then he was out with the football and I think they must have grown apart,' says Peter. His parents carried on living together but they didn't get on at all; in fact, their marriage was over. I know this hit him very hard because my parents' marriage also ended at the same time and we went through it together. Neither of us actually said much about it, just bits here and there, but we both felt it badly.

'I remember thinking his mother was having a difficult time with her husband because she aged a lot during those years; she looked as if she was very stressed and unhappy. She looks very different these days when she is out beside Colin. Now he is doing so well, she is getting everything she deserves.'

Colin told Robin Lane Fox that, as a young teenager, at only about 12 or 13, he had become his mother's 'adviser', as her marriage crumbled. It wasn't a normal role for a young lad, and it hardly enabled him to maintain a good relationship with his father. He was in the position of having to choose between his parents and, as his father was gradually pushed further out of the family circle, he effectively lost him.

This fissure between his parents bit deep into Colin and created a hole inside him somewhere, a gap that has affected his entire emotional life since.

Around that time, he began to be plagued by insomnia, from which he still suffers. 'I haven't slept much since I was maybe 12,' he says. 'I used to wait up for my dad to come home. He'd come back from work at about midnight. I was always up waiting for him. He didn't mind and I remember him saying, "You're going to be a night watchman when you grow up."'

At this time, he first took an interest in films as a way of escape from all the tensions of real life around him. 'I also used to sit up 'til all hours with my sister Catherine, watching movies on TV,' he says. 'We really liked Hitchcock films and I had this huge love of videos. I used to sit up and watch all types of films – serious, silly, independent. The first one I ever bought was in 1987, *The Lost Boys*, by Joel Schumacher.'

Apart from the coincidence of his later connection with Schumacher, the film's theme about alienated boys, who sleep all day, party all night, never grow old and never die, was oddly prophetic for his own life.

Not sleeping and upset by the tensions at home, his school work and his love of football fell away. He couldn't concentrate on academic work and football was to do with Dad, someone he was rejecting. 'He never had any fixed aims at school,' says Peter.

As many boys do under pressure, he took flight, inwardly and externally. By all accounts, though, Colin remained a 'kind and perfect gentleman', if not an actual saint, until the age of 13, when he says he became a skinhead and went into full-scale revolt. 'I was 14 when I started with drugs,' he insists. From this time, he loved to project this image of himself as an angry, risk-taking outsider. 'The first time was at my friend's house and we made a concoction of booze –

Cointreau, gin, vodka – put it all in a tankard and got sick as fucking dogs. Then, when my friend's brother came home, he gave us this lump of fucking brown stuff. We knew it was hash and, at 14, the fear, oh, I was scared. For all intents and purposes, I might have been smoking heroin.'

But he loved the fear and the risk. 'Anyway, he put the hash in a Bic pen, burned it and we sucked it and soon we were out of our fucking minds. But I probably didn't buy any hash myself until I was 15 or so.

'Castleknock is a fairly wild place,' he adds, 'maybe because the young people there have plenty of money from a young age, and they are often spoiled rotten, used to having whatever they want... they are all party animals.'

He is possibly exaggerating the availability of drugs. Between school and football, he can't have gone into Dublin much, and there were no drug-pushers at the school gates then or now. If what he says of his behaviour is true, he must have gone to great lengths to find a really bad crowd to fall in with.

He did lose touch with sensible, easy-going Peter, and took up with a much wilder boy. 'I had this really good mate called Eliot,' he says. 'He was a huge fucking drinker, popping back the Guinness to beat the band. I used to smoke fucking joints like they were fucking candy.'

He claims he started taking large amounts of Ecstasy every weekend. 'I was a real E-head, too, popping about 15 at the weekend. It was really a way of life. I used them as if they were candy for about two or three years on the Dublin scene. I got really into it. It became my scene, my way of life, not a weekend-warrior thing. The mates I was hanging out with were real E-heads.

'Eliot knew I was an E-head and one night he said, "You're always taking them fucking wanker pills, you fucking tosser. Why don't you have a fucking drink?"'

They were too young to drink in Myo's Pub in Castleknock, now decorated with bright Spanish tiles and converted into a respectable eatery, so he and his pals took to drinking in the local fields behind the pub. Later, they discovered The End, a nightclub on the Phoenix Park racecourse, where 15-year-olds could get in with false ID and party the night away. He also discovered sex; not as something sacred, as his priest on Sunday and the teachers at Castleknock might have preferred, but centred around masturbation.

He'd always dreamed of drawing lovely, unobtainable girls into his life. 'When I was about eight, I discovered Marilyn Monroe,' he says. 'I'd never seen anything like her. I fell madly in love with her and dreamed about giving her my M &Ms. I dreamed about her.'

But by the time he was a teenager, he also saw sex as something more brutal and much less romantic. 'I always wanked with trashy magazines,' he says, 'and I've always loved porno movies... they're great, great fun. I've been buying them since I was about 14, since I went on a school trip to London and we took a visit to Soho. I was like, "Oh, my God, there is sex everywhere. This is great, this is heaven."'

He had girls on his mind all the time but, in reality, was too shy to approach them. 'When I was 14, I was in a summer school and I remember fancying the fuck out of this beautiful blonde,' he recalls. 'But she looked at me like I was 12 years old, with my baby face. I asked one of my mates to put in a good word with her about me. He came back and said, "She thinks you are really cute, but you are just not her type."

'Fucking bastards. I have never, from that day to this, felt I had any great understanding of how to charm women or anything like that.'

His mother's love was his only certainty. 'No matter what Colin got up to at school, or what trouble he was in, he'd always win his ma over,' says a former classmate. 'He'd give her a hug and say, "Ah, Ma, you know I love you." And she'd just end up laughing. I think she is and always has been the love of his life.'

No matter how bad his behaviour, he never had any problems getting generous amounts of pocket money from Rita. 'My ma was always great,' he says.

When Colin was about 16, he discovered that most seedy of modern amenities, phone sex lines. 'They're terrible fucking things,' he says. 'I remember calling them from the downstairs living room of my parents' house, trying to whack off. When it didn't work, I had to hang up, go upstairs, grab a fucking porno magazine and finish it off with that. You'd want to be in some kind of funky place with a bird with a cigarette hanging from her mouth.'

Later, his mother lent him her VW Golf so he could enjoy real freedom and take a proper 'bird', out. Once he gained some confidence, it was a small step from charming his mother to using his magic on other women. Just as girls who are loved by their dads often grow up to be adored by men, so the same thing works for boys. If your mum loves you that much, you can't go wrong. Even other people's mothers will love you.

'My mother always loved Colin,' says another of his school friends. 'She always said he was so gentle and mannerly. She was always eager to meet him. He always listened to what she said and was always polite and interested in her.'

But managing real love was more difficult. The girl he most wanted beside him in the passenger seat of the VW was no mere 'bird', but someone carefully brought up and extremely bright.

'When I was 16, I fell in love with Amelia Mantero, the daughter of our neighbours,' he says. 'She was a beautiful girl; her father was Portuguese and her mother was Irish. We'd known each other for years; her brothers Tony and Chico are still my best friends. She was the real deal for me... I was in love with her, besotted by her. I am soft about those things.'

But he can't have offered her a very attractive prospect, unless she was into bad boys, 'gurriers', and dope-heads, which, sadly for him, she wasn't.

'I got into trouble for drugs,' he says. 'I got caught with substances, I got caught smoking joints and stealing coke and ten packs of cigarettes from a shop. Growing-up things.'

He says that, in his late teens, he was also arrested for drunken driving at the wheel of Rita's car and spent the night sobering up in a police cell.

Tragically and typically, he didn't lose his virginity with Amelia, but with a stranger, an older woman. 'It was 4.00am and Eliot was nearly comatose so we went to a club,' he says, 'a place we'd always gone to, a gay club in Dublin called Shaft. It stayed open into the wee hours, and I met this Australian woman there aged about 36 and she basically said to me, "Do you want to go back to my place and fuck?"

'We were lying on her bed and kissing. Then she got up and got out some champagne, which I fucking hate. I took a sip and, as I did, she reached under the bed and brought out a basket containing about 400 different condoms, all different colours and flavours. I thought, I am in fucking trouble here. But it was OK, I was OK, for about four hours straight, without a condom, idiot that I was. I thought I'd found the Holy Grail.'

This sounds like the stuff of schoolboy fantasy rather than the often mundane reality of first-time sex, but, however it happened, he'd lost his virginity and managed to break almost every rule of the Catholic Church at the same time. Sex, stealing, drinking and taking drugs was not quite the kind of behaviour for a boy who was going anywhere, academically or on the sports field.

'There are certain lads with a lot of talent, but when they get to 16 you lose them to women and drink,' says Tony Jordan sadly, sounding like a man who has seen it happen all too often. 'Colin was in that category. If you don't behave in football, you end up in one place only, at home or on the sideline.

'At 16, he dropped out. He was chasing girls and it was difficult to get him out of bed for matches on a Sunday morning. He was out late and just couldn't make it at 10.00am.'

Colin is philosophical. 'My da was realistic,' he says. 'One day, he said to me, "You are just not hungry enough to make it in football... one day, some girl will grab you by the short and curlies and the football will be over."

'Sure enough, I got a bird, started drinking and smoking and started missing training on Tuesday night. And that was the end of my football. It kind of went downhill. I was smoking a bit of reef. You know, you roll your first joint, drink your first beer, discover the girls and, well, that was it. I loved football but I couldn't make the training any more.'

He was just not turning out to be the kind of boy that Castleknock Celtic or Castleknock College, the 'nursery of saints', wanted. 'I was not getting on great at school,' he says. 'My mother got a letter saying I was getting in too many fights. Then I heard there was this gang of 20 blokes looking for me. That was one Halloween when I had got into a bit of a skirmish at school. Boarding school was suggested and I thought, Fuck, I'll go away for a while and get out of the situation.'

After he sat his Junior Certificate, it was agreed with his parents that he would leave Castleknock and try somewhere else, so he went to a boarding school, the familiar last resort of desperate parents.

He enrolled at Gormanston College, whose motto is 'DEI

GLORIAE, HIBERNIAE HONORI', 'To the glory of God and the honour of Ireland'. A private school run by Franciscan monks, situated on the bleak Co Meath coastline, 20 miles from Dublin, it should have been well away from trouble. Its prospectus promises its 604 pupils, boys and girls, that the staff will be 'firm but fair', in an atmosphere where students are directed towards 'reverence for Gospel values'. Again, its best-known old boys are politicians and footballers.

Colin was utterly miserable and suddenly seemed to notice that Amelia, his true love, was far away. 'When I went to boarding school, I only saw her once a week, on a Sunday,' he says. 'I wanted to spend every second with her, but I was in that school with a bunch of fuckin' dudes, playing table tennis and bartering for fucking Coke bottles.'

Amelia is now married, still living in Castleknock and a practising barrister in the central Dublin law courts. Colin hadn't a hope with her.

He was no longer much of a catch for an ambitious, middle-class girl; he had even lost his prowess at football. All those childhood dreams had come to nothing. Although he sounds blasé about it now, it was a painful lesson to learn, and he was now stuck in a boarding school, and hating it. 'I had no education,' he says. 'School had to be endured.'

The privileged son of wealthy parents, unlike his father at the same age, he had no idea what he wanted to do and no obvious talents to exploit. After one year, there was a parting of the ways with the Franciscans, who, although they began teaching in 1210, had probably never experienced such a difficult pupil.

'I wasn't going to many classes,' he says. 'I was taking three-hour lunches and meeting Eliot and all the lads in the pool hall having a couple of pints, then going back to class, the smell of beer on our breath.'

His last attempt at education was at Bruce College, then in

the centre of Dublin, now moved to the country. The motto there was 'REPEAT AND DO BETTER'. A private college founded in 1984, it specialises in enabling weaker students to achieve Leaving Certificates through intensive revision courses. In other words, it's a crammer.

'He didn't go there because he wanted a brilliant Leaving Cert,' says one of his friends from the time. 'He was just fed up with the whole school thing. He didn't want to wear a uniform and he liked the fact that the college was right in the town, where all the action was. He just wanted to get his Leaving Cert done with as little hassle as possible.'

One of his friends there was Dublin character Gavin Lambe-Murphy, a socialite who later became well known in Dublin for boasting about his 'friends', the English 'It' girls, Tara Palmer-Tomkinson and Lady Victoria Hervey.

'He was like me, an absolute messer,' says Gavin proudly. 'We just used to doss about and go to a pool hall near the school and, about once a week, the headmaster would appear and tell us that there was more to life than playing pool and going to POD, a really funky nightclub we liked in Dublin.

'We were once suspended for four days for throwing rubbers at each other and messing around in a study period.' Another friend remembers them drawing Christmas trees on an exam paper instead of answering the questions.

'The last school I was in was particularly strict,' says Colin indignantly. 'Security cameras in the fucking study hall! We'd wire ourselves to our stereos, put them on and go to sleep. A study supervisor grabbed me one day and I threw him up against the wall. I said, "You touch me again and I'll fucking rip your head off."

'I'll never forget packing my bags that day and feeling like a fucking rock star. I'd been fucking looking forward to getting kicked out of the fucking dump. My mother was worried, but I knew I'd be all right.'

It was once said about the film star Louise Brookes that beautiful people make their own rules. At least they can work out a separate agenda. Colin wasn't too worried about school because he was already thinking about making money from modelling. He knew enough about life so far to know how far good looks and charm could get you.

Like most teenagers, he was acutely image-conscious. His older brother, who bravely came out as gay while he was still at school, was very stylish, and Colin constantly experimented with different styles of dress and had his ears pierced several times. 'No matter what he wore he always looked good,' says a friend, 'and he knew he could get away with anything.'

He had inherited his parents' good looks. 'I owe my parents everything,' he said later, 'because they gave me this face.'

CHAPTER THREE

CAREER MOVES ON A STAGE

Even for someone with a face as handsome as Colin's, life wasn't all fun: he'd left college at 17 with no qualifications and an unrequited love for Amelia; he'd wanted to be a footballer but that hadn't worked out; he'd let his father down, although his father didn't admit to it; his mother, who saw him as special, wanted him to enter a profession such as law, but he didn't have the qualifications for university. He thought about being a journalist, perhaps a writer, but those things are difficult to achieve, especially if your confidence is low.

He became seriously depressed for the first time. It was the onset of what he calls his 'melancholy side', which still dogs him. 'I was only going one way… down,' he says.

He began seeing an expensive psychotherapist in Dublin. 'I ended up on the couch and he told me to write down everything I was taking, all the drugs and all the drink. In one week, I counted 20 Es, four grams of coke, six of speed, half-an-ounce of hash, three bottles of Jack Daniel's, 12 bottles of red wine, 60 pints of Carlsberg and 40 fags a day.

'When I gave him the list, he read it, looked at me and said, "Do you wonder you're depressed... have you read your own shopping list?"

'I saw him for six months. I went to his office and spat the shit out. I just vomited for six months, once a week. He didn't say much, just listened to me, and that was grand. I just needed someone to talk to.'

The solution he found in the short term was to put his problems behind him and take off across the other side of the world. In 1993, he flew to Australia with two childhood friends, Paul and Stephen, and £10,000 in his back pocket from Rita.

The idea of backpacking was exciting but, again, things fell rather flat. Instead of feeling like wild colonial boys with the wind in their hair, they found themselves getting respectable jobs. 'We were supposed to travel,' he says, 'but we got a job in a clothes shop then in a bank and only left Sydney twice for two day-trips. We eventually got fired for taking a four-hour lunch break in a pub. I remember the manager coming across the road. We tried to scarper, but everything seemed to go in slow-motion and, before we got the chance, the door opened and there we were, all fired on the spot.

'I'll never forget it. We were there with a big television screen, watching it, although there was nothing on it because it was two o'clock in the afternoon, and we were having a great time.'

You get a sense that, despite the wild-boy image, he didn't enjoy failing in school and he didn't really like getting fired. He really needed to feel worthwhile.

For a time, the boys waited on tables. A Sydney woman interviewed recently by the BBC still remembers vividly his real-life role as a waiter. 'He was so good-looking,' she sighs. 'I knew from the day I met him that he was different from the rest. Although he was only about 18, he just oozed with sexuality. A few girls from work went ga-ga over him... and some older ladies as well.'

The lads spent a lot of time at Bondi Beach, crashing on people's couches, then they rented a one-bedroom apartment on Taylor Square, Sydney. It was cramped and Colin was plagued by insomnia.

'I could never sleep,' he says, 'and things were worse because Paul had the couch and me and Steph shared the bed. He would always be snoring and throwing his leg over me and calling me Rachel, because he missed his girlfriend.'

Colin also continued his strange old habit of going into gay bars. 'I would always get out of bed at three in the morning,' he says, 'pull on my tracksuit bottoms and walk into this shitty gay bar called The Judgement, have three or four pints and stay there and read. It was good, and I've done that ever since.'

Photographer Stuart Campbell met Farrell through a mutual friend and ended up giving him a place to stay when he first arrived in Sydney. 'He slept on my couch in Bondi for a few nights,' Campbell recalls. 'Colin mentioned that he wanted to be an actor so I offered to take his pictures. He was totally, absolutely charming.'

The portfolio contained black-and-white pictures, semi-nude, more cheese than beefcake, moody, displaying a peek-a-boo charm, some with Colin dressed strangely in beret and home-knitted sweater. But it was a very professional job, which would have cost an aspiring model about £200, but Campbell gave it to Colin for free.

When he didn't get much modelling work, he took a job as a waiter. Girls who had the pleasure of being served by him when he was waiting tables still treasure some very fond memories.

While shooting the snaps at the old Colgate Palmolive factory in Balmain, west of the city centre, Campbell introduced Colin to Tony Knight, a highly influential teacher and a director for the National Institute of Dramatic Art (NIDA), which is part of Sydney University. Among its graduates are Russell Crowe, Geoffrey Rush and Cate Blanchett.

'He asked me about acting and about NIDA,' says Tony. 'He was a very polite and nice young man and I gave him what help I could.'

Knight had contacts at The Performance Space, a radical theatre on Cleveland Street in Redfern, a rundown suburb of south Sydney. He suggested that Colin might go there and try out his acting skills.

Opened in 1980 as a theatre with a studio and two art galleries, and sited at a traditional meeting place for Aboriginal people, The Space now calls itself 'a place for exchange and cultural mapping'. In 1995, when Colin was there, performances included *Dolls Vomit* and *The Politics of Belly Dancing*. There were also numerous body and movement workshops on offer.

He relished this free, totally experimental approach to work. After all, it was real acting but it was also a bit of a game. A video of the time shows lot of young acting hopefuls at The Performance Space school, waving their arms about pretending to be trees, feeling the connections with each other. 'It was perfect for someone who'd never done more than shout, "Bang, you're dead..." in games of cowboys and Indians in the back garden,' he says, forgetting about his youthful adaptation of 'Escape from Colditz'.

He joined the hastily formed Fireweb Productions Company, consisting of 19 male actors who were mostly college friends, and eight musicians. On 4 October 1995, Colin made his acting debut in *Kelly's Reign*, written by Michael Hurse, Nicholas Reid and Richard Sutherland. It was a dramatic portrayal of the life and times of Ned Kelly, the great Australian outlaw and folk hero, using video projection screens, background sounds, naturalistic bush lighting and even the smell of gum leaves. All it lacked were real kangaroos.

The play went into great detail about Ned's life. It was described by the director Kristen Boys as 'the whole story about the human spirit and choices in life'. They dug up some fascinating facts about Kelly. According to this version, the fearsome bushwhacker was a foot fetishist, who was obsessively proud of his own feet. He kept them very clean, even when on the run with hundreds of state troopers after him, and would show them off on any occasion he could, even at his trial.

One gang member, Joe Byrne, was an opium addict, and the Kelly gang liked to dress up in drag even when riding out to commit bank raids. None of this was ever revealed in the 1970s film starring Mick Jagger.

Photos show Colin in costume, looking very exotic, with a silk waistcoat and white breeches, his hair drawn back in a bow, more like a Regency dandy than a late-19th-century Australian outlaw. The photos are interesting in the way that he stares at the camera in a cool, confident way, perhaps more like a model or a pop singer than an actor in character, but he looks very professional.

On the first night of performance, the video projection screen sadly broke down several times. Michael Graham, a critic for a local paper, wrote that he felt he was watching an 'annual school play', and felt 'let down by the technical hitches with the large-screen video projection'. He also complained about the actors' diction. 'I lost much of the quickly shouted Irish dialogue,' he wrote, 'and battled as well as I could to follow the storyline, but all the actors gave well-rounded performances.'

He also graciously thanked the company for bringing the adventures of Ned Kelly back into the public mind, for better or worse.

Writer Richard Sutherland, who played Byrne, also seemed a bit faint-hearted about the project. 'We did it because we're all young male actors so we can relate to the Kelly gang,' he told critics. 'And we don't get much work, so it kept us going.'

Funded by the Australia Council and the NSW Ministry for the Arts, the show lasted two weeks, from 4 to 15 October, and Colin was paid $300 a week. But it wasn't the money that mattered. 'The part was rubbish,' he says, 'but it was the first time I got to work with a bunch of actors.'

Sadly, Colin was the only one of that bunch of earnest young hopefuls who went on to get not just regular work but fame and commercial success.

In Sydney, he not only got to work on a professional stage for the first time but also discovered that there were some limits to which he would not go, even in the Bohemian world of Australian theatre. 'One day, I was acting in a children's community play but I was stoned on marijuana, out of my fucking head, and I didn't like myself for that. I decided never to do that again and it was the only time I've ever worked while I have been under the influence of drugs or drink.'

He'd begun his life as an actor and already had certain rules for himself in his head. No matter what his nocturnal activities might lead to, he has always prided himself on showing up on time and knowing his lines.

By going all the way across the world, he had discovered his future. His Australian odyssey was turning out to be highly fruitful, although it came to an unfortunate end. One night, walking home through Sydney, he was suddenly arrested, handcuffed, searched, photographed, fingerprinted and questioned roughly by police for four hours. 'I was taken in for suspected murder,' he recalls. 'I was a wild lad but murder was never one of my pastimes.'

It was a case of mistaken identity, but the event upset him

and, not long after, he flew back home. He has never been back to Australia since.

Back in Dublin, aged 19, now long-haired and artistic-looking, he set out on a new road as an aspiring actor. 'I remember meeting Colin when he came back from Australia and he said he wanted to go to drama school,' says a neighbour. 'It struck a chord with me, because I always thought he was ambitious and determined, and he was.'

His mother backed him wholeheartedly but his more hard-headed father was not quite so sure. 'I told my dad I had decided that I really wanted to be an actor and he roared laughing,' says Colin. 'His attitude was, "What do you want to be doing that play-acting lark for?" but in my belly I knew it was the right thing for me. Once I started getting pay cheques, he changed his mind and slapped me on the back.'

Dublin is a very small world, where people are either related or connected by marriage, football club or friends. His sports-mad father couldn't help him much with theatrical contacts, but, not long after he got back to Ireland, Colin met the young Ronan Keating, who told him about an audition coming up for a boy band. Louis Walsh, from Kiltimagh in Co Mayo, had been promoting bands since the age of 15. Most of his groups resembled Status Quo, but now he wanted to create an Irish version of Take That, the successful English boy band. He held an open audition at the Ormond Centre, on Dublin's Ormond Quay.

'I would have done anything for money back then,' Colin explains. 'I mean, I loved buying drugs and going to bars. I thought, if I had a job as a singer, I would get free drugs, Ecstasy, coke, whatever. I was a fucking kid.'

Three hundred young boys who could sing and dance turned up and Louis selected five who couldn't do any of those things, some might say. Ronan was chosen but, despite his extremely boyish looks, Colin was not.

'I sang George fucking Michael's "Careless Whisper", a couple of times,' says Colin, 'but it wasn't on the cards, man. They threw me out on my ass. I guess I wasn't meant to be a teeny-bopper singer.'

He'd missed out on a huge chance. A year later, the first single by the group christened Boyzone made number three in the Irish charts. Two years later, they were voted Most Promising Band by *Smash Hits* magazine. They became the first group ever to get their first six singles into the British top three, knocking Kylie Minogue off her perch, and they were also the first Irish band to have four number-one hits in the UK. Since then, they've had four number-one albums selling over 12 million copies.

They quickly became millionaires, but then so did Colin, so who cares what happened back then? Well, Colin still does. Walsh insists that he didn't get the gig because he couldn't sing well enough, but Colin still strongly denies this. 'It's not like Louis tells it,' he says. 'I auditioned for the part but it didn't work out. I had terrible rhythm at the time but my singing voice was as good as the rest of them. In fact, I turned them down because I really wanted to become an actor, not a pop singer. I can hold a tune – it was Boyzone's loss.'

Making the best of it, he signed on with Assets Model Agency in Lower Leeson Street, Dublin. Most of the grand 18th-century terraced houses on this road have since been turned into offices and small businesses. Notices on their Georgian façades offer such things as 'Irish Corporate Outsourcing' and, appropriately enough, as Ireland plunges into the global economy, next door there is a society for tackling 'stress-related depression'.

Assets, next to the Legs nightclub, occupies a dingy basement under one of these grand buildings. Despite looking rather shabby, the agency was the alma mater of Chris de Burgh's beautiful daughter Rosanna Davidson, Miss World in

2004, and Amanda Byram, host of *The Big Breakfast* and of Miss World 2003. It was opened in 1990 by Mags Humphries (who also runs the Miss Ireland Contest) and Derek Daniels. 'He [Colin] just came in one day and asked if he could become a model,' says Mags, a determined-looking ash blonde who gives the impression that she's a highly experienced professional. 'I never thought he'd be in films one day. I thought he would probably join a boy band because he was so drop-dead gorgeous and just the type that young girls adore. He was absolutely gorgeous… you would take him home with you, sure, you would if you could.

'He was very quiet and polite and extremely gorgeous-looking, a very, very pretty boy, with long hair and big chocolate-brown eyes. He was pretty and he wasn't afraid to have a go. He was shy to talk to, here in the office, but he wasn't shy in front of the camera at all. He would just look at it directly, embrace it, if you like, make a pose… most lads can't really do that, not without a lot of encouragement. He seemed to know right from the start just what was required.'

The first job she got him was for a Cadbury's chocolate bar, known in Ireland as a 'Moro'. 'It was my first real pay cheque,' says Colin. 'Over £1,000 in cash. I went out and bought myself this revolting but cool pair of Harley Davidson motorbike boots that cost about half the money I'd earned. It was a mad extravagance, and I haven't done anything like that since. My dad wasn't pleased about the boots but he began to think that maybe showbusiness was a good idea.'

'I think he got a big buzz from the work,' says Mags. 'We often used to put him into ads where there was some dancing involved. He would dance for fashion shows. He did a catwalk show at Jury's Hotel. He did OK… he was having fun.'

In fact, he now says that, while he was modelling, he first began dabbling with hard drugs – paid for by the modelling jobs. He told GQ magazine, 'I smoked heroin a couple of times, but I knew what I was doing. For some reason, it seemed pretty fucking nice at the time.'

Mags saw a beautiful young model in front of her, but his description of himself at that time is harsh. 'I was a chancer, a hustler,' he says, 'out of my tits on Ecstasy for a year. There is footage of me in a red G-string advertising Christmas underwear. I did it because they paid an extra £10, the cost of one E tablet. I was going one way – down. I was very self-destructive, and I still am.'

Perhaps to cheer him up, his brother Eamon gave him a pair of 'lucky' boxer shorts covered in shamrocks, with 'THE LUCK OF THE IRISH' written around the waist band. He now wears them on the first day of every film he makes. 'They are my lucky charm,' he says. 'If I don't have them with me, I won't come out of my trailer – I'd rather shoot myself. They're starting to get a bit old now but I could never part with them.'

To Mags and his friends, he seemed cheerful enough and, whether it was drugs, or just the effect of more experience and some travel, he was increasingly confident with girls. 'Colin definitely didn't just go out with anyone,' says Gavin Lambe-Murphy. 'He liked good-looking, confident, popular girls with a bit of class.'

Dublin was a small, delightful pool where particularly beautiful and ambitious types stand out and, for the first time, Colin realised he was among them, and could take his pick of them. After the sultry but unobtainable Amelia Mantero came Glenda Gilson, a niece of Irish MP Liam Lawler. Colin had already known her as a neighbour in Castleknock when they were younger, but they met again at Asset's Agency when she was 16 and he was 21. She was one of the prettiest girls around, recently voted by *Showbiz Ireland* magazine 'the best-looking Irish woman ever'.

Five foot ten inches tall, slightly taller than Colin, she was slim, bust size 34B, dress size 10, with slanting green eyes and the long, dark mane of hair that Colin likes so much. They are rather alike in colouring, or would be if she didn't have a permanent tan, and both have strong, dark eyebrows.

For some reason, Glenda was and is the talk of the town. Her eyebrows come in for a good deal of unkind comment on Internet discussion boards, specifically set up for people to give their opinion on her. Not many people would bother to email in their views on the EU constitution, but lots of them are eager to have a go at Glenda.

In fact, she attracts almost as many bitchy comments as Sinead O'Connor, known in Ireland somewhat facetiously as 'Father O'Connor', who was recently voted 'Publicity-Seeker of the Year'.

In November 2004, Glenda allegedly received telephone 'death threats' at her home and at the Assets Agency. She was advised by the police not to say anything until a suspect had been identified. In fact, the menacing caller simply kept saying he 'was sick and tired of seeing her picture in the paper'.

But, despite the carping critics, Glenda has always known that her rightful place was distinctly on view, preferably next to a dazzlingly attractive or at least dazzlingly powerful man. She was Colin's first real 'good-time' girl. Soon, they were out enjoying clubs and bars, regularly dancing at POD, a trendy nightclub on St Stephen's Green, or Reynard's Night Club, a dive on South Frederick Street owned by Colin's uncle, the dark, burly, bearded Robbie Fox, who looks like a bouncer.

They also had a mutual love of cinema. Having studied film and TV at the Ballyfermot Senior College, Dublin, Glenda says, 'I always preferred the flicks and a good film on TV to the soaps, any day. My favourite films are the *Godfather* series because I love Al Pacino – in anything he's done, really.'

When she started dating Colin, she can have had no idea

how significant Al Pacino would one day be for him. It would have been a teenage fantasy to think that either of them might one day appear in a film alongside the Hollywood legend.

Glenda is a very feisty girl, needing a strong, determined man who is content to be chiefly focused on her. Colin says that, although he is romantic, he 'doesn't do flowers and chocolate', and he was perhaps not attentive enough; consequently, they were not a romantic couple for very long. Having gained in confidence and discovered a taste for models, he was soon seen around the clubs with Siona Ryan, who became known as 'Ireland's It girl'.

Whereas 'It' girls in England usually have titles and country estates, Siona, from rural Co Wicklow, was a waitress in Dublin, who became part of the short-lived group Girlzone. When that finished, she released a solo record with the unsubtle title 'Do You Want to Funk?'.

She was spotted by the artist formerly known as Prince at POD nightclub. She and Colin made a decorative couple but both quickly moved on. She has now found a sort of fame as the host of Friday night at the Ministry of Sound club in London.

Glenda has become Ireland's first and only 'supermodel', although her catwalks are mainly in Ireland. 'Supermodel, my arse!' as someone recently put it on the Internet discussion board. She is also Dublin's number-one, A-list party girl, seen regularly at The Spy Bar, The Dakota and Lilly's Bordello, with the likes of Bono, former Miss World Rosanna Davison and Georgina Ahern, who is surely even a couple of rungs above Glenda on the A-list ladder, as the daughter of Taoiseach Bertie Ahern, and wife of Westlife's Nicky Byrne.

Despite losing Colin, Glenda has never lost her place as a hometown celebrity. She then met Brian O'Driscoll, the captain of the Irish rugby team, at a ball at Dublin's Burlington Hotel. He is a national hero in Ireland... or was.

Some people rather resented his glamorous new partner's political connections and, as they took to the town together, they became known as 'Posh and Wrecked'. Her tan got stronger, he got an outlandish haircut and began endorsing O_2, Adidas and Powerade and put on excess weight. After being voted both 'Ireland's Sexiest Male' and 'Ireland's Ugliest Man' in 2003, he decided he needed to concentrate more on the game and broke up with Glenda.

Not wasting any time, she was soon seen out with Mark Kershaw, the motor-racing-enthusiast son of millionaire businessman Alan Kershaw. For a time, she joined the Formula 1 crowd, then moved on to top US rapper Snoop Dogg, whom she met at the Spirit Club, where his eyes were strangely attracted to the transparent dress she was wearing.

To cool things down, she invited him to Reynard's where he offered to rent out the club for the whole night, but Robbie Fox wasn't prepared to play along.

When he left Dublin, he offered Glenda use of his private jet. Despite this, she returned to O'Driscoll. They are now regularly seen 'engaging in public displays of affection' in the exclusive Club 92 at Leopardstown Racecourse. In front-page headlines, society and sports pages, they constantly vie with Georgina and Nicky for the title of 'Ireland's first couple'.

Dublin is an international, cosmopolitan city but, in so many ways, also has the feel of a small, close-knit town. With little in the way of competition, Colin could easily have stayed there and become half of one of its leading couples. It would have been a good life – encouraging gossip and entertaining the townsfolk with his photo in the local papers every Sunday morning. But he always said Dublin was claustrophobic, and he was more genuinely ambitious than any of the other young folk around him.

For the time being, though, living at home with his mum, modelling by day and dating models by night was not a bad life. And there was not much modelling about, even for him. 'We had a problem because he was a bit young,' says Mags. 'Ireland is not London or Milan; our youth market wasn't that well developed. This is an older market... people here liked to see boys aged 23 and upwards. There was not so much work for the younger boys.

'You put the younger ones on the books then you have to wait for them to grow up a bit, and he was very young-looking, even for his age. Pretty boys like that don't usually age well at all, but he has. He looks like a real man now.'

His most interesting work during this time was for Wrangler, the great jeans emporium, who hired him from Assets and put the emphasis on the 'ass'. O'Leary PR were asked by Wrangler to come up with a line-dancing stunt to help sell a line of jeans.

'Wrangler jeans introduced this form of dance to Ireland,' says Mari O'Leary, Managing Director of O'Leary PR. 'Country and Western music was huge at that time, in the mid-'90s, and the cowboy look and the line-dancing became a real fad.'

They held an open audition for the 'Step In Line' dance troupe and Colin was offered the job.

'It was a case of good arse, good face... and the dancing followed. You needed people with good bums for that job,' she says laughing. 'He was a perfect size 32 round the waist and 32 inside leg; not tall, but very well-proportioned.'

'He had good rhythm, could dance-ish, and he was very pleasant, so he got the job,' says Mari. 'It was a very successful promotion and built the Wrangler brand in Eire.'

A video of the time shows him dancing in the troupe dressed in tight black pants, black shirt and Stetson, shaking his booty and looking incredibly camp.

'I looked exactly like one of the Village People's idea of what a cowboy is,' he says, shuddering at the memory.

'His dancing was OK but he had the gift of the gab,' recalls Lisa Mooney, now 'line-dancing world champion'. She had a lesson from him in 1994. 'He was good at getting people on the floor and getting them motivated.'

Part of the time, the work was at Dublin's fashionable Break for the Border nightclub, the Spawell Hotel and the Tosca Restaurant, but most of it was way out in the sticks. 'It wasn't a cushy job at all,' says Mari. 'They were paid 50 and they had to travel all over Ireland by bus to places like Cork and Co Meath way out in the countryside. They sometimes had to travel six hours to a venue, give a two-hour session then it would be six to eight hours back, five nights a week.'

They frequently travelled as far as Limerick in the west of Ireland, to Doc's nightclub, in the dank basement of an old mill. The wife of the manager, Norma Kennedy, remembers Colin well. 'He was a beautiful-looking boy,' she says. 'I was always watching him dance. He was very flirtatious and good fun. Everyone loved him and you couldn't keep your eyes off his rear end. At the end of the night, I'd give them tea and sandwiches and they'd go off in the bus, all the way back to Dublin.

'It took me a long time after to twig that Colin the dancer was also Colin Farrell the film star. To me, he was like the good-looking boy next door.'

If he was uncomfortable on the bus, or embarrassed in his tight jeans, Colin could possibly have consoled himself with the thought that, at the time, Boyzone were also on the road, travelling all round Ireland in a battered transit van.

When that work finished, he got jobs painting warehouses and more waiting on tables. At night, he was still a regular 'Jackeen', enjoying all the cities' popular haunts, spending his hard-earned cash at POD, where he would take to the floor dressed in a red bandana and dance to Techno, Electro, House, Hip Hop and Monster Rap.

He was also a regular at Reynard's. 'It is a great place,' says Mags. 'Robbie Fox has been around for years and he really looks after people. He is always on the door and takes you inside, makes you feel at home.'

Well-off due to his parents, but not doing anything serious – 'a fairly lazy bastard', as he said himself – Colin was going nowhere fast, but there was one person prepared to push him. The ever-protective Eamon, perhaps the best-looking of the family, had come out as gay – or 'light on his loafers', as they say in Dublin, a jokey reference to an effeminate, mincing walk – and was a popular local character, busy building up his career as a successful dance teacher. Eventually, in 1994, he opened his own school, The Factory, in Barrow Street near the town centre.

He was one person that Colin always respected. 'He had a very hard time at school,' says Colin, 'standing up for who he was and what he was. Dublin is still fairly unforgiving, but much more liberal than it was.

'He always stood up for what he believed in, although he never tried to push it in people's faces. He is a very warm man and was never bitter about what happened to him. He taught me love and understanding and he's one of those people that it's good to be around. He is also the one who instilled a sense of self in me... he is a very strong man.'

Eamon was determined to stop his younger brother's endless drift, to get him to fight back against apathy and self-doubt and do something positive with his life. At the time, Colin was working as a waiter at the trendy Elephant and Castle restaurant in the Temple Bar area, which was popular with lawyers, actors and writers.

'He was cocky but a good laugh,' says one of his fellow waiters. 'He seemed to know many of the well-known people who came in to eat. His brother Eamon is quite a flamboyant fella and I think Colin knew people through him, and a lot of the girls who came in fancied Colin. They wanted to know everything about him, weighing him up. He was bright and very streetwise... you felt he was unusually sharp, but he didn't put on any airs and graces, never went round saying he was going to be an actor or anything like that. The whole staff often used to go on all-night benders, then we'd wind up at one another's flats. He was a total party boy like that.'

'The Elephant was a great place,' says Colin, 'but one night, between shifts, I had a drink with my brother and told him I felt my career was going nowhere. I was getting bored and fed up. He said, "Why don't we just step across the road to the drama school, and sign you up?" He had always encouraged me about acting. I was so fed up at that time that, when he suggested college, I just thought, What the hell! Eamon paid the £20 audition fee. My side of the bargain was just to show up for the audition.'

So Colin entered yet another elite educational establishment. The Gaiety School of Acting is Ireland's premier theatre school. Catherine Farrell had already been there and Colin was easily accepted on their two-year acting course, costing £2,500 a year.

His tutor was Patrick Sutton, who'd been very involved with youth theatre in England. 'Colin just walked in the door and I saw his energy and charisma right away,' says Patrick. 'It was great. Everyone was mesmerised by his presence. When young people walk through the door, I usually know whether they have got "it" or not, and he had it in spades – presence, energy, charisma, sex appeal, looks – but he also had talent, and without that you don't get far. You can tell if someone has talent.

'There was a confidence about him and you see it now on film, especially in the tiniest moments, which make a film worth watching. There is something there that is not about showing off, but about keeping something back, something private.'

The school was flourishing with an extraordinary array of talent and determination. In the two years before Colin's arrival at the school, it had had students such as the extraordinarily handsome actor Stuart Townsend, who is now firmly established in Hollywood. The son of a professional golfer from County Dublin, Townsend supported himself by boxing until he won a part in the film *Trojan Eddie* in 1996.

He was cast as Aragorn in *The Lord of the Rings: The Fellowship of the Ring*, but was replaced after four days of shooting because, as an elfin-faced Irish lad, he looked too young. Undaunted, he went on to make *Queen of the Damned* in 2002 and perhaps, better still from a male perspective, moved in with actress Charlize Theron who thanked him by name in her 2004 Oscar acceptance speech.

The beautiful actress Eva Birthistle, from Derry in Northern Ireland, was one year ahead of Colin. She has made a series of acclaimed independent films and is now in Hollywood. There was also Catherine Walker, now a leading light at the RSC in London, and Don Wycherley, a fluent Irish speaker from the little town of Skibereen in West Cork, who has appeared in *Ballykissangel* and 15 films, including *Michael Collins* with Liam Neeson.

There was a professional atmosphere in the school; students were expected to focus and work hard. Irish education is still about discipline and rigour, and Patrick doesn't take any prisoners. Like a genuine father, he won't single out any of his past pupils for praise – he is proud of all of them. 'Of course most of my former students are working,' he says challengingly, as if they wouldn't dare not to. He is proud not just of them, but also of the Irish tradition which has produced them.

For the last 200 years, Ireland has produced many great dramatists and magical actors, from Oscar Wilde to Gabriel Byrne and Pierce Brosnan. But, for years, the Irish image on film was of pugnacious fighting fools like James Cagney, beautiful victims like Maureen O'Hara or Greer Garson, or feckless charmers like Peter O'Toole. But about 15 years ago, things changed. The Irish economy, the 'Celtic Tiger', was suddenly unleashed. According to the Economic Intelligence Unit, Ireland now has the best quality of life of any country in the world, and is now the fourth-richest country per capita income.

By the time that Colin began making films, Ireland had become the key economic and cultural link between the EU and the USA, catapulted from an economic back-water straight into the high-tech ocean. The population began booming for the first time since 1845, and this new confidence naturally had a big effect on the arts. While the middle classes felt rightly proud to belong to a new dynamic Ireland and an even more energised Dublin, original and edgy stars like Bob Geldof, Fiona Shaw, Sinead O'Connor, Bono and Colm Meaney have also felt more confident to express other aspects of Irish culture.

From the film *Eat the Peach* in 1986, a black comedy about a wall of death rider, and *The Commitments* in 1991 to the black comedy *Adam & Paul* in 2005, a whole new, realistic image of the Irish on screen has become possible.

Colin and his generation, including Stuart Townsend and Cillian Murphy, have been part of the steady rise of dark, naturalistic drama, destroying the old rural image on film – the amiable drunk, the poetic dreamer playing the melodion down by the bog, the pretty girl milking a cow with a song on her lip – and replacing it with something far more complex, urban, disorientating and detached from the traditional values of family, church and land.

CHAPTER FOUR
FILM START

Patrick's judgement about Colin being worth watching was eventually proved to be correct, but he was far from the finished product at this stage. Despite Eamon and Catherine's encouragement at the Gaiety School, things didn't start too well.

The teachers accused Colin of muttering, and he often felt inferior and shy. 'There was one guy in the class who was awesomely good,' he recalls. 'His range and his ability to slip into different roles was just phenomenal. Then I would get up, not really knowing what the fuck I was doing, speak too quickly and sit down again.'

He did manage to get into some first-year productions, though, including *Blood Brothers*, *Lady Windermere's Fan* and *Philadelphia, Here I Come*. Sadly, there are no photos, as the school keeps all first-year work under wraps and refuses to allow it ever to be seen by the public.

He was not happy, always one of those people who prefer to learn on their feet by doing things out in the big wide world rather than testing things out in theory in the classroom. He wanted a lot more risk than was offered in the teaching environment, or by Edwardian drawing-room comedies and musicals.

While still at the school, through word of mouth, he made his film début as an unaccredited extra in *The Disappearance of Finbar*, an Irish–Swedish production directed by feminist film-maker Sue Clayton. It was naturally very low budget but intriguing, the story of the effect on a group of Irish children when Finbar, played by Jonathan Rhys Meyers, bounces a ball down the road and never comes back, a theme of child disappearance taken up by Clint Eastwood in his ponderous but award-winning *Mystic River*.

In March the following year, Colin won his first, brief film role in Owen McPolin's low-budget feature *Drinking Crude*, made in Kerry. Against a thumping rock soundtrack, this was a highly entertaining parody of the road film. Paul, played by Andrew Scott, is a character rather like Colin, a drifting, spoiled, middle-class youth, frustrated with life in boring, conservative Ireland. He emigrates to London and bumps into a shifty Scotsman, James Quarton, who agrees to help him. He then finds himself cleaning out oil tankers and, to his horror, his work takes him right back to Ireland.

Paul also has a difficult on-screen relationship with an arrogant Scottish 30-something woman, played brilliantly by Eva Birthistle, also making her film début. She and Colin knew each other from the Gaiety School and they began a passionate love affair. 'I have loved two women in my life – one a blonde, the other a brunette,' he later said. Eva was the blonde, and Amelia Mantero the brunette.

Like Colin, Eva came from a moneyed background. Born Eva Marie, she was brought up in a very select area of Londonderry. Her parents' home, a grand, Victorian detached house, sits at the top of a steep, winding drive with spectacular views over the River Foyle. A delicate beauty, but tough, with an aura of being in charge of things, she might be termed the first of his 'leading' ladies, long before he set eyes on Amelia, Britney, Angelina or Kate.

Drinking Crude received rave reviews when it was shown at the 1997 Montreal World Film Festival. Colin was now appearing with some of the best young acting talent in Ireland in films of low budget and high quality. With all this work available to him, after 18 months, he quit the Gaiety School.

'He worked very hard,' says Patrick. 'I could see he had talent and we had no real problem with him. He sometimes squared up to me and I squared up to him, but we got on well. The idea of a movie career was ever present for him. He is a good-looking guy and people were knocking on the door.'

Colin takes a more dramatic and less forgiving view of what happened than Patrick. 'I didn't think that I should have to pay £2,500,' he says, 'and take years out of my life to be told I was crap. At drama school, they break you down and then build you up into the actor they think you should be, but I don't buy into that at all.'

He might not have excelled in the classroom, but he knew he had what it takes to get work. A student friend observed, 'I remember him saying he was only at drama school in order to get work and, now that he was getting it, he was leaving.

'Other people in the class said he was wrong, that he should fully learn his craft and get all the training available before launching himself, but he didn't see it like that.'

His work in *Drinking Crude* caught the eye of agent Lisa Cook of the Lisa Richards Agency, who signed him up. With their advice, he made an audition video, playing the part of a louche record producer. The agency sent this to Hubbard Casting who invited him over to London to see them.

Hubbard, originally from Dublin, was a man with a keen instinct. He chose Kate Winslet for her first major film,

Heavenly Creatures, discovered Rhys Ifans, later to star in the film *Notting Hill*, in a pool hall in Cork, and he also cast *The Lord of the Rings*. At that time, he was looking for a good-looking boy aged between 19 and 24 for the Irish TV film *Falling for a Dancer*.

'When I saw that small tape, I thought, Wow,' says Hubbard, a man who sees thousands of these audition reels a week. 'When I see a tape, I think, Will this person make me look good in front of a director?'

Richard Standeven, the director of the proposed series, was also delighted with what he saw. 'I was looking for a good-looking guy with a mysterious, moody look and, when I saw his tape, I thought, That's the guy. Let's not see anyone else, but I sent Colin out of the room to wait before I said I'd made a decision.'

Outside in the corridor, Colin need not have worried; Standeven was smitten. Like Patrick Sutton, he instantly recognised Colin's dramatic charisma, his ability to make even small things powerful. 'The best actors use their eyes and mouths,' he says. 'That is what most viewers at home look at. Colin did that naturally, it was quite amazing to watch it happen. I knew he was going to make a good actor and I think he knew it, too. He was a natural at it, he enjoyed it, he had few doubts about it. There was an element of shyness but you get that on a film set. He knew he'd found what he was looking for.'

Colin landed the role, along with a pay packet of £15,000 a week. It was his first commercial job.

Falling for a Dancer was a mini-series of four episodes made by BBC Northern Ireland and the Irish broadcasting company RTE. It was based on the best-selling romances by Deirdre Purcell, who also wrote the script. Beginning in 1937, the mini-series – or 'misery series', as it might better be called – tells the story of Beth Sullivan, a solicitor's daughter from

Cork City, played by the young English actress Elisabeth Dermot-Walsh.

At 19, she gets pregnant by a strolling player, an English cad called George, who is rather in the Hugh Grant mould. Her parents, a frigid couple seething with hostility towards each other and her, reject her, and she is threatened with going into one of the Magdalene laundries, the Irish concentration camps for girls who broke the rules by having illegitimate babies.

Rather than face this and be separated from her child, she agrees to marry an older man, Cornelius 'Neely' Scollard, who takes her away to live in the rugged Beara Peninsula, in south-west Ireland. The area is illuminated by having Bantry Bay on one side to the south, and Kenmare Bay to the north, but in this film you don't see the glories of the scenery, as it is mostly shot in heavy rain.

In her Beara home, Beth finds her new husband already has three children and a small baby, and a psychotic temperament. It's all rather predictable, but there are some interesting exchanges between Beth and Neeley which reveal how he is from the old rural tradition, while she is from the new world of the metropolis and the cinema. Of course, they can never understand each other. He is unfortunately the type of Irish farmer who sews himself into his clothes for about nine months of the year and smells strongly of old cheese. The words 'time for bed' have never sounded so ominous.

As soon as Beth arrives in her new home – in fact, before she even gets out of the car – her handsome neighbour Mossie Sheenan falls deeply in love with her. He stares at her so persistently in the driving mirror that it is surprising they don't drive over a cliff. Mossie is played brilliantly by Liam Cunningham, with a beautiful lilting Beara accent. It is a terrible part as the lovelorn local, but he gives it great poignancy as, for the rest of the 200 minutes of the film, he gazes at her longingly from the hillside or the field.

In European cinema, men crackle, smoulder and sometimes flame with passion, but in Irish films like this, perhaps because of the damp, rather than ignite, they tend to glower and occasionally steam. There is a great deal of misunderstanding, brutality and glowering, then things become even more complicated when Colin appears as Daniel McCarthy, a spirited young local. We first see him in a church parade, his small, square face framed by a stiff, starched collar. He looks full of mischief as he sets his eye on one of Beth's grumpy stepdaughters.

Meanwhile, Beth, now 25, increasingly frustrated, goes off into the village and meets George again. Of course, her whole life has changed for the worse, while his hasn't been affected one jot. Dangerously attractive men seem to inhabit every corner of this remote outpost.

When she arrives home late, Neeley rapes her. She runs out of the house and plunges into a local bog to wash, and, when she emerges in a clinging wet dress, there is young Colin looking at her.

'You have a beautiful body,' he tells her memorably, and their love affair begins. Later, when they dance together at a party, everyone is upset – his brother, her husband, stepdaughter, sex-starved friend, Mossie – who glowers even more – the local priest and gossiping neighbours. The rest of the story revolves around the events set in train by this public display of desire.

Colin is ideal for the part of a natural country boy finding himself quickly out of his depth, falling in love with an older woman. He also felt a little out of his depth in the role. He is remembered as being rather subdued on set. Later, he admitted he'd felt intimidated by the whole thing, but you wouldn't know it. 'I was so nervous that I nearly had to wear a nappy,' he recalls. 'But I learned more on that shoot in two months than I'd learn in drama school for the rest of my life.'

Despite the stomach-churning nerves, he moves easily in the part from natural, unaffected and sweetly romantic country lad to someone becoming angry and overly intense. After obsessively roaming the local hills, rabbit-hunting in the middle of the night, Colin's character shoots Neeley dead and Beth finds herself at the centre of a court case.

After falling for a man like Hugh Grant, marrying a mad rapist and having two desirable men driven to distraction by passion for her, at least she can't claim that life at the back of beyond is ever dull, apart from having a cabin full of teenagers, a baby that never gets any older and no indoor plumbing.

The series was by no means Thomas Hardy, or Dennis Potter… or John B Keane, who made *The Field*. The plot twists are unlikely and overwrought, babies keep appearing without any explanation, and there is a terrible crashing score bashed out constantly by the Irish Film Orchestra.

Some of the speech is very odd, too. Elisabeth Dermot-Walsh, just out of an English drama school, sounds far too posh. She later went on to the more appropriate role of Princess Elizabeth in the TV production *Bertie and Elizabeth*.

There are frequent anachronisms in the language as well. 'Oh, don't patronise me,' Colin cries when he turns up in Beth's barn while on the run for murder. Hardly something you'd expect to hear from the mouth of a wee peasant boy.

Towards the end, his character becomes hard to fathom. When the noble Mossie lies for him in court and saves his neck, he appears to be furiously ungrateful. Then, after ending up in bed with Beth's stepdaughter, he selfishly abandons her.

Although the characterisation is rather ropey, Colin pulls it off, acting through every unlikely event with great conviction.

Patrick Sutton from the Gaiety School was generous about his performance. 'It was his first break and he was magnetic in it,' he says. 'I am delighted for him. I think that boy has a hotline to the heavens and there was someone up there secretly telling him to go for it.'

The series was a worldwide hit, shown in the USA on their Romance Classics station and in Canada on the Women's TV Network. It won the San Francisco Film Society Golden Gate Award in 1999.

Although he was not a leading player in the series, Colin's face appeared on the book cover, in publicity shots and on the video jacket, something which was to happen to him repeatedly over the next few years even while he was still only taking on the lesser roles. In the film world, it has always been a case of 'have looks, will travel'.

The marketing men and the viewers liked him. A glance at the reviews from that time on the Internet shows that Colin had been slowly building up his own female fan club, and that they were now looking out for him on screen.

His father might have laughed, but this series proved to Colin that his gut feeling about acting was sound. It was right for him, and he was right for it. The material rewards for finding his way in life at last came almost immediately. He bought himself an MG soft-top, a Mercedes for Rita and a VW Golf for brother Eamon.

From gloomy Beara, a place of dark brooding passions, it was only a short step to the sunny uplands of the ever-smiling *Ballykissangel*, then the most popular series on TV.

We are in a small church at the rehearsal for a baptism. The family is gathered round the font; there is the sound of softly lilting Irish voices. But the father of the baby is full of doubts about the whole thing and he suddenly bolts, leaving mother, baby, godparents and bewildered young priest standing staring after him.

Cue jocular theme tune, a bus with Ballykissangel on the front trundling through a village, a Catholic festival procession and some Irish girls' knees bobbing up and down under pretty skirts in a traditional dance.

This was the start of the *Ballykissangel* episode, broadcast on 11 October 1998, which first brought Colin Farrell – or Col Farrell, as he then called himself – to wide public view in the UK.

It wasn't much of a view at first. He is seen lurking down by a stream looking furtive and dishevelled, attached by a string to Razor, his tubby grey Connemara pony. His short, damp hair seems to have been chewed and, with a bag on his back, he looks every inch the urban cowboy.

We are quite a long way into the episode before he actually speaks. 'Could be worse,' he mutters, as he ties up the horse and takes shelter inside an old hovel.

'Danny was supposed to have ridden bareback from Dublin,' says Colin. 'He was a working-class guy who had come to find his uncle Eamonn Byrne, whom he'd never met before. He thought that the police wanted to impound his horse because he had no proper stabling for it in Dublin, so he ended up in Ballykissangel living with his uncle.'

This was quite a clever element to add to the story because, in Ireland, horses still cross the divide between urban and rural. In Dublin, it is possible to see children riding horses bareback among the city traffic. There are stories of horses seen going up in lifts on the rundown housing estates in Ballymun, and coming to the door of houses with their owners. There is also a distinct brand of youthful rebellion in Ireland that takes place on horseback rather than motorbikes.

'There wasn't much similarity between me and Danny,' says Colin, 'except in age. He was not a complex character, just a young fella who'd ended up in a place he'd never been before, dealing with a new place and new people. I'd done that myself, living in Australia, so I could relate to his problems fairly easily.'

The bareback horse carried him into Ballykissangel and into public view as Danny, a lost boy that fans of the series still remember. The episodes he was in over the next year, 400 minutes of them, made him, if not exactly famous, a well-known, well-liked face.

Even a small part in *Ballykissangel* – his name was fourth from the end on the credits – meant the kind of instant success and money that few actors, even from Patrick Sutton's stable, ever find. This was a golden chance for Colin – a hit show that was popular in England and Ireland and finding a following in the USA.

By the time Colin joined the cast, *Ballykissangel* had become a national phenomenon in the UK and Ireland. Full of witty exchanges, it was always a real community piece with even the smaller characters being extremely well written and acted. Its success might lie in the way it offered an image of close community at a time when most people were losing that experience in their own lives.

Wherever its magic lay, the series was a huge hit, amassing 14.5 million viewers a week, making it the BBC's highest-rated weekly drama for 15 years. Even in 2005, six years after the series ended, a train was still leaving Connolly Station in Dublin every week for the 'Ballykissangel Tour'.

When there was a wedding scene, people wrote in asking how they could make copies of the dress for their own nuptials. The local church suddenly had a booming congregation, mostly people from England who'd rarely been to church before. The local priest had to order new visitors' books and thousands of extra votive candles.

Just as many people converted to Catholicism after seeing *Brideshead Revisited* dramatised on BBC TV in 1981, Deborah Jones, the editor of the *Catholic Herald*, thought that the programme had somehow helped to restore the credibility of the Church after numerous unpleasant sex scandals.

Some of the actors in the earlier series, though, had been quite disturbed by the extent of the show's popularity. 'We were out filming once and a man came up to me and said, "Assumpta, can I touch you?"' says Dervla Kirwan, who was in the first series. 'He wasn't strange or anything and the moment seemed unreal.'

Stephen Tompkinson, who played a young English priest, recalls that he kept getting molested by women from the tourist buses that poured in. 'They'd grab parts of my anatomy while photos were being taken,' he says. 'It was like a Chippendales concert.'

Based entirely on situation and character, *Ballykissangel* was perhaps the last Sunday series of real quality, without a mysterious corpse, murderous vicar or Nazi uniform in sight. It also avoided any Irish pitfalls and stereotyping; unlike *Falling for a Dancer*, *Ballykissangel* was no hackneyed tale of the Emerald Isle, no evocation of 'Irelantis', the imaginary lost world of an Ireland that never existed.

It was originally created and written by Kieran Prendiville, who won a BAFTA award for his BBC series *Care*, about a victim of child abuse. He is not a sentimental writer. 'I would have been mortified if the characters had been clichéd or stagey,' says Kieran flatly. 'And the actors wouldn't have done it.'

A former sports journalist from Fleet Street, who worked on *Man Alive*, the first popular BBC documentary series, he had also been involved in the early days of *That's Life*, wrote for *Boon*, *The Bill* and created *Roughnecks*, a successful BBC drama about life on a North Sea oil rig.

'I first got the idea for *Ballykissangel* when I was leaning over the guard rail of an oil rig just inside the Arctic Circle being sick into the sea,' he says. 'Writing *Roughnecks* was tough; I needed to be on the rig to experience the life and learn all about it, but by episode four I was fed up and I just wanted to be somewhere else, away from the noise of machinery and the smell of diesel oil.

'The men on the rig weren't particularly friendly either. They were very reserved, as they had been turned over by a tabloid paper and mistrusted my being there. I just kept thinking about Ireland and the lovely places my father used to take us to on holiday.'

He'd been born in Killorglin, near Ballykissanne in County Kerry, but his father, a GP, had taken the family to Rochdale when Kieran was a boy. Stuck out in the freezing North Sea, he escaped in his mind back to those days in Ireland.

'I remembered an Ireland full of talkers and chancers,' he says, 'but I didn't see the series being some old story about comical Ireland and its funny ways. What I always wanted to do was explore the collision between people's ideas and expectations of rural Ireland and what really goes on there.

'It is a place where, these days, Rupert Murdoch speaks to more people through TV than the Pope ever did through the Church. When I was a child, it would take you two days to get from Rochdale to Kerry; now it is about an hour's flight. The kids there all wear trainers and speak the lingo of *NYPD Blue*, in a Kerry accent. The series was about this clash of the rural idyll and the true reality of it.'

By the fourth series, the scriptwriters were looking for someone new to play a real rough diamond, a refugee from the city. Irish casting agents Frank and Nuala Moiselle invited Colin to audition for the role of Danny at the Royal Marine Hotel in Dublin. His lucky underpants played up because he became a bag of nerves, mumbled his lines and said he left feeling 'about an inch tall'. Not for the last time, he relayed the bad news to his mother that he hadn't got the part.

A week later, he was surprised to hear he was wrong. The Moiselles were delighted by his dark, Celtic good looks, his soft Guinness-brown eyes and delicate mouth, which made him look as if he would be gentle when stroked, dangerous when provoked.

Disaffected, he looked sulky rather than intimidating, and he was obviously cute, if not quite 'sweet', appealing to young girls who would fancy him, and older women who would fancy him and also want to mother him.

'We needed a young, good-looking actor who could ride bareback,' says producer Chris Clough, 'not that easy to find.'

He'd learned to ride as a boy in Phoenix Park. He liked horses, and you can see by the way the horse nuzzles his fingers that they like him, and so he was just right to play the edgy, sexy Danny.

'He had presence to burn,' Kieran remembers. 'The guy had something, although I'm not able to say what. It was that intangible quality that makes someone a success on screen.'

When he began the show, Clough warned him that it wasn't going to be an extensive period of work, hardly the equivalent of getting signed up for a major role in *The Archers* or *Emmerdale*, just a few episodes, then he'd probably be back on the dole or working in a bar.

But, for Colin, any real work was worth having. 'I told him that, if I started thinking about security, mortgages, Visa cards and all that rubbish, I'd be finished as an actor at 22,' he says. 'I refused to be scared off. I never thought ahead to where I might get to. I just let one job tumble into the next.'

It was a very happy time for him and a gentle start to his career. 'It was like a day job,' he says. 'I'd go to work at 8.00am and we'd finish at 6.00pm, just as a lot of my friends in Dublin were finishing work. We'd all go off up the pub. It wasn't like they'd say, "Wow, you're in a TV series," there was no big bog about it.'

He certainly didn't expect or get any star treatment. 'When he joined *Ballykissangel*, there was no fuss about him at all as an actor,' says one friend. 'I remember thinking it was strange that he had such a small role in it. There was a lot more fuss about some of the other actors, such as Cillian Murphy.'

'He was charming and a normal member of the ensemble,' says Clough.

At this time, he was nothing like the person who became famous. He was no longer acting out his role as wild, drug-taking teenager and he had not yet created the aggressive Irish persona that he was to adopt in Hollywood. He was still just himself, a boy feeling his way.

'We all had a few good nights out, but I didn't see Colin drunk or see him approach any girls at any time,' says Clough.

In Fitzgerald's Bar, owner Gerald Kelly confirms this. 'I never saw him with any girls,' he says. 'He was too shy, very quiet.'

No one saw any sign of the hell-raiser that he was to be once he got to LA. He was interested in nothing but doing the work well. 'Despite his lack of experience, he was terribly professional,' says another acquaintance.

Muriel and Harry Williams, the agricultural advisers on the programme, trained him to work with the farm animals for the series. 'He was very good with the sheep,' she says.

'I think he could have been a shepherd if he'd wanted,' says Harry. 'He learned how to spot maggots on them very quickly.'

His uncle Eamonn in the series was played by Birdy Sweeney, who got his nickname aged 11, after his early career mimicking birds on Radio Ulster. He looked rather like a little old lady, and was a pig farmer, involving Colin in some new experiences.

'I remember he had to learn to handle some newborn piglets, standing inside a filthy sty,' says Harry. 'The heat was bad because of the lights, there was a horrible smell and lots of flies. He only had a few moments to do the scene because the piglets had to be handed back to their mother fairly quickly. But Colin was concentrating so hard and it wasn't until the director shouted "Cut!" that he let us know that the sow had been urinating on him all the time he was standing there.

'He got on well with everyone on set, a really cheerful person. I met him again three years later and he looked very different. More trim, honed, more the image of an American actor, but he was still very friendly, giving me a real hug.'

It was a happy experience all round. Colin fitted in well, he had regular money, there was no pressure from fame and he understood the other people in the cast.

'I particularly loved working with Birdy Sweeney, who played my uncle,' he says. 'He was such a gorgeous, gorgeous man, my ma's favourite character by a mile.'

Colin's only problem in the series, which was to be very rare in his future career, was one of non-romance with his co-star. 'It was difficult when myself and Kate McEnery, who plays Emma Dillon, were getting it together and they had built up this romance,' he says. 'It was a problem because I was good mates with her and it's difficult for us to snog.

'We had a laugh about it, but it's fairly unnatural. You just feel there is no way in the world it could be sexy. They have to make something of it in the editing suite afterwards.'

Colin made his final appearance in an episode called *Behind Bars* on 31 October 1999, starring James Ellis as a crazed UFO fanatic. It was still good Sunday-night fare, although getting a bit silly and losing some of its earlier edge. Danny is living happily with Birdy, Trixie his collie bitch and his horse. But things go wrong, the weather turns rough, the village is hit by a bad storm and ends up looking like a flooded disaster zone. Emma's father's cottage is hit by lightning and he decides to return to England, a marriage breaks up and Trixie disappears.

But all ends happily; the villagers rally round to restore the cottage, providing mugs of tea and trays of cakes. Colin finds Trixie alive and well, and the whole village meets for a communal dance, when Colin is seen as just a face in the crowd.

Sadly, in April 1998, Birdy Sweeney died aged 68 of a suspected heart attack, so that storyline came to an end. Colin had to leave the series, but for some he will forever remain the disgruntled boy on a frisky grey pony. A lot of lives were changed by the success of the series.

Although Kieran had tried hard to create a realistic scenario, and the writers who followed him kept to this, the public had other ideas. Shot at the Ardmore Studios in Bray, near Dublin, *Ballykissangel* was set in the lush vale of Avoca, south of Dublin, and the whole village of Avoca was refurbished for the series; it even gained EU grants to help keep up the image of the imaginary place, so that no tourist would go away disappointed.

Not surprisingly, the village quickly acquired a fictional *Brigadoon* quality. At worst, it resembles 'Ballykettle', a fantasy Irish village selling its wares on the Internet, including plaster leprechauns, 'heritage crystal' and teapots representing 'aspects of village life', such as 'Tinkie O'Reilly's Jewellery Shop' and even 'Maggie Crotty's knitwear'.

But the locals could not be blamed for seizing their chance. A former mining area when the series started, it had high unemployment, then 400,000 visitors a year began to descend on the place, all looking for Ballykissangel.

'It was a village in decline,' says Jim McCabe of the Avoca Tourist Board. 'Now we get tourists from all over the world, from as far away as Australia and New Zealand.'

'It amazes me that people will travel all this way to see a fictional village,' says Dervla Kirwan.

By the time Colin joined the series, the whole place had been transformed. Unemployed villagers were paid as extras; a hugely profitable gift shop had opened; the rundown supermarket had morphed into a 'craft shop'; and another grocery shop recorded a 30 per cent increase in trade as it started to sell *Ballykissangel* pens, baseball caps and T-shirts.

The pub changed its name to the one in the series, and photos of the stars and printed T-shirts adorned the bar, selling at nearly £10 a time. Even the local weavers, established in 1723, who obstinately refused to change their name from the Avoca Handweavers to anything resembling Ballykissangel, benefited from an increase in business, and Razor didn't do too badly either. He went on to be ridden bareback by Geri Halliwell in a Spice Girls video.

Ballykissangel brought Colin all kind of rewards. He could now wallow in credit cards and mortgages if he wished. Trading in his vintage MG with plastic bumpers, he bought a flashy red sports car, and also became a property owner for the first time, not in a fashionable part of London or LA, but very close to home. 'I will always live in Dublin,' he said romantically. 'Whether I'm smart or dumb, it's made me who I am.'

He bought a long, low, one-bedroom cottage in Ringsend, Dublin 4, which was also once known as 'Ray Town', after the abundance of flatfish caught in the local harbour. For a century, it was home to dock workers, and is graced by two huge chimneys and a power generator popularly called 'the pigeon house'.

According to one local, until quite recently, the whole area was 'a lot of rat-infested pits'. But it is now part of one of the top-ten most expensive real estate belts in the world.

Rich kids, whose parents probably live in Dublin 8 near the park, new money, media folk and popular radio presenters are all buying up the area and are scathingly known to less fortunate outsiders as 'The Dublin 4 Brigade'. They are seen as the high-handed dictators of taste and style to the rest of the country.

It is also a quiet seaside town where you see old men in baseball caps walking their dogs on leads, an unusual sight as, in the rest of Dublin, where pet-owning is not established, you hardly see a domestic animal.

A short walk from a sandy beach and the Irish Sea, Colin's beloved home forms a corner of Chapel Avenue. Among other small, sturdy cottages, many painted cream, brown and lime green, some given pretty curtains and fancy pebbledash, Colin's is probably the plainest, just stark white, with two narrow windows and no adornments.

Despite being cramped and gardenless, they are all in high demand. One undeveloped property in a street adjoining Chapel Avenue was on sale in March 2005 for €390,000.

While he was away, a local workman was busy installing some cream porcelain tiles. 'Colin loves this cottage,' he told me, 'he has a very sentimental attachment to the place. Wherever he goes or whatever he does, he always says, "This is the only house in the world." It is pretty much the same as when he bought it, but he keeps it very nice. He wants somewhere cosy to come back to, somewhere that is certainly not like a hotel.'

By buying the cottage, he put roots down in the area. His local became John Clarke and Sons, an elegantly painted pub that, from the outside, could be a bistro or even a delicatessen. It was once a small bar serving the locals with Guinness and live music, but in 1998 it almost trebled in size. The music went and in came Art Nouveau statues and lamp bowls, rustic Irish paintings and food from 'Cleary's Kitchen', advertised on a wooden blackboard and, in case you missed it, 'Clarke's House Food and Drink' is written in the obligatory, quaint Irish script over the café area.

Rather than the black stuff, the cuisine can now be washed down with fine teas and special coffees. 'Colin, his brother and sisters come in,' says Vincent the barman. 'They are a lovely family, very down to earth. They'll have a few Carlsbergs here then head off into town.'

Locals like to show that they are in the know, and ahead of any game that might be on. And they don't want to be too admiring of a local boy made good. 'Colin sounds quite broad Dublin these days,' says Vincent, 'but we all know that people from Castleknock don't talk like that; it's probably to do with the people he hung about with, and I think he is determined not to appear better than anyone else. But everyone knows he is really posher than he makes out.'

In fact, they like his wild behaviour. 'The thing is, the Irish are a nation of knockers,' says Vincent. 'We don't really like other people to have success. In America, they like people to do well, but here we don't give anyone any dues. The only reason that Colin gets away with it, being a famous film star, is because of his laddishness. It endears him to people, especially the ladies.'

Doro Corrigan, the waitress in the bar, was less analytical about him. She practically fainted at the mention of his name. 'My friend Glenda Pugh is mad about Colin,' she said, her face flushed. 'She met him at a football match in Dublin, and had a picture taken with him. He put his arm around her. She's never stopped talking about it.'

If the local ladies see him as adorable, the men prefer to think of him as a local character, a bit of a lad, and that does him very well; at least, no jealous male has punched him yet.

Everyone knows that Colin's cottage is just round the corner in the next street. 'The owner doesn't let his daughter walk round the back there at night because Colin lives there,' says Vincent. 'After all, she is a good-looking 22-year-old.'

Whatever people might say in pubs, he was now that glorious thing for a young actor, a household name. But, despite his success in *Ballykissangel*, essentially a cosy Sunday-teatime show, he had not gone soft; he was still after risky, hard-edged projects and his next move was light years away from the image of Irish picture-postcard whimsy.

The War Zone for FilmFour Productions, the film arm of Channel 4, was based on a novel by Alexander Stuart about incest, which he wrote in a black depression after his son was diagnosed with cancer.

It was south London actor Tim Roth's directorial début. 'The book was scary but I had a gut reaction to it,' says Roth, who resembles a pint-sized version of Sean Penn. 'I wanted to make a grown-up film about children, without any of the preaching or offering any solutions. I wanted to tell a story about what people do to children within the family, how the actions of an adult can destroy generations. It's an immensely important story. It could be your next-door neighbours... your wife... it could be you.'

Mum and Dad are played by a pregnant Tilda Swinton, looking like a cross between the Virgin Mary and a hammerhead shark, and Ray Winstone, playing his usual blunt Cockney geezer, with lots of ugly, jerky movements. The kids, selected from 2,500 who showed up for the audition, were Lara Belmont, aged 18, playing Jessie, who was spotted while she was shopping in Portobello Market, and Tom, 15, played by Freddie Cunliffe. Colin – using the name 'Colin J Farrell', the middle name James after his beloved maternal grandfather – played Nick, Jessie's boyfriend.

The story is about a family who relocate from London to the Devon coast. It's a disaster for them and the scenery, filmed mostly in the rain, looks like Craggy Island in *Father*

Ted. It is a miserable place, and they are a sad family. Roth describes it as 'a sad film... deeply, deeply sad'.

The project was heavily influenced by the Danish film *Festen*, or *Celebration*, which came out the year before, a bitter story about incest and denial, noted for its relentless, unblinking realism.

Most of the characters in Roth's film slop about looking so damp and wear socks of such length and thickness that sex would normally be out of the question, but Tom returns home one day to find Jessie in the bath with Dad. She denies that there was anything going on but, hunting through photographs, he finds lurid, naked images of his father and sister together.

Agitated and upset, he turns on his sister, burns her with a cigarette end, then starts spying on her, tracking her down to an old wartime bunker where he sees her being raped by Dad.

The children are allowed to carry the film, and Colin shows his screen presence, although this is partly due to his being much better-looking than any of the other youngsters. He also starts out with an Irish accent, but when he takes Jessie to the beach, he turns West Country. Jessie says she likes his accent, but doesn't say which one.

Cunliffe, as the intense Tom, really provided the moral centre of the film, the only person with any certainty and conviction as Dad betrays his family and they all despair. But the film suffers from not being edited tightly enough, from its first interminable scene showing Tom cycling up a long road in the rain to the long-held shot when the family car crashes; there are many pointless longeurs which add to a sense of gloom. With all the characters, except Colin's Nick, cold, wet, lonely and with apparently little to do, you can almost see a case for incest, which is not the aim of the story.

The film won a slew of awards, including Most Promising

Newcomer for Lara, whom Roth compared to Ingrid Bergman, Best British Independent Film of 1999, Best Performance in an Independent Film by Ray Winstone and Best Director for Tim Roth.

It seems odd that none of the talented young participants has done much since... except, of course, for the good-looking boy in the bar.

For Colin, the film had been an important experience. Although he hadn't yet settled on a professional name, it proved to him that he could cope with filming, even if it meant two weeks of rehearsals mostly in pelting rain and putting up with the humourless Roth 'pushing people hard', as Cunliffe put it. At the same time, he was having his first experience of being recognised in the street, in Dublin and London, because of *Ballykissangel*.

A couple more TV parts followed, including a tiny one in a BBC production of *David Copperfield*, made for a 'Christmas audience' and stuffed with stars such as Dame Maggie Smith and Sir Ian McKellen. His scenes as a Victorian milkman were sadly deleted.

Back in London, he became involved in the theatre again for the first time since Sydney. In July 1998, his agent got him a part in a play at the Donmar Warehouse, in Covent Garden, one of London's most fashionable and successful venues. Appropriately for Colin, the theatre had once been a hop warehouse and brewery.

Donmar takes its name from the impresario Donald Albery and the great ballerina Margot Fonteyn, who used it as a rehearsal studio for the London Festival Ballet in the 1960s. It gained its real prestige as a theatre throughout the 1970s and 1980s as an alternative venue for the Royal Shakespeare Company, and became the West End home for Britain's most innovative touring companies.

Anyone who was anyone went 'up the Donmar

Warehouse', the 'warehouse' bit adding extra frisson, with its image of an audience sitting on sacks of grain or packing cases. It was rather stark and rough-looking, and uncomfortable, but then most London theatres are. In 1990, it was taken over by the young director Sam Mendes, who later worked with Kevin Spacey so brilliantly on the film *American Beauty*.

On stage at the Donmar, Colin, still only 23, was at the heart of the most intensive and competitive theatrical culture in the world, and he was able to prove that he could really hack it.

In *A Little World of our Own*, by award-winning young playwright Gary Mitchell, he played a mentally handicapped teenager. The 'little world' refers to Rathcoole, a bleak council estate in Protestant north Belfast housing 20,000 people, with one road in and another out, a closed and dangerous community.

Colin played Richard, a damaged Protestant boy who falls in love with a Catholic girl who disappears. The play tackles the continuingly disastrous relations between Protestants and Catholics, and the despair of impoverished Protestant families.

Nicholas de Jong, the leading drama critic of the London *Evening Standard*, commended Colin's work: 'The performances of Stuart Graham's hardman Ray and Colin Farrell as his flailing, adolescent sibling are eloquently powered by fury and pain.'

He also came to the notice of other powerful and influential observers from the theatre community. One night, while taking a break from rehearsals for his forthcoming role in Eugene O'Neill's great but garrulous play *The Iceman Cometh*, Kevin Spacey saw Colin's performance. The play wasn't a great hit, but Colin stood out, at least for Spacey. 'About four minutes into the production,' he says, 'my friends and I began looking at each other and saying, "Who the fuck is this kid?"'

The next day, Spacey took Colin out for lunch. 'Sometimes you meet young people who have an almost dangerous level of ambition,' he says, 'but Colin never struck me that way. He talked a lot about his family.'

They got on well, and the young actor couldn't have had a more influential admirer. Spacey, who had won one Oscar for Best Supporting Actor in *The Usual Suspects*, and was about to win another Best Actor Award outright for his role in *American Beauty*, was widely considered the most interesting actor in the world at that time. Despite his success in film, he had recently moved away from Hollywood and had fallen in love with the English theatre. Determined to grab it by the throat, he was playing the lead in *Iceman...*, one of the most difficult challenges in the theatre for any actor, in one of the most risky and demanding modern roles, which was really a three-and-a-quarter-hour monologue.

The production had been a hit at the fashionable Almeida Theatre in Islington, and then at the Old Vic, where dangerous things seemed to happen every night. A full bottle of whisky broke on stage when Spacey as Harry slammed it down too hard; a chair splintered when he kicked it across the stage with too much force; one night, the performance was halted when a mobile phone went off in the audience and, as the audience member foolishly answered the phone, Spacey stopped mid-sentence, came downstage to the front and said, 'Tell them you're busy.'

It was a great time for the London theatre, and for Spacey who was fêted and in his element.

Although Colin now knew he could succeed on stage before the most critical audience in the western world, he really always wanted to be a film star, and he told Spacey that that was where his ambitions lay. 'I was always influenced by Steve McQueen, Brando, Monte Clift, Ernest Borgnine,' he says. 'I've seen them in how many fucking movies.'

Just looking at himself in the mirror and knowing how others reacted to his looks probably also gave him a hint that he could do well on screen. Spacey thought so, too. Stills taken at the time show him looking at Colin as if he couldn't quite believe what he'd found, rather like a thirsty man looking at a long, cool pint of Guinness.

He launched Colin from stage and cosy small screen into cinema orbit by offering him a part in his next film, *Ordinary Decent Criminal*, made in Dublin. The film tells the bizarre story of Martin Cahill, played by Spacey, a Dublin gangster and folk hero, known in Ireland as 'The General', because of his meticulous planning of every crime.

Colin accepted a fee of only £1,000 for the chance to act with Spacey, but he was also keen to get into close proximity with actress Linda Fiorentino who was also cast in a lead role. As a boy, he had been infatuated with the lean, dark, rather boyish actress.

'I used to fucking whack off looking at pictures of her,' he says, 'especially when she was in *The Last Seduction*.'

In that 1994 film, Fiorentino plays a besuited saleswoman who calls her co-workers 'eunuchs'. Driven by cruel, relentless sexual aggression, she becomes a kind of anti-hero, a role usually only given to men, and, eventually, the man who loves her complains that she is only interested in sex while he longs for a normal domestic relationship.

In this twist on normal sexual politics, and unlike most wicked women on screen, Fiorentino gets away with all her evil schemes without a moment's regret. Dominant, overpowering and remorseless, she represents the kind of complete sexual role reversal that many men fear, but the idea of a woman being totally in control obviously appealed strongly to Colin. She was dangerous, but undemanding emotionally, and he liked that.

As soon as he met her on the film set, he tried to provoke a reaction from her, which might have been rather self-destructive if she'd taken it the wrong way. However, he trusted to his cheeky Irish charm with the lady... and it worked.

'When I met her on the film set, I told her about what I used to do, about the wanking,' he says. 'She quite liked the idea. At least I didn't get a slap in the face, so she took it all right.' She was probably bemused by Colin, Ireland, the film and her role in it, which amounted to almost nothing.

Colin didn't get anywhere near her on screen or off, but at least this was his chance to get his beautiful face on to the big screen, playing alongside people he admired. He has the small role of Alec, a scruffy, hoodlum van driver, a real 'gurrier', a combination of all the bad boys and hoodlums that he'd ever longed to be.

He isn't seen much in the film, but still manages to bring great intensity to his driving. Well into the film, when standing in a bar, he delivers the immortal line, 'I couldn't give a shite, man,' his considered view on a painting by Caravaggio that Cahill has stolen.

The police prove to be even worse philistines when they shoot him and other gang members dead through the painting, wrecking the canvas.

But it wasn't just Colin who went rather unnoticed in the film; almost everyone was eclipsed by Spacey, who dominates everything as Michael Patrick Lynch, or rather Martin Cahill.

Ordinary Decent Criminal was the third film made about him, following *Vicious Circle*, a successful TV film written by Kieran Prendiville; John Boorman's 1998 film *The General*, starring Jon Voight, now most famous as Angelina Jolie's father, with Brendan Gleeson and Adrian Dunbar. In

2003, he would come up yet again in Joel Schumacher's film *Veronica Guerin*.

Cahill's haul from bank robberies, art-gallery thefts and home burglaries was estimated at nearly £60 million. And, it turns out, one of his burglary victims was John Boorman. He also had an interesting sex life, living with both his wife Christine, her sister Lisa and their four children. After the IRA murdered him in August 1994, for interfering in their drug business, it turned out that he had also had a child with his wife's second sister.

It was Cahill's potent mix of violence, humour and generosity that made him such a legend, but none of this quite comes over in this version directed by Thaddeus O'Sullivan, as Spacey plays him as a sophisticated family man, more like a middle-class liberal schoolteacher experimenting with different lifestyle choices, than a hood who is capable of extreme violence.

It's as if he hasn't got to grips with the black humour he was trying to create by playing the character in a light-hearted way. And, because of this strange, uneasy playing, the film doesn't make much sense. The women don't help either – Linda Fiorentino and Helen Baxendale, last seen as everyone's idea of a perfect girlfriend in *Cold Feet*, the ITV soap opera, just don't cut it as gangsters' molls or as Dublin housewives.

In the film, Cahill divides his time between his women and glides about on an old motorbike, enjoys plotting heists, thinking as much about the showmanship as the loot involved. He decides to steal a painting by the Italian master Caravaggio worth £30m from a Dublin gallery, echoing Cahill's real robbery in 1986 of paintings worth £30m from a private house in County Wicklow.

He hires a tour bus, driven by Colin. Spacey puts on irritating retro clothing, including checked trilby and dark shades. There is a lot of jaunty music and the robbery is a success, apparently as much a fashion statement and art installation as a crime.

The police are hopping mad. 'The cheek of the man,' says Commissioner Daley, played by Patrick Malahide.

DS Noel Quigley, the coolly elegant Stephen Dillane, becomes obsessed with the master criminal, but somehow his quarry always gets away. Eventually, Cahill 'dies' in a hale of bullets during a bank robbery but, when his wife and mistress come to identify the body, his head is too badly disfigured so they are asked to do the job by looking at his blue and lifeless penis. As they walk away, they seem to be laughing – perhaps recognising that the male appendage unmistakably belongs to someone else.

In the final scene, Cahill is shown living as a fugitive in the 'wild west', Connemara perhaps, where he is unknown but happy, back to stealing sweets from the local shop as he did as a boy.

One of the most interesting aspects of the film is seeing Irish actor David Kelly in the role of a priest. Kelly is probably best known to UK audiences for his role as O'Reilly, the disastrous builder who is savagely chastised by Sybil in *Fawlty Towers*. Still working in his seventies in 2005, he has a role in the new version of *Willy Wonka*, starring Johnny Depp.

The results of *Ordinary Decent Criminal* must have been disappointing to the whole cast. Only Colin and the other twitchy members of the gang manage to convince as disaffected corner boys and chancers, with Colin gleefully taking on the police. And, although his part was tiny, his dark, brooding face and his name appear on all the film posters. His pretty face had preceded him again on the road to fame.

The IRA had disliked Boorman's film *The General*, as it drew attention to their racketeering, but this film upset everyone. It is still actively disliked in Dublin. When it is mentioned in O'Donoghue's Bar on St Stephen's Green, there is a general murmur of disgust. 'The whole city was waiting on it,' said one local journalist, 'and they were all disappointed. It didn't ring true at all.'

'Limp and uninspiring,' said another. 'Spacey has no charisma.' There was a general mood of puzzlement about why he had wanted to play a Dublin man in the first place and, inevitably, people wondered sarcastically whether there weren't enough good Irish actors around. One thing they all seemed to agree on was that one young Irish actor, in the form of Colin, was certainly able to hold his own on the screen, and they were eager for him to take on larger parts in future.

CHAPTER FIVE

PLAYING WITH THE BIG BOYS

He'd been in a hit TV show, been a success on stage and made a film with some well-known stars. By 2000, things were happening fast but, in any career, no matter how promising, showing up for interviews is very important.

When Joel Schumacher, the director of the 1997 hit film *Batman and Robin*, held an open casting session in London, he was looking for fresh, young talent to play the lead role in *Tigerland*, a Vietnam war flick. He saw 40 young, desperate hopefuls, but Colin wasn't among them because he managed to turn up just as Schumacher was leaving. They spoke for only five minutes as the director was putting on his coat, but he generously offered to look at an audition video some other time if Colin sent one in.

'I thought, Well, fuck that fancy director,' says Colin. 'That's a plane ticket to London wasted.'

He headed back to Ireland, where he told his mother, 'He was a nice man but I didn't get the part.' He may have sounded unconcerned but he wasn't going to let the first

Hollywood director he'd ever met get away that easily. Back at the cottage on Chapel Avenue, he made a desperate attempt to recoup his loss by making a video of himself in the part of Roland Bozz, the randy Texan youth who is the lead character in the film. He did it using his sister Catherine's hand-held video camera; the lighting was very poor and his only prop was a Camel Light cigarette and his attempt at an accent.

Schumacher loved the tape and Michael McGruther, who wrote the script for *Tigerland*, was also impressed. 'I saw his tape and I thought he was the guy, he was Bozz,' says McGruther. 'He was really in character... he'd worked on the part and he was Bozz.'

Two weeks later, Colin got the call. As he was sitting up in the early hours watching a video, a voice down the phone from California demanded to know, 'Hey, kid, wanna make a movie?'

For better or worse, he was on his way to the great dream factory. The following week, he found himself in a room at the Holiday Inn, 120 Colorado Avenue, Santa Monica, 12 miles from the airport and nine miles from all the action of downtown LA.

On his first afternoon, he wandered down from the pier towards Venice Beach, clutching a six-pack of beer. On the way, he won a teddy bear on a fairground stall, then he stood looking out to sea. 'It was a sad image,' he says mysteriously. 'It wasn't a bad place. I wasn't that hard up, but I remember looking at other hotels, all lit up like Christmas trees and wondering if I would ever get to stay in anywhere like them.

'I finished my beer and went back to my hotel not knowing if anything that was going on would ever lead to anything.'

He says he was there because of his 'passion' for acting, not just out of pure ambition. 'For the Irish, success is not so much about money and material things,' he says, 'success is over-rated. For us, it is more about telling stories and having a laugh.'

But America had been the land of promise for countless thousands of young Irishmen before him and, even if he told himself he was just going there for a bit of a jaunt, it was also a chance in a million and he knew it.

Kevin Spacey had made him visible to Hollywood, and he had very practically got him representation at the Creative Artists Agency – CAA – the dynamic Hollywood talent agency in Beverly Hills, headed by Richard Lovett, reckoned to be the most powerful man in Hollywood. He numbers among his select clients the most popular stars on screen, including Tom Cruise, Tom Hanks, Sting and Bruce Springsteen, plus a host of beautiful, talented actresses such as Cameron Diaz, Nicole Kidman, Sandra Bullock, Renée Zellweger, Gwyneth Paltrow, Julia Roberts, Catherine Zeta-Jones, Angelina Jolie and Drew Barrymore.

The girls sound like a wish-list on Colin's bedside table, and he calls CAA 'the Mother Ship'. It has been the emporium of all his dreams, but others have called it 'the vacuum', as it sucks up all the top talent and agents in Hollywood. Some critics have pointed out that, although it holds most of the top stars, its directors and writers lists aren't in the same league – its ethos is competition, big bucks and commercial success.

On his second day in the USA, Colin made his way to Wilshire Boulevard, to find the CAA's headquarters. It's not easy to miss, with an impressive structure of glass and steel by IM Pei, a pre-eminent architect who has designed museums and art galleries all over the world, including a pyramid at the Louvre in Paris, and the John F Kennedy Library in Boston.

When he describes the place, Colin, from Georgian Dublin, loves to sound as if he had never been in a fine building before. But perhaps he'd never been in such a big one before.

'I walked into the lobby… well, that's what I called it. I really got hung because it was "an atrium". I didn't even know what a fucking atrium is. But it was, "No, sir. This is an atrium…" Fine!

'It must have been Monday because they were having their Monday-morning power fucking breakfast and power lunch. So it's double power on Monday and I was there for the second half of it.

'My agent brought me into this room like I am the Queen fuckin' Mother, and there were 25 quite attractive human beings. Very well dressed. Blue suits. Very smart. Diet Cokes and half-eaten salads on the table. When we came in, they all stood up at the exact same moment, and I stood there and shook all their hands, and as soon as they said one name it would go in one of my ears and out the other. Some names bounced off without going in at all. I didn't remember one name. I was so fucking nervous, I was trembling.

'They asked me to sit at the table, then I grasped a glass of water so suddenly the spotlight was on me. I had the floor. Then I got one of the worst attacks of verbal diarrhoea I've ever had to this day. I rabbited on for 15 minutes. It was scary as fuck. I mean, I was 22, I didn't even know what it was about.'

Far from home, Colin quickly made an interesting discovery. 'It is easier for me to get laid in LA, for sure,' he says with his famous candour. 'I put myself up at the Holiday Inn in Santa Monica and used to go on my own each night to the Third Street Promenade area. Some nights, I'd come home on my own, some nights with a girl, sometimes I'd have a room full of fucking strangers and we'd get pissed and stoned and laid.'

It is clear that he was used to seeing sex as a commodity, and this helped him to feel less alone in a strange town and those people of the night who came back to his hotel room were the last people to know him before he became famous.

'Those were great times,' he recalls, 'particularly as the people I spent my evenings with were either bored or lonely like I was. They laughed at my jokes because they thought I was actually funny. Now the lines have got crossed. People start treating you the way they do because of your name and position, whatever that may be.'

Sexually active by night, he needed to be charming and entertaining by day. He was soon swept up by the film crowd, eager for new blood, new people, especially exotic types from Europe. After an uneasy start at CAA, soon he was never alone or looking for company and the invitations just piled up. He played the Hollywood party scene, and got it right.

Scruffy as any urban waif, he mingled easily with the very well dressed and, above all, he played the Irish card. The myth of the wild Irish beauty has always haunted the English and American mind. You can see it in films like *I See a Dark Stranger* (1946), where a staid English officer falls for Bridie Quilty, a beautiful but volatile Irish nationalist, and in *The Quiet Man* (1952), where John Wayne goes home to Ireland and tries to claim his flame-haired colleen. There also lingers the romantic idea of the Irish character, apparently untameable, not susceptible to the rules that govern everyone else. This has been represented over the years in rugged actors like James Cagney and Spencer Tracy, and later by Richard Harris and Liam Neeson. Being irascibly Irish in Hollywood was and remains a valuable asset.

'Being Irish has done me no disservice in Hollywood,' says Colin. 'I am fairly Irish, you know what I mean, I wear it on my sleeve, and, if I do play it up, it is to remind me where I'm from, and to get a laugh.'

To cope with his sudden entry into this new society of highly polished but very insular people, who knew most of what they knew from film and TV rather than travel, he started speaking like his character Danny Byrne in *Ballykissangel* again and created a whole 'Irish' carapace which protected him from being truly known by anyone.

He is not the first actor to do this, of course. Cary Grant famously said that everyone wanted to be Cary Grant, and even he wanted to be Cary Grant.

As a youth, for whatever reason, deeply unhappy with reality, Colin had created a new self – the hard-drinking, all-swearing rebel. Now he added to that again by trowelling on the Irish dimension. Creating his own myth, sensing what people want, what pleases them and going with it. Soon, even his own family hardly recognised him. Brother Eamon has been quoted as saying that, when he visits him in LA, he no longer understands him, as he is more 'Irish' now, living in Hollywood, than he ever was at home in Dublin.

This new guise worked. At his first Hollywood parties, he would arrive looking like a nervous wreck, almost too paralysed with fear to speak. He'd have a drink, usually Johnny Walker whisky, 'a gargle', as he calls it, and the next thing, there he'd be, the wild Irish boy, charming the trousers off all the right people, like Mr and Mrs Tom Cruise.

'Jesus' – or 'Be-Jaysus', as he probably said it – 'You're much more attractive in real life than you are on the screen,' he gushed at Cruise when they first met. The effect was immediate. The buttoned-up Cruise was fascinated by the young Irishman.

'He cut a swathe through Hollywood,' says Joel Schumacher. 'At one party, I heard him talking to his agent's assistant, a very attractive girl. He was saying to her, "Do you really mean you have never seen an uncircumcised penis?"'

Colin loves enlightening Hollywood ladies. 'They are fucking fascinated with a foreskin, aren't they?' he asks interviewers with a certain faux naivety. 'In Ireland, we don't get the tip of our fucking knobs chopped off. I fucking completely disagree with that. People in America say it's much cleaner to have no foreskin. I say, have you never heard of a fucking shower, or Q Tips, or whatever you want to do with the fucking thing?

'I remember at that party about 20 people standing about and that agent from CAA talking to me. Somehow, the subject of circumcision came up. She said, "I just don't understand the foreskin. I've never seen one." So I whipped out my dick and said, "Here, that's all it is, a bit of skin."

'I did a little puppetry of the penis sort of thing and showed her what it was about. You would have thought she was at a circus the way she was looking at me.'

That is what he wanted and he began a strange pattern of childish behaviour, giving the previously sheltered ladies of Hollywood a lot more joyful surprises along the way. During the filming of *Alexander*, Angelina Jolie would eventually change her hotel because of his incessant willy-waving. Not since the days of Errol Flynn had there been so much discussion and speculation about a film star's male member.

As well as popularity in the pants department, Colin now had a mentor in Joel Schumacher. 'I wouldn't have done it if Joel hadn't picked me out of obscurity,' he says. 'Everything goes back to him.'

Schumacher was trying out new ground. He met Colin at a time when he was starting what was almost a second career after a difficult time in Hollywood. After starting out as a costume designer, working for Woody Allen, he became a scriptwriter working on *Carwash* and *The Wiz*, and then had a couple of teen hits with *St Elmo's Fire*, *The Lost Boys* and a remake of *Cousins*.

In the 1990s, he was offered higher-profile work, such as *Flatliners*, some John Grisham adaptations, then the blockbusters *Batman Forever*, which was a huge success, and *Batman and Robin*, which was a disaster and hated by most critics. His reputation went into a decline, so he had wisely decided to shift his attention to smaller, cheaper projects. The first of these was *Tigerland*.

Before he started work on the film, Colin visited Texas to research the accent he would use as US gurrier Roland Bozz. He did his research in the Golden Spoke bar, in Austin, watching country bands and chatting to the locals. He also explored the kind of women that the bed-hopping Bozz might have slept with.

'What a fucking lovely place,' he says dreamily. 'I was in Austin, might have been three weeks, might have been six, and everyone was a very drunk one and a very good one. Beautiful women, so many of them. It was like an ant farm.'

He'd begun in America the way he intended to carry on, but it wasn't all fun. There is always a fly, even in the Farrell ointment. Before he started work on *Tigerland*, he had to break off from his indoor games and fly to Florida to join a boot camp to get him in the mood for the brutality of the film.

'We had to create a military experience,' says Michael McGruther. 'There were two military instructors and they were really on us hard core for a few nights. We went out and hiked, went on manoeuvres, we were booby-trapped by them. It was all meant to create realness and Joel wanted us all to bond.'

Generous and easy-going, Colin is good at making friends, but he is not so keen on the paraphernalia that happens before you make a blockbuster. 'I find physical training for film roles the most tedious waste of time. It's so boring. I'd prefer to be sitting in a pub with a few strangers talkin' shit than looking at meself in the mirror runnin' on a treadmill.'

Although he hated going to the gym and doing any kind of organised exercise, he took it all with good grace and

McGruther, who is used to the demands of US film actors, was astonished at how easy-going he was.

'Colin was the most happy-go-lucky guy around,' he says, 'calling out people's names, "Hey, hey, how are you!" He liked everyone to be included. He's a regular guy. I don't think he is the next Tom Cruise... he is the next Colin Farrell.'

As the bad boy Bozz, he got his face literally rubbed in the mud, but where there's muck there's brass and he was paid his first £100,000 fee for the film.

It is also a wonderful part, set in 1971 during America's worst agony over the Vietnam War. He plays a youth who is conscripted into the army and is determined to make trouble, for himself and others.

The *Tigerland* of the title is a terrible military theme park in Louisiana where 'the dumb fucking grunts', or rookie soldiers, get their final infantry training before they are put on the plane for South-East Asia and the reality of war.

During his infantry training, when we are informed that the USA has 'the best soldiers on the planet', Bozz sets about sabotaging things; he seems to be a 'fool who is fighting the system and wants out', but he is more than that. Among a mêlée of damaged and bad people, he is really a modern saint, the first time Colin had been called on to play one since he left Castleknock College. He is angry and difficult but fatally imaginative about other people's suffering, and tries to help men who are even worse off than he is. Despite his bravado and vulnerability, he is ultimately moral and self-sacrificing.

The question he poses is: how does a clever and humane person deal with the degrading madness of war, without being court-martialled, deserting or becoming a beast himself?

This is one of the central and enduring narratives of European cinema and theatre, from *Journey's End*, written as a play in 1929 and made into a film in 1930, to *The Parchute*, the BBC play by David Mercer and *The Bofors Gun* in the

1960s, *Colonel Redl* and *Observe the Sons of Ulster Marching Towards the Somme* in the 1980s, even down to *Blackadder Goes Forth* in the 1990s. It's *Sergeant Bilko* without the laughs, and one critic even compared Colin's role as Bozz to the lead in *One Flew Over the Cuckoo's Nest*, in its tale of one smart man against a callous, incompetent institution.

Any successful work of art succeeds on several levels and in unexpected ways, and *Tigerland* manages to show not just the brutality and stupidity of the army, but also its glamour, its attractions as a defining male experience. It is an anti-war film, but it might not stop anyone joining up, at least not romantics who are attracted to the idea of total risk.

Shot with hand-held 16mm cameras, the film wreaks of authenticity. There is not a false note, with no intrusive music; instead, Nathan Larson's subtle soundtrack, with its oriental hollow and whining sounds, subtly builds up the atmosphere of foreboding. There is also some poignant *a cappella* singing from a group of black actors led by Tory Kittles.

Sadly, the film did not receive a major release, but it was a critical success, with Colin named the Best Actor of the Year by the Boston Society of Film Critics. It also won him the London Critics Circle Award as British Newcomer of the Year, an odd accolade as he is no more British than George Bush.

It also created another discussion about his private parts. There is a shower scene in the film in which he only appeared above the waist, but he told a reporter, 'My bits looked the size of a cashew nut.'

Schumacher had taken a risk casting an unknown in a leading role; he had been proved to have had inspired judgement, but Colin was slightly stunned by his own good fortune. 'Thousands of actors in the world could have played Bozz as well as me, if not better,' he told a reporter. 'It's just luck… fucking luck. It's just me having the avenue to stumble into a theatre school in Dublin one day, then, you know, meeting Joel Schumacher in London, doing a play in London that Kevin Spacey saw because he was doing a play there, too... Then there was the agency who signed me based on Spacey seeing me. Come on. Give me a fucking break. Luck? Yeah, man.'

He has the luck of Zorro and, once again, his face, scrubbed clean and luminously beautiful, was up on the film poster, showing his delicate, youthful profile against a dark landscape. It was now impossible for anyone in the film world not to know who he was.

Schumacher's next project with Colin was *American Outlaws*, a *Young Guns* spin-off. Colin naturally saw it as another step upwards in his career and they both hoped for box-office success with this one.

Before filming started, Colin and the other young actors had to spend six weeks at a ranch observing the work of a group of real cowboys, and learning to ride Western-style. He hadn't been on a horse since Razor in *Ballykissangel*; now he was up on Milagro who was 21 years old and no trouble at all, and his riding teacher, Terry Leonard, had once worked with John Wayne.

In this, another film about young men embroiled in serious conflict, Colin plays the legendary Jesse James, the ruthless outlaw, who was, in fact, an angry Irish yahoo whose family came from *Ballybunnion*, a small town on the north Kerry coast. For any non-believers, there is still a pub there named after him.

Jesse rides with his older brother Frank, and their pal Bob Younger, played by beefy, big-jawed Scott Caan, the son of actor James Caan, who appeared in the *Godfather* films. Like Colin, Scott had grown up with a father who spent all his spare time coaching his son in football. Both had once been promising athletes who'd 'let Dad down' by becoming actors.

The film opens with the three boys fighting for the rebel

General Lee and, although they look about as effective a fighting force as a boy band, they take on major parts of Lincoln's Union Army, armed with only rifles against cannon and Gattling guns.

The James boys were among 20,000 Irishmen who fought for the Confederacy. It seems odd that Irish people who'd fled from the cruelty and oppression in their own land should take up arms in the USA for the right to own slaves, but issues like that are not raised in the film – in fact, no issues at all are raised in this film, which remains at the level of a Saturday-afternoon fantasy for teenagers.

After the victory of the North, Jesse and Bob form a partisan band to protect their land from carpet-baggers and fat-cat railroad men moving in and spoiling their way of life.

The villain, Alan Pinkerton, a US government agent, is played by former James Bond Timothy Dalton, looking as if he is sucking a lemon. He and the other railroad magnates are unfeasibly evil, while Colin as Jesse isn't allowed to be a bad boy at all. It is hard to believe that the Schumacher who'd just made the brash, honest *Tigerland* was involved with anything as shallow as this.

Jesse James was, to put it mildly, disturbed… some would say psychotic. Colin does a strong line in just that type of character. If they could have recreated and developed Alec from *Ordinary Decent Criminal*, reprieved Private Bozz or allowed Colin to create the vicious and unpredictable character he was to play in *Intermission* two years later, then the film might really have had something. Instead, it sticks to the subject of teen love with Jesse, a good lad whom any mother would be proud of, falling for Zee Mimms (Ali Larter), a neighbour's pretty blonde daughter.

Larter looks like a preppy college girl and is rather stiff, but Colin fell for her. 'She is the only person I've ever really kissed on screen,' he says. 'We nearly swallowed each other.'

'It is quite natural for an actor to fall in love with his leading lady during a play or a film,' the actor Richard Burton once said, adding, 'It's harmless, because he can always walk away.' He, of course, walked away until he met Elizabeth Taylor on the set of *Cleopatra*, whereupon he changed his mind.

Colin found he had the same susceptibility to his female co-stars as Burton, and the same attitude when the show was over. But, as Jesse, he is a clean, upright, noble boy, with no complications, fighting for his family land, his girl and his mother, played by Kathy Bates like a slightly crazed Sunday school teacher.

There is a lot of mayhem as he and his gang, who really just want to be farmers, are forced to rob banks to support themselves. A lot of banks are robbed, perspiring, bug-eyed bank-tellers plead, large men are thrown through windows without getting cut, and the film is both violent and cheesy.

It all ends happily, no one gets hurt and the young couple ride off together back to their farmstead. In fact, of course, Jesse never settled down and was quickly shot by Younger.

The film flopped and went straight to video in the UK. 'It was just bad film-making,' says Colin, adding, in his nonchalant way, 'A pile of shit.' But he did walk away with the boots and jacket he'd worn on set, and he still wears them to this day.

Scott Caan's career has been slow since the picture. In 2005, he filmed *Into the Blue* with Jessica Alba and Paul Walker, a water-centric Bahamian thriller about divers.

Colin may have been disappointed with *American Outlaws*, but it didn't affect his upwardly mobile direction one jot. He continued his ascent through Tinsel Town by good connections, lucky chances, looks and charm. As he put it, 'I know that I skipped at least 100 rungs on the ladder.'

But even for a young film star, love is not as easy to negotiate as a career and, for it to flourish, it relies on a lot more than luck and charm. Colin chose a particularly dramatic moment to fall in love with the lovely dark-haired English actress Amelia Warner. Like him, she was a rising star. After small parts on TV, she'd starred as Lorna Doone in a BBC Sunday serial, then, in a rise almost as astonishingly swift as Colin's, she won a leading roll in *Quills*, a controversial historical drama about the Marquis de Sade, starring Geoffrey Rush, Kate Winslet and Joaquin Phoenix.

In the film, she plays Simone, a cross between Jane Eyre and Snow White, who is married off to a cruel doctor, played by Michael Caine, with less conviction than someone attending a fancy-dress party. Simone was not a well-written part. We are never sure of what she is up to and, towards the end of the picture, her character simply disappears... but it launched her film career.

'We met just before *Quills* came out,' says Colin. 'I can tell you the exact moment I fell in love with her. Holy fuck, she's beautiful. It was at the première, on the red carpet. I stepped back because it wasn't my night, it was hers. So I step back and she steps forward and looks at all the lights and cameras, then looks back at me with this killer fucking "help me" look on her face, and she reached out for me and that was it. Right through the heart. I'd been in love twice in my life... this was the third time and it was the true fucking thing.'

She remembers it all a bit differently, as not quite such a dazzling flash in the pan. She says they met through mutual friends in Los Angeles, and they knew each other for a good while before they fell in love. At the time, she was studying for her A-levels in London. Despite working on *Lorna Doone*, and hanging around on a film set waiting while Colin was working, she eventually got two As and a B. Then, in February 2001, he attended the *Quills* première with her in LA and fell in love with her, and they became a real couple soon after.

After the première, he had her name shortened to the affectionate 'Millie' and tattooed on his left ring finger above the knuckle, so everyone he met could know of his devotion. 'I didn't know that Pamela Anderson and Tommy Lee had also done it,' he said later, sounding uncharacteristically snobbish. 'I had no idea. I wouldn't be fucking following in their trends, thank you.'

Or perhaps he has more personal reasons for apparently disliking Tommy Lee, making reference to his own feelings of physical inadequacy again. 'He's supposed to be hung like a donkey,' he says. 'They call him T-bone. He has a huge fucking cock. Good for him. I'd follow that trend if I could, but it's physically impossible. Two inches, hard as a rock. Write that down.'

Whatever his shortcomings, as young, up-and-coming stars, they looked just perfect together – both dark, pale-skinned, luminous-eyed and perfectly featured, like brother and sister in a Shakespeare play.

After *Lorna* and *Quills*, Amelia was, like Colin, deemed by everyone to be 'the next big thing', and it must have seemed to their increasing number of fans that they were a perfect match. Colin thought so, too. 'I was madly in love,' he says, 'I asked her to marry me.'

They married on 17 July 2001, on an idyllic beach in Bora Bora, the most romantic island in French Polynesia, serenaded by ukulele players. It was a filmgoer's fantasy come true, a real-life *Blue Lagoon*, but she is not clear what happened in reality. 'We just went to the activities desk and said, "We want to go jet-skiing and shark feeding and we want to get married." They said, "Cool. We'll do sharks on Monday, jet-skiing Tuesday and we can fit in a wedding on Wednesday." It wasn't really legally binding, it was just something we did for us.'

Together on the island, they loved passionately, attracted

and excited by their differences. Strangely, it turned out that each was the mirror image of the other, pretending to be what the other really was.

In interviews, Amelia speaks beautiful BBC English, like a privately educated young lady but, in fact, she was brought up on a tough council estate by a single mother and went to State schools. Her parents never married. Amelia never identifies her father, a musician who lives in Yorkshire, but she sees him and her half-siblings Thomas and Sarah. Her mother, the actress Annette Ekblom, who, despite her name, comes from the Wirral in Cheshire, was just 23 and living in Liverpool when Amelia was born. Six years later, they moved to London. She grew up on a council estate overlooking Ladbroke Grove in overcrowded west London.

Like most actresses, her mother struggled for years until, eventually, she found regular work playing Debbie Gordon in *Brookside*. She is now starring as Patricia Davey in *Peak Practice*. But, while Amelia was growing up, she had to scrimp to afford her school uniforms and school trips.

Talented academically and at drama, when she was ten Amelia won a scholarship to board at the Royal Masonic School, and realised for the first time how poor she was in comparison to her friends. 'I never thought anything of it until I went to stay with someone for the weekend,' she says. 'They had a huge house with electronic gates. That was the first time I thought, Oh, shit, I'm not the same as everyone else.

'I got really embarrassed if people wanted to come back to our flat, although some of the people who did thought it was really cool. For a while, I thought I was living two lives; it was weird, because my friends on the estate spoke a certain way and behaved a certain way, and the ones at school spoke and behaved completely differently.'

It is not surprising that Colin saw such shuddering uncertainty in her on the night of the film première, a real trembling waif now turned into a fairy princess. While he had been playing at rags to riches, pretending to come from a working-class background, she had been living the real thing.

They really had nothing in common apart from a very troubled past and, despite the beauty of Bora Bora, they soon found to their shock that there was little to keep them together. 'I thought I'd spend the rest of my life with that girl,' he says, 'but it didn't last long. We fell in love very hard, loved for a year but then we fell out of love equally fast, as people often do. It was that simple and complicated and that flippant and spontaneous.

'But it was tough being in love and then finding yourself not in love as you once were, that was a jagged little pill for me to swallow. I just couldn't understand it. I couldn't understand how I felt so different. It's sad when a relationship dies. It is a death.'

In November 2001, just four months after their South Sea island wedding, their love ran out like the tide and she asked him for a divorce. They'd had one of the shortest marriages in Hollywood history. There were rumours that he had been unfaithful. 'He didn't do anything wrong,' she says protectively. 'I loved him so much. I had the most amazing times of my life with him. He was a fantastic partner, but we were too young. I had stuff to do and he had stuff to do and it just didn't work out. It was really sad.'

The odds were against them anyway; Amelia was only 19 and girls who marry at 20 or earlier are more likely to divorce than those who wed after 25. The children of divorced or separated parents are also more likely to have broken marriages themselves, but, if they'd looked at each other closely, or listened to each other, they would have realised that they were set in opposite directions; their aims in life were different. They didn't even want to live in the same town.

'I love London. I love English people,' says Amelia. 'I love the weather.' She enjoys hanging round, looking chic in antique Portobello Road grunge, buying her clothes from market stalls and attending local community events. 'I don't even want to talk about how I hate LA,' she says. 'It's such a weird place. If it were my choice, I wouldn't spend a day there. Everything shuts at 11.00pm and everyone thinks they are so crazy, wild and liberal... but they're not.'

Colin, too, has his reservations about living in the eternal summer of LA. 'I miss the greyness, leaves on the ground,' he says. 'I wish it was more overcast in LA, too much sun is depressing. I miss Irish people, Irish pubs, the canal, fish and chips with curry sauce on the side. Over here, people watch each other day and night to see what they're wearing and how they behave, and being an individual isn't that important.'

But apart from the 100-degree temperatures and the dullness of the people, LA is vital to his career – it is, after all, the only place to be for someone who aims to be an A-list film star. It is also the place, far removed from home, that offers him complete licence to live in just the way he wants and to explore himself and his needs. As a boy, he'd struggled with relationships; as a teenager, he'd gone into a rather nihilistic world of porn magazines and drugs. In his early career, he'd fallen in love with women he couldn't bond with. But now he was in LA, a 'Pornopolis' where all the old bonds of obligation were broken and he could allow himself any amount of freedom to experiment.

It's the town where anyone who wants to can, as he puts it, order whores like pizza. Colin's own preference unbelievably to those of us in Europe, is for US girls with their French-manicured nails and Brazilian-waxed landing strips, to rough, hairy European types. Once he saw LA, he decided that, although the girls in Dublin's fair city were pretty enough, they were not in the same league as Californian girls. In 2003, he told *Playboy* magazine, 'I ate a lot of pussy at home, but I never saw a vagina until I came here; they were all well covered at home. In Ireland, the birds are all clean... it's just that a lot of them have big, hairy pussies.

'Girls in Ireland are great fun, they can drink all night and fucking get pissed out of their minds, but they are not as hugely into grooming as they are over here, which is not a fucking problem at all – just different flavours of the same lollypop.

'In Ireland, there is not so much importance placed on physical appearance, more on what someone is like. In Ireland, we think that to have the prettiest toes in the world and the most beautifully groomed pussy does not an interesting, generous, intelligent person make.'

It's not surprising that interesting and intelligent Amelia, in her thrift-store gowns, stayed back in London, while he took to romancing well-waxed women in the bar of the Château Marmont.

'He's become a bit of a womaniser since he has been in Hollywood,' says Glenda Gilson, with some understatement. And then, as if admitting defeat, she adds, 'And let's face it, who can blame him?'

Going to LA, he was entering an enchanted land, like Odysseus on the remote island of Ogygia, he was soon enchanted, captivated by the place, and couldn't leave it for long. He now leads the life of a film star, while Amelia says she'd 'hate to be a big star. I want to make good films, and I have to be careful... I don't want my life to change. I really don't want to be a movie star. I think there are ways of doing this work, staying below the radar, so you can still walk down the street and not get hassled. If you are out there all the time with your bodyguards, drawing attention to yourself, then you're opening yourself up for people to think they know you.'

The way they handle the press also shows how different

their attitudes are. While Colin was inveigling himself into men's magazines describing varieties of 'pussy', calling every film he did a 'cock fest', and telling a reporter from *Cosmopolitan* magazine, which first featured hunky male nude centrefolds, that he'd like 'another three inches below', Amelia was saying little about her private life because she feels it's very important to 'choose the kind of press you do very carefully'.

She was the second Amelia to trouble his heart, and brought him no more lasting happiness than the first.

The fact that he treated marriage so flippantly and spontaneously, getting into it on a whim, shows how far he'd come from his Irish background, a boy brought up by Catholic priests and teachers to whom the institution of marriage is sacred. Until 27 February 1997, divorce was forbidden in Ireland and is now only allowed after four years apart. His own parents separated but have never divorced. In Ireland, only 20 per cent of couples seek divorce, but in California the figure is over 50 per cent.

Colin was either still in full revolt against his parents' marriage, which had taken so many agonised years to come apart, or he was plunging further into the entirely new culture of Hollywood, where marriage is treated like a short-term contract and it is not unheard of for stars to wake up the day after a wedding and phone for divorce papers before getting out of bed. Divorce is integral to the legend of the place. Liz Taylor famously wed eight times, Lana Turner seven, Zsa Zsa Gabor nine; J-Lo is already clocking them up.

Part of the privilege of being rich and famous was being able to marry in haste and repent with alacrity. Drew Barrymore, nicknamed 'Marrymore', decided to marry bar owner Jeremy Thomas the day she met him, and left him after 19 days. In 1977, Cher lasted for nine days with rock singer Gregg Allman before filing for divorce. She famously said that life with him was like 'visiting Disneyland on speed'. Dennis Hopper's marriage to Mamas and Papas beauty Michelle Phillips in 1979 lasted eight days.

Among the present generation, Colin and Amelia were following in the footsteps of Jennifer Lopez and Chris Judd, who lasted as man and wife for 13 months. In 2001, she married comic actor Tom Green, but they parted five months later. Nicholas Cage was wed to Lisa Marie Presley for three months, 15 days; and Robin Givens married her tennis coach for one day.

But perhaps Britney Spears took the nuptial biscuit when, in January 2004, she stayed hitched to her childhood friend Jason Alexander for just 55 hours, after a wedding in the Little White Wedding Chapel in Las Vegas, where the bride dressed in blue jeans and a baseball cap.

Now aged 23, she is married to Kevin Federline, one of the dancers in her tour group, who has two children by another relationship. At the time of writing, they've been together for a lengthy six months, but recent reports suggest that, in July 2004, while they were still engaged, she left him out of her 27-page will, leaving all her $100 million fortune to her immediate family and a few friends. So there is obviously not much trust there.

But, in Hollywood, proximity is everything and love is mainly about beauty and the buzz that it brings. The whole culture mitigates against any lasting relationships. According to Anne Roiphe, author of *Marriage: A Fine Predicament*, attractive, charismatic people, the type who strive to become stars, are always seeking confirmation of their adorability, of qualities like youth and beauty that are bound to fade. Colin snatched at marriage at a time when he was plunging into this world of ephemera, the pitiful facelift and the surgically enhanced vagina.

The acting profession itself makes successful marriage

difficult. Actors often have to spend weeks apart on different film sets. Brad Pitt and Jennifer Aniston recently blamed this for the failure of their four-year marriage which began so gloriously with a million-dollar fairytale wedding.

Glenda Gilson suggested that spending too much time apart was a possible reason why Colin's marriage failed. 'He's a big-time romantic,' she says. 'When he falls in love, he falls deeply and he would stick by you. He wouldn't have gone off with anyone else when he was with Amelia, he's not that type of guy. I think the split might have been something to do with him spending a lot of time filming away in LA, while she was wanting to get her career off the ground in England.'

The pressures of being a rich, famous aspiring film star are intense, and everyone has their own particular problems, too.

'I think we were too young to be married,' Colin says. She was perhaps seeking a father-figure, having never had a father in her life, but he was too young to fulfil those needs, and perhaps remains so, because he is still his mother's little boy.

'If there were an article about me in a newspaper saying 'IRISH ACTOR FOUND WITH PROSTITUTE IN LA HOTEL, my mother wouldn't say, "I can't believe that," she'd say, "Did you pay by cheque or fucking cash… and did you keep a receipt?"' Colin says proudly. 'She knows I'm not a fucking bad guy.'

That's OK then – but why bring Mother into it? Why is her approbation, almost her permission to misbehave, still so important to him, even when he is with strangers in hotel rooms in downtown LA?

From his description of his mother's attitudes, she always supports him, never reproves him or makes him feel bad about himself, and that is what he wants. 'My mother has the patience of a saint,' he says. 'She reads the headlines and her eyes roll to heaven and she goes, "Oh, God." But then she takes the paper, rips out the story and puts it in the scrapbook.'

'She knows her little fella, her little boy. She knows I am a messer. But I think I have a good heart. I'm very attached to her. My mother... she's me drinking partner, she's me best mate, she's me wife,' he says. 'She fucking worries about me too much.' It is as if he has never made a proper separation from her.

This kind of relationship can have a distinct upside for a man. Freud once said that a man who is his mother's favourite, as he was himself, is likely to do well in whatever profession he chooses. Doting mother love gives any boy an extra boost of confidence which can make him a powerful fighting force in the outside world, a captain of industry, a great artist, an actor who fills up the screen. He is also very often a great success with women, feeling secure from an early age that he can please them. They hold no terrors for him, as he knows they will succumb to his charm. But a man who loves his mother may secretly have very ambivalent feelings about all those women who aren't Mum. He will look for his mother in all of them; he will probably want to settle down with someone very like her but, because of the incest taboo, he may not be so relaxed about sleeping with her, and will probably only enjoy sex with women who do not resemble her at all, women he does not love or respect.

'There is safety in the idea of getting a high-class hooker who is going to keep her fucking mouth shut,' he says almost defiantly, not meaning that she might talk to the press, but that she, of all women, will be safely unemotional. 'You do what you want to do behind closed doors and they don't really become involved or embroiled in your personal life. I'm very fucking flippant with all that shit and I couldn't really give a shit what other people think of me.'

It seems that, after his marriage failed and he became yet more famous, more loved by strangers, he made the complete split between sex and love. As he often told reporters, 'I am into sex, not love. I've always been a firm believer that casual sex is a fucking good thing.'

Affection, loyalty and family were placed on one side, sex on quite another. 'I've got this guy thing going on now. I've been in love, but you can substitute that with what your body needs physically,' he says. 'Save your love and give it to your friends and family.'

When someone accused him of having one type of woman in his mind for sex and another for settling down, and never letting them overlap, he agreed. 'Well, it didn't work,' he said, 'so I stepped away from love.' The reporter pointed out what a disappointing message that was for half the human race to hear. 'Not the half that wants to get fucked,' he replied, ignoring the possibility of emotion.

Too much mother-love may produce a highly successful man who is charming to women he doesn't know well, but it can be disastrous for close personal relationships. Being in love with a real woman, even one as pretty as Amelia, will be difficult because she will have her own needs. Confused about the role of sex in a loving relationship, used to being loved entirely as 'the little fella', he has no incentive to grow up and, as a little boy, he will be a nightmare for any woman who tries to love him.

A woman who takes on a mother's boy won't be able to compete with Mum, and he will always have to have everything his own way, including an absolute tolerance for his whims and temper tantrums. 'Being in love is tough but it's gorgeous,' he says, which sums up what he might go through and put his partner through.

Craving closeness but unable to handle it, he will swing between offering affection and intimacy, wanting to be almost overwhelmed by the other person, but after this comes a sudden withdrawal, a distancing that is cruel and bewildering to the other person.

'Whatever I'm addicted to in the person, what makes it electric and engaging, is also a destructive force,' he says.

Amelia, at just 19, was a lamb to the slaughter. Even if she had been wise enough to know what she was getting into, she would hardly have had the experience to cope. 'She said I was a nightmare,' he says, 'which is the broad consensus.'

He interprets this need for distance as boredom and a need for freedom or, as he puts it, 'I need to be surprised a lot. How can you have a relationship that is not about ownership but about absolute freedom at the same time?'

He circles around the issue of dependence, how to be with someone without being possessed by them, how to merge into another person yet at the same time remain free and autonomous, issues which have dominated his life since childhood when he was so close to his mother.

As the marriage failed, he began to show unbridled passion for certain actresses in the lobby of the Château Marmont, went charging from bed to bed, proving whatever he needed to prove to himself in a twilight world, where nothing is real and everything is ersatz, including names, breasts, eyelashes… even lips. He has dealt with the loneliness created by a lack of true intimacy by creating idealised figures, from Marilyn Monroe to the women he works with, and by casual sex with strangers.

'You are talking to someone who was married for four fucking months,' he says bitterly. 'Since then, I just haven't been in the mood for a long-term relationship… maybe I was burned more than I realised.' He knows something is wrong but can't put it right. 'How can I have an easier path?' he asks plaintively, as if giving himself to someone else, apart from his mother, is just too painful and risky.

The situation is probably worse for anyone who lives on planet Hollywood, where so much ideal, unobtainable beauty is on show, and so much accessible temptation is on sale. And in such a sexually competitive and self-serving society, a lot of people get hurt. Jane Fonda recently revealed that she caught her husband Ted Turner being unfaithful in the first month of their marriage and their relationship never really recovered, and, according to many reports, Jennifer Aniston is distraught about losing her husband Brad Pitt. As if just losing him wasn't bad enough, she has to see him spread all over the newspapers clutched in the extraordinarily long, sinewy arms of Angelina Jolie.

All Colin has left of his marriage is the tattoo of his wife's name. 'I'll probably keep it for ever,' he says. 'I'd sooner skip laser treatment and all that. It is part of my past. But if I fell in love again, and it was a problem to someone, or if I ever get married again – God forbid – I'll have a look at getting rid of it.'

Amelia has put all romantic feelings behind her, too, for the time being. 'I am not really a boyfriend type of girl,' she says, which is sad from someone who looks like many a young man's ideal girlfriend. 'I've got some people who take really good care of me, but that's all for now.'

Like Colin, she is also ready to experiment with practical alternatives to love, and has decided that it's safer to take care of herself. 'Last Christmas, I bulk-bought vibrators for all my friends,' she says. 'I think every woman should have one. I can't believe they haven't already. They always say, "Oh, I couldn't possibly buy one for myself. But then if someone else were to get me one..."'

After the marriage, she found refuge in work with its ready-made relationships. Like Colin, her life is now mostly about work. They both find the process of film-making in the little enclosed world of the set reassuring. 'It's weird, but, when you are on set,' she says, 'and the cameras aren't on, you get intimidated by people, scared and nervous, but then once the cameras are on and you've got your line, and your relationship with the other person in the part, all that nervousness goes away. Once you're doing it, you've known each other for years.'

But her once highly promising career definitely suffered. 'I'd disappeared for a whole year,' she says. 'When I came back, none of it really made any sense. It took me at least a year to get back into it – it was really hard.

'You could say I was heartbroken. When you're acting, you have this ready-made social life – all you do is go down to the hotel bar and there are your friends. But then I'd get home and feel really depressed. And it's hard to describe to your real friends what you've been through... it's a different life and it's very weird.

'Now I love the time I spend at home. I like to make sure that I see my friends and spend proper time with everybody; you can't take anything for granted.'

Her career is on the up again and, in 2005, she appears in two major films, *Love's Brother* with Adam Garcia, and *Winter Passing*, opposite Ed Harris, who, in 2000, directed the award-winning film *Pollock*, about the artist Jackson Pollock.

There is still a residue of warmth between Amelia and Colin. Glenda, who remains in close touch with Colin, says they are still friends. 'We don't meet every weekend and go to the pub,' Colin says. 'She is in London and I've been spending a lot of time working in LA. I loved her so much, and I don't want her to ever think that I'm not at the end of the phone. I wouldn't like that.'

Two months after the marriage ended, headlines screamed, 'FARRELL HAS GONE HAZEL NUTS!' In Dublin over Christmas, he had begun dating singer and model Hazel Kareswarren. Once the lead singer with the Dublin band Dove, she became a model, and went on Ireland's *The Late Late Show* to talk about her 'wonderful' breast implants. That fling came to a halt when he had to fly to Canada to start filming *The Recruit*.

Hazel said she was moving to London to concentrate on her singing career. Instead, she stayed in Ireland, got married and had two babies. 'She doesn't talk about Colin at all now,' said a friend of hers. 'That is another life entirely. She's got two children now and, if his name comes up, her husband gets furious.'

Back in LA for the New Year, he was seen with *Playboy* magazine's new 'Playmate of the Month' Nicole Narain. She was shorter than his usual taste, at only five foot four, but coming from British Guyana she had the soft curves, café au lait skin and thick, dark locks that he loves.

She'd been discovered by a *Playboy* photographer in a club in Chicago in 1998 and became one of their lingerie models. Then she moved to LA and graduated to *Playmate*, and became a genuine playmate to the likes of Colin, Nicolas Cage and Jerry Springer.

Her association with Colin didn't get her into pictures but she became a *Playboy* 'video nudie cutie', and now gets herself photographed a lot with celebrities who turn up at the Mansion Nightclub in Miami Beach. She also sells signed copies of nude photos of herself on the Internet for $25 each. A sweet girl who loves animals, who gives the impression of not being particularly bright, she is a survivor, swimming with sharks but avoiding, as she says, 'anyone controlling'.

After his steamy winter, in August he was seen 'playing tonsil tennis' on an aeroplane with lissom, darkly tanned Californian swimsuit model Josie Maran, pronounced 'Mair-an'. They met at an airport, made love on the plane and the affair lasted a few weeks. Five foot seven with chestnut hair and chocolate-brown eyes, she was an ambitious girl who'd been modelling since the age of 12, but keeps up a faux naivety about her own attractions. 'It's like I'm still figuring out why people would want to look at me,' she says. 'Maybe it's generic beauty, but it's weird to be valued for something I was born with.'

She learned to live with it and told a reporter, 'I love talking about sex. I'm good at loving. My dream is to have sex twice a day. Every time I get it, I want more. Guys are, like, "Whoa, slow down." With most guys, when it's time to stop I'm like, "No, it's not!" They can't keep up with me.'

She also stressed that she wasn't looking for marriage or even a long-term relationship. What more could a young Irishman abroad, just out of a sad marriage, ask for? Not only did she look like his ideal woman but also said her dream is 'to live on a beach and enjoy the good life'. In fact, she lives in Manhattan, and craves modelling contracts and a film career. She has been the face of Maybelline and Neutrogena, won a small role in a Canadian comedy film, *The Mallory Effect*, in 2002 and a small part as a club hostess in *The Aviator*.

She came to wider public notice in the USA by welcoming street magician David Blaine out of a block of ice after he'd been frozen in there for three days. They became a couple, which was no bad move, as Blaine, who has also dated Madonna in his time, is Hollywood's favourite trickster, performing stunts at parties for Al Pacino, Jack Nicholson, Mike Tyson and President Clinton.

But, at the end of that month, cruel headlines began to appear, such as 'SOME NEWS FOR AMELIA', and, much to the delight of gloating gossip columnists, Colin started seeing blonde, blue-eyed soap star Maeve Quinlan, who plays Megan Conley in the US daytime series *The Brave and the Beautiful*.

They were first spotted together one night at Château Marmont. 'They almost eat each other everywhere they go,' said one eyewitness. 'Even in the hotel lobby, their passion is unbridled.'

She does not resemble his usual girlfriends, being a 'Veronika the Viking' type rather than softly undulating and darker-skinned. But the attraction between them was irresistible. Not only had she been voted one of soap's Most Beautiful People, but also her parents came from Ireland. They still have property in Dublin and Wicklow and she has both US and Irish citizenship. Their rapport was instant, the kind that only comes when two fellow countrymen meet far from home. At a time when he was feeling insecure, she was also nine years older than Colin and physically very strong. He loved and needed her independence.

Before taking to acting, she'd been a professional tennis player. Seeded 85th in the world, she'd played at Wimbledon against Navratilova when she lost 6–4, 6–2, and competed in the US, French and Australian Opens. She'd given up the international tennis circuit because it made her too lonely. After the end of a tempestuous marriage in 1996 to Tom Sizemore – he was well known as a tough-guy actor and George Clooney look-a-bit-alike, having had parts in *Natural Born Killers*, *Saving Private Ryan* and *Pearl Harbour* – she was lonely again and looking for someone to love, but not too much.

'Maeve thinks the world of Colin, but she has had enough of marriage to last a lifetime,' said a friend of hers. She'd needed all her beauty and bravery to survive marriage to Sizemore. Throughout his career and his marriage to Maeve, he'd fought a constant battle with drugs. He said that Steven Spielberg had tested him for drugs every day throughout the filming of *Private Ryan*, and swore that if any drugs were found, even on the last day of filming, he'd cut Sizemore from the film and reshoot the whole thing.

Despite such support, in 2005 Sizemore twice tried to use an artificial penis to avoid being drug-tested by the police, and was caught out each time.

In January 1997, the police were called to their home in LA and Maeve claimed he had assaulted her. He was arrested then released on $50,000 bail and admitted he was addicted to heroin and crack cocaine. The marriage ended soon afterwards. He then became temporarily engaged to Heidi Fleiss, LA's number-one call girl who served three years in 1997 for a list of crimes including 'attempted pandering', or procuring prostitutes to serve her Hollywood clients.

Colin must have seemed like plain sailing after Tom, but they did not provide any lasting consolation to each other. Unlucky in love maybe, but he was a winner at everything else that mattered to him.

Having identified the part luck had played in his early career, Colin was about to get another big slice handed to him on a plate. In 2002, Ed Norton, a handsome young actor who had appeared in *Primal Fear*, and who had been chosen to star alongside Bruce Willis in the film *Hart's War*, suddenly dropped out. The film was to be directed by Gregory Hoblit, who was best known for his TV work on *NYPD Blue*, *Hill Street Blues* and *LA Law*. He and his backers at MGM urgently needed someone to step in fast.

It had to be someone who could sustain the large part of Lt Tommy Hart, aged 24, the same age as Colin, a privileged youth who had trained as a lawyer at the prestigious Yale University, but ended up a prisoner of war in Europe. The actor chosen had to carry almost the whole film. He also needed to be charismatic and good-looking... not that easy to find at short notice.

Hoblit had seen Colin's performance in *Tigerland* and he showed a print of the film to other producers and to Bruce Willis. Everyone liked what they saw. 'Colin just jumped off the screen. He was exactly what we were looking for,' says producer David Foster. 'It was very much a coming-of-age story, with a tremendous character arc for an actor to play.

Colin possessed at once both the youthfulness and the maturity as an actor to pull it off.

'As the new kid on the block, he had to step into that and grow from it, in terms of his acting and his character. It's a case of life imitating art. His journey happens on the set and on the screen, and it's fascinating to watch.

'I think it's exciting that many audiences will have few expectations of Colin. 'He's been in a few movies, but for many filmgoers the movie will introduce him and his character at the same time. There is a unique sense of discovery that happens with a new performer as talented as Colin, and I think audiences will really respond to him.'

They urgently needed him and he was perfect for the role – so this time he could name his price, which turned out to be £1.5 million. After such a short ascent to fame and fortune, Colin was a bit overwhelmed by the position he was now in, as a leading player next to cult hero Bruce Willis. He spoke to Hoblit about his feelings of unease about being paid what he called 'silly money' (for what turned out, fittingly, to be a rather silly film) and the apparent unfairness of all this success.

Why had he been chosen to play Tommy Hart and not the others? 'He said, "Will all that money infect things?"' says Hoblit. 'I said, "I know it is out there, and some guys might be saying, 'Why him, why not me, why am I not playing Tommy Hart?'" But I told him to make that feeling go away by not acting like a movie star and, after a few days, those feelings will go away.

'He's a really secure guy, with a solid set of values and a good family behind him. Money makes some people feel better than other people, but he is secure and knows who he is, and he knows he is a lucky guy.'

He was now working with A-list stars, something that was stunning for a boy who had once been rather star-struck. 'I've been really lucky,' he said, 'I haven't had a big film released in America, yet I am given a film part next to Bruce Willis. I grew up watching him in *Die Hard*, so it feels mad sitting opposite him in a room. It's unreal. And then you do the first scene and he fluffs a line, and he gave me advice, telling me to stick to my own guns and not take it too seriously.'

He also had to take in the strange rituals of Hollywood, in particular 'Method' acting, feeling the part yourself, rather than just learning the lines and pretending to be someone else. Although it was only mentioned in passing in the film that Tommy Hart went to Yale, before filming began, Colin, in order to 'feel' the part, had to spend time at Yale familiarising himself with Ivy League campus life, as if he couldn't possibly have imagined what it was like to be a privileged, well-educated young man.

Hoblit seemed doubtful that anyone as famous as Willis, playing Col William McNamara , could really be expected to act. 'I'm incredibly grateful to Willis because he's so right for the role,' he said. 'Bruce is a very good actor with a strong sense of leadership. That's something you can't fully "act". You have to have it. He's matured into someone who commands respect and can wear the uniform. Bruce just has the right bearing to be McNamara. He brings a real intensity to the set, both as an actor and because of who he is.'

Willis was pleased to be in the film. 'I've been a student of World War II for a long time,' he said ominously. 'I thought this was a great script, taut and exciting.'

Yet, throughout, he looks as if he really doesn't want to be there and rarely took any interest in the script.

Colin, always on time and word perfect, was fascinated by this new attitude to the acting craft. 'Don't get me wrong,' he says, 'Bruce is the loveliest fucking fellow. But the fucker couldn't remember a line to save his life. Or he learns them then fucks them up a lot. But it's funny and you slag him about it. One day, there was a scene where I said, "Objection, Your Honour." He looked at the script supervisor and said, "Line?"

'She whispered back, "Sustained," and he looked back at her and whispered back, "Sustained?"

'Later, I said to him, "You better go home now and get an early night. You have a word to learn tomorrow." He looked over at me and went, "Fuck you, you Irish prick."'

With this banter going on – Colin teasing the older man – they got on really well and, during a break in filming, Willis lent Colin his private jet so he could fly home for the Irish Film Festival.

It is perhaps no surprise that they became such pals. Apart from the fact that both have a riotous sense of humour, Willis had won in the Hollywood lottery, just as Colin was doing, and neither man could believe his luck. Willis had started life as the stuttering, insecure son of a welder. Like Colin, he had dropped out of school, got into all kinds of trouble, become a truck driver and a bit-part actor, then through the power of one big ABC TV hit, *Moonlighting*, opposite Cybill Shepherd, he'd become a multi-millionaire actor, getting nearly $20 million a picture.

For a decade before he had to play the older guy in *Hart's War*, he and his wife Demi had been Hollywood's hottest couple, playing out the American dream like no one else. Both were originally from the wrong side of the tracks, but by the time Colin met them they could boast an apartment in Manhattan, a luxurious home in Malibu and a whole town in Idaho which they'd bought together for $8 million. They were no longer hot favourites for film parts, but they were still Hollywood aristocracy.

Making the film, in the countryside of the Czech Republic, was tough. Most filming took place at night in temperatures often below freezing, over six weeks, and Willis found it

In 1995, Colin is pictured a long way from home as he poses for photos in Sydney, Australia.

As a line dancing instructor at the Break the Border pub in Dublin, Colin shows that the road to the top is never smooth.

Above: The camera loved Colin even in this hat as he models in Sydney, Australia, in 1995.

© *Rex Features*.

Below: With the cast of the 1998 TV series *Falling for a Dancer*.

© *Empics*.

Above: Colin with co-star Matthew Davies in the 2000 film *Tigerland*.

Below: Getting to play out his rebellious streak in 2001's *American Outlaws*.

Above: In his 2002 role in *Hart's War*, Colin looks sombre next to co-star Bruce Willis.

Below: Alongside Tom Cruise and Neal McDonough, Colin gets to grips with the advanced technology of 2002's blockbuster *Minority Report*.

Above: Colin is worried about his hair on the David Letterman show in 1993.

© *Getty Images.*

Below: At the 2003 Ireland Music Awards, Colin is in awe of rock icon Bono.

© *Getty Images.*

In the 2003 film *Daredevil*, Colin shows his menacing side as the hero's nemesis Bullseye.

© *Rex Features.*

Above left: Colin proves his acting credentials in 2003's ambitious *Phone Booth*.

© *Rex Features*.

Above right: As Jim Street in *S.W.A.T*, showing how good he looks in uniform.

© *Rex Features*.

Below: Alongside Al Pacino in the 2003 film *The Recruit*.

© *Rex Features*.

particularly demanding. 'No matter how good a mood I was in, about ten minutes before our car arrived at the set I would start to get depressed,' says Bruce Willis. 'I wasn't sure why until I realised it was the camp itself, which was bleak and miserable. It made this one of the most physically demanding roles I've done.'

Colin, accompanied by sister Claudine as his paid assistant, didn't find it so physically difficult. He didn't expect any luxuries, and his imagination was stirred by the idea of life lived in the close confinement in a POW camp.

The camp, a character in its own right, and one of the least wooden elements of the film, was built around a former Red Army barracks near the village of Milovice, an hour's drive from Prague.

'The camp experience was intense, to say the least,' he says. 'It gave us, in the smallest sense, an idea of what the prisoners had to contend with. Along with the obvious physical hardship, they endured extreme mental stress. Constant surveillance from the guards, no privacy, no moments to yourself. There was no sense of the future because they couldn't see past tomorrow.'

On the first night of filming, a blizzard created a stunning vista for a wide shot in which 1,500 soldiers are being marched on a moonlit night through the woods and into the eerily lit camp. There were also some real physical dangers. The Russians had left over 300 live landmines behind them when they left. All had to be made safe and removed before filming could start.

Colin was more bothered by Prague than the countryside. Some filming was done in the Barrandov Studios in Prague, a site once requisitioned by Hitler's film-makers to make Nazi propaganda films after they'd invaded Czechoslovakia. Late one night, he and the producer David Ladd were attacked in the street by a group of gypsies. Ladd had his money, phone and camera stolen, but Colin was able to fight them off. 'Prague is a mad, mad city,' he says, 'there is fucking darkness to be found there. I couldn't wait to get out and I'll never go back.'

But the cinema audience only sees the camp itself. Cold, confining and austere, a little like Castleknock College, it is an uncompromising place where the Germans act like prefects and constantly make the men stop playing poker or get out of their warm beds to attend roll call.

When they released it, 20th Century Fox gave *Hart's War* the weighty tag line: 'Beyond courage, beyond honor'. They might also have added 'beyond belief'.

It is a real prison-camp yarn. Inside the wire, all are subject to the whim of one man, German Colonel Werner Visser, played rather alluringly by Marcel Lures, who adopts a soft Mittel-European accent, suggesting a man with whom you might well have had tea and pastries in better times. His authority is absolute, or so he thinks. Firm but fair, he's no horrible Hun, but he hasn't heard of the Geneva Convention or, if he has, he doesn't let it prey too much on his mind. When challenged by McNamara for disregarding the rules of war, his response is icy and final: 'Look around you, Colonel. This is not Geneva.'

Lures gives one of the best performances in the film, as a man bored and fed up with the situation they all find themselves in, not unlike Willis.

As the camp's highest-ranking American officer, McNamara is silently waiting for his moment to strike back at the enemy. Here the film gets into very dark waters. Two black US airmen come into the camp, Lt Archer and Lt Lincoln Scott from the 99th Airborne Division, a Negro section of the US Airforce. They are immediately singled out for bad treatment by the enlisted men in 'Rio', or Barracks 27, who call them 'niggers and flying bell hops', worse terms than those used by the Germans, who call them '*Schwartzers*'.

As an officer, Colin is forced by McNamara to move in there to try to keep order as racial tensions start simmering like a cornpone stew.

The racists are led by Sergeant Vic Bedford, an unpleasant black-marketeer. There is quite a lot of bitching in the barracks and the Germans make things worse by putting on films showing Aryan girls performing gymnastics, which no one seems to want to watch. While they are all being forced to watch the film, Lt Archer is framed by someone putting a stolen tent spike into his bed, to make it look as if he was trying to escape. He is hauled off and executed.

When McNamara rouses himself to complain, Colonel Visser accuses the Americans of being racist. A fine one to talk, but, when Bedford is found dead by the night latrine and the other Negro officer is accused of his murder, Colin's character demands a fair trial for him.

Visser is sceptical and starts going on about lynching in Alabama again, but the trial goes ahead, with Colin as the defence council. As a lawyer, Colin as Tommy looks more like a choirboy. There are a lot of profile shots of him in the courtroom scenes, showing the surprising delicacy of his tip-tilted nose. He had probably never looked better on screen, at least with a lot of clothes on, his cold, stone-white face looking almost luminous against his soot-black brows, five-o'clock shadow and dull, olive-green uniform, a vintage army original loaned by a costumier in Los Angeles.

Tommy Hart doesn't do too well against the defence, and he visits Visser, who turns out to have been at Yale, too, 'Class of '28,' he says wistfully. He also has a love of the BBC and Negro jazz. A bit of a softy at heart, when he is not executing people without trial. He obviously has an interest in Tommy, which could be sexual, but this is not explored; the men give each other pats, slaps and bear hugs now and then, but we

COLIN FARRELL: LIVING DANGEROUSLY

never understand how they really feel about each other.

Visser's feelings are mainly paternal and all the main characters, even the Negro officers, apparently have fathers who fought with distinction in the First World War, and some of them are fathers themselves, worrying or grieving over their sons.

Confused paternal feelings as well as war and racism become themes in the film. After accepting a book on law from Visser, Tommy does better in court and McNamara is furiously angry. Visser brings up Alabama again. It's a pity they don't organise a proper debate, but instead there is a lot of muttering and brooding.

Then, during a break from the trial, Tommy discovers what he was not supposed to know, that, in fact, McNamara is planning a major escape through a tunnel.

If the camp was as much a character as a setting, then the tunnel is a star. Lit by electric light, high and broad with a perfect support structure, it appears to have been designed and built by a crack team of civil engineers. No claustrophobia or crawling along on your belly in the dirt for these boys; it is wide enough for them to walk out upright holding hands in a crocodile.

The murder of Bedford and the trial is all a ruse to distract the Germans while 35 men escape along the tunnel, and blow up a nearby munitions plant which is disguised as a shoe factory. 'Everything here is a lie,' as Tommy puts it to McNamara.

The Germans, even apparently the gunners in the watch towers, are transfixed by the trial and the escape goes ahead unnoticed. While Tommy goes on fighting for Scott's life, men come up like moles beyond the wire. Then the escape is discovered and all the people taking part in the trial are ordered to line up to be shot. The escaping men are presumably loaded with TNT as the munitions factory is blown up a few moments later, and McNamara trades his life for those of his men. Visser, irritated beyond belief, shoots him dead, and all the men weep and salute.

Visser gives Tommy a lingering, rather contrite look and goes off back to his BBC news reports and his jazz records.

Colin's voiceover then tells us that the war ended three months later, Lt Scott got home safely and was able to teach his son about honour.

This film, which cost $80 million, was really a wasted chance. Author John Katzenbach wrote the novel *Hart's War* in 2001, based on the experiences of his father, who spent 27 months as a prisoner-of-war during World War II. However, once it reached the desks of Hollywood producers such as David Ladd and David Foster, it was quickly taken away from Katzenbach and given to a committee of writers. It was meant to be 'an opportunity to write an open love letter to the men who served and suffered during World War II... a cinematic tip of the hat.'

You can see that they exhaustively researched the daily life of soldiers and the hardships of men in captivity, from their maggot soup to their nocturnal farting contests, but somewhere along the line the human interest and the credibility of the story vaulted over the wire or dug itself out.

Hoblit, however, was pleased with the end product. 'I thought the story was loaded with wonderful characters whose lives I wanted to explore. Certainly, this film has lots of impressive bells and whistles – airplanes and explosions and stunts – but at its core it's an intimate story of men interacting under duress. That's the most enjoyable thing for me as a director – working with great words and great actors, people just talking to each other.'

In fact, there is not enough talking to each other at all, just a lot of speeches about duty and honour so that the film becomes a strange mishmash of *To Kill a Mockingbird*,

Conduct Unbecoming, The Great Escape, The Wooden Horse, Slaughterhouse Five, Saving Private Ryan and *Driving Miss Daisy*, all rolled unhappily into one.

The film nosedived at the box office. But it had been an outstanding lead role for Colin (he won Best Actor at the Shanghai International Film Festival Golden Globe Awards) and he shone on screen, not only delivering a rather sensitive, intense performance as young Tommy, but somehow managing to bring some integrity to what was an impossible yarn. He also gained a philosophical attitude towards working on big-budget films.

Willis had kindly advised him not to take things too seriously, and he could see that was important. 'You're in a multi-million-dollar movie with Bruce Willis, and then you think, What has happened to it? But there is no rhyme or reason. The good thing about movie acting is there is no science to getting it right or wrong, or else every movie would be a hit. I work hard, I take the money and I take it all with a pinch of salt. And I realise I am a lucky little cock.'

He became more relaxed about the money he earned from what he called 'a silly way to make a living'. At home in Dublin, he celebrated becoming a millionaire rather cautiously by buying two cottages on Tritonville Road, close to his first cottage in Ringsend, including one for brother Eamon, and he helped his mother buy a terraced house in Albert College Road, Glasnevin, in Dublin 9, about a mile from her former home in Castleknock.

He also bought five new flats at Spencer Quays in Dublin, paying £1.5 million for the investment. The glossy brochure for the Spencer development shows beautiful people with wraparound teeth sipping orange juice and lying gracefully on couches while using the latest laptops, hinting at the kind of lifestyle that Colin at least was about to enjoy.

The whole city from the suburbs to the airport is currently

being turned into a building site, as the city undergoes the most extensive urban-regeneration programme in Europe, costing 2.5 billion euros. Tower blocks are being replaced with masses of 'residential units'; even old Georgian buildings such as the one housing the waxworks are being swept away in the effort to transform the once reticent ancient capital into a gleaming global hub, or at least something along the lines of Seattle or Vancouver.

Property was an increasingly wise investment and Colin is what is known in Irish slang as a 'cute hoor', a term defined by Colin Murphy in his book of Irish slang, as 'a suspiciously resourceful gentleman'.

He now knew his price and what was required. 'I've got good genes,' he said, his own life proving that anatomy was destiny. 'I've got my parents to thank for where I am now. They are fucking beautiful and they've given me a face which Hollywood thinks it can use to sell $80 million movies.'

'I've got to admit that I am not hard on the eye, although I hate looking at myself.'

But then he adds in his usual self-deprecating way that is probably the only thing that keeps him from being assaulted by other jealous males, 'but when I see my face on a billboard, I love it. I won't masturbate to anything else.'

The mention of masturbation does suggest a certain amount of loneliness. A coming man, he was coming alone, and soon he was back living alone in LA. When a reporter at the time asked him how he spent his evenings, he said, 'Usually in a hotel room reading a script. I'd be in trouble if I lived here permanently,' he told another reporter. 'I'm just a normal Irish person and LA is the loneliest city in the world. I've been in a room with 100 people and never felt so alone. And how do you get out of a place while remaining there geographically? I can understand how some actors get screwed up on drugs. You get all these people floating round being nice and you don't know what is real and what isn't. I am trying to figure it all out.'

This was a far cry from his original thrill at being in a hotel in Santa Monica and inviting strangers back. His dreams had all come true and it was now a matter of living with them.

CHAPTER SIX

GREAT REPORT FOR
THE NEW RECRUIT

Just four days after his gruelling weeks in the Czech Republic, he found himself on a film set with Steven Spielberg – in 2005 voted the world's greatest film director by 10,000 readers of *Empire* magazine – and Tom Cruise, the most successful movie star alive.

Minority Report was based on a short story by the extraordinary science-fiction seer Philip K Dick, whose novel *Do Androids Dream of Electric Sheep?* had been turned into the cult film *Blade Runner*.

Directed by Sir Ridley Scott, it made stars out of Harrison Ford and Daryl Hannah, and created a whole new genre of science fiction, based on real anxieties about the future with its fears of genetic engineering and advanced methods of surveillance and social control, not to mention terrifying shopping malls.

Minority Report is about a cop, played by Cruise, working in Washington in 2054, in a division of the police department that arrests killers before they commit the crimes, courtesy of some future-viewing technology, and some Martian mutants who have prophetic powers. Cruise's character has the tables turned on him when he is accused of a future crime and must find out what brought it about and stop it before it can happen.

Powerful and convincing, it was to be the breakthrough film for Colin. He got $2.5 million up front and this was the film in which anyone who hadn't already heard of him sat up and said, 'Who is that?' adding unanimously, 'He is *gorgeous*. We want more of him.'

He won his role as Detective Danny Witwer by luck, yet again. 'Matt Damon was supposed to do the part originally,' he says, 'but, because of his work on *Bourne Identity*, he couldn't make it, so I was lucky enough to get the call from Spielberg. He'd seen one of my films. And I went over and spent 20 minutes talking with him and sharing a sardine sandwich with him and I got offered the part. I'm not a part stealer but I am a sweeper-up.'

Dutch actor Yorick van Wageningen, 41, and Javier Bardem had also been considered for the role of Danny. Alas, poor Yorick, his agent did not act speedily enough to get him a work permit for the USA, so he had to drop out, and Bardem said he didn't want to 'just run around chasing Tom Cruise'.

Spielberg wanted Colin precisely because he didn't think he would chase his biggest star around. 'I wanted to find somebody that could hold the floor with Tom,' he told a reporter on the CBS *Early Show*, just before the film was released. 'I wanted to find an actor that you would actually look at and listen to and be compelled by. I didn't want Tom to suck all the air out of the room. So I tried to find somebody very, very strong to play all of the scenes with him. Colin was able to stand up and hold his own with Tom, which is a credit to Colin.'

So Colin found himself on a film set with Tom Cruise, not yet 40 years old, but having already amassed a fortune in the realm of $45 million. His films had grossed about $2.5 billion worldwide, leagues ahead of Pacino and even Jack Nicholson.

Minority Report was originally planned as a direct sequel to *Total Recall*, with Tom Cruise's character played by Arnold Schwarzenegger. But Spielberg, who had inherited the project from someone else, wanted only Cruise, even though he cost at least a million dollars more than the muscle-bound Austrian.

This was a long-awaited collaboration for Spielberg and Cruise and, in part, it would be a project about their mutual admiration. The great director wanted that particular actor simply because he liked him. 'I like his style,' he explained. And Cruise had been watching Spielberg for years.

'I loved *Jaws*,' says Cruise, in his sunny schoolboy way. 'It scared me so much I jumped over three people sitting near me in the cinema. And I saw *ET* with my family. Spielberg has given us so much cinema joy, he's an amazing artist and an amazing person. Everyone wants to work with him. I cherished every moment.'

Spielberg and Cruise together were seen as so powerful that they could have whatever they wanted and do whatever they wished. Fox didn't see them as employees, but as partners, men who would share in every dollar as soon as it came in.

To keep costs below the $100 million mark – they were likely to be huge because of the special effects – Spielberg and Cruise turned down any salary in exchange for 15% of the box-office takings. This system, only open to Hollywood greats in the league of Jack Nicholson and Tom Cruise, is called 'first dollar'. The director and the lead actor would get 30 cents between them for every dollar Fox collected from ticket sales. This left the studio with 70 cents out of every dollar to cover production and marketing. Studios get half the price of every ticket bought for a film.

But they still needed to take $180 million in the USA alone to make any real money on it, and only 18 films in the previous three years had achieved that.

It was no sure thing, even with Spielberg's prodigious talent and reputation and Cruise's winning smile, but the studios were prepared to take the risk – after all, their names alone would attract massive audiences, especially overseas. They could also provide a valuable captive audience as the people who came to see them would also see all the trailers on the screen for forthcoming films.

Colin was now stepping into a film world that was almost beyond ordinary risk. This was going to be a different style of film from anything he'd experienced before; this was upper-class Hollywood at play.

English actress Samantha Morton, best known for her Oscar-nominated role in Woody Allen's *Sweet and Lowdown* in 1999, was brought in, an exotic outsider like Colin. She candidly summed up the value of her part in *Minority Report*, saying, 'Working with someone as powerful as Spielberg is a luxury. On one level, a film set is just a film set, but beyond that there is another magic I had never experienced before. That magic is when people have the money to be free to do what they want to do. So often, the frustrations on a film set are, "We can't afford to do that. We haven't enough time." To have the time and the energy and dedication to be able to do what you want is just a luxury.'

This was film-making at its most enjoyable – as part of a selected elite, an aristocracy who didn't have to worry about the usual considerations of money or time, because there was plenty of both.

Having gathered all the right people together, including classy European actor Max Von Sydow, once famous for his work with Ingmar Bergman, people could relax, take tea, be nice to each other and explore ideas, like students at a film college. They also had licence to put themselves into the film in an intimate, personal way.

Tom Cruise began filming only days after completing work on *Vanilla Sky*, with Cameron Diaz and his new love Penelope Cruz. As an in-joke, Cameron Crowe, his director in that film, appears in *Minority Report* as a commuter on a train and Cameron Diaz also turns up as an extra on the train.

Characters were called after people that Cruise and Spielberg admired, such as Agatha Christie, Dashiell Hammett, who wrote *The Maltese Falcon*, and Arthur Conan Doyle, the creator of Sherlock Holmes. Von Sydow's character is named after writer Anthony Burgess who wrote *A Clockwork Orange*, which became the first great futuristic film of the sound era.

Colin was now among powerful players having fun with private little games. But there were serious considerations, of course. At the time, great as they were, Spielberg and Cruise were both rather bruised, so they had a lot resting on the success of the film.

Spielberg had just made the disastrous film *AI*, which had only earned $78.5 million at the box office, while Cruise had broken up with his wife Nicole who was fast becoming more famous than her ex-partner. They had appeared together three years previously in the hugely disappointing, if not embarrassing fiasco of *Eyes Wide Shut*, Stanley Kubrick's last film.

Now both men needed something good to work on, something that had the smell of success. Colin came along with less baggage, not yet internationally famous, and for him the project was an enormous challenge. For once, he wasn't likely to eclipse everyone else on screen; he was now up against the gleaming smile of Tom Cruise, American's Mr Wonderful, the man Oliver Stone once called 'the kid off the

Wheaties box', whom another writer recently termed 'a guy with a halo turned on at all times'.

It would have been a tough job for any young actor. On his first day working with Cruise, he described himself as 'shit scared'.

'The first day I arrived, I completely forgot I'd have to do a scene staring into Tom Cruise's eyes,' he says. 'I had a meltdown; I did many takes.'

Colin as Danny looks like Daniel McCarthy from *Falling for a Dancer*, with slick black hair oiled down and stiff collar, but this is an American Dan, who, although he sounds vaguely Irish, chews gum while he talks and lifts his top lip in a kind of Elvis leer.

It is not really a very assured performance but he makes a brave stab at it and largely wins. 'I just came in with a certain attitude and a certain confidence that the character has in himself and his knowledge,' he says. 'I don't know anything about being a federal agent or any legalistic jargon.' He played it off the cuff but was obviously a little shy. He also found that, after a heavy night out 'on the batter', the next day he found it was almost impossible to say the line, 'Surely you understand the fundamental questionability of pre-crime methodology?'

A film of the actors on set shows Colin looking a little jittery, and Spielberg looking like a jolly schoolteacher going through some of his lines with him, in a deliberately funny camp voice, making light of the whole thing.

'Steven is incredibly open,' says Colin. 'While being incredibly smart, he sees everything through a child's eyes, and he gets so excited about new ideas. Every idea of mine, even if they were mediocre at best, he would say, "Try that." It makes you just want to do the best job you can for him.'

Cruise agreed. 'Steven's always bouncing ideas around,' he said, 'coming up with new ways of doing things. There's a sequence in the film with all these mechanical spiders and I guess I thought it would all be planned out in advance. But he uses all sorts of stuff as a starting point and the speed at which he thinks of new ideas was dizzying to me.'

Dick's work is also full of ideas, which have been used by Hollywood in *Blade Runner* and *Total Recall*, but, in terms of sophistication, *Minority Report* is way ahead of these previous films. Not as dark as *Blade Runner*, and based more in reality, it deals with disturbing ethical matters which affect everyone and increasingly threaten us in the future with the advancement of genetic engineering. Like *Blade Runner*, it creates a Dystopian world in the future, but not a place of chaos. This time everything is orderly, a place that looks like faded picture postcards, a kind of 1930s dinginess sometimes alleviated by the sickly colours of fast-food outlets, where reality is similar to our own but just slightly distorted enough to be worrying.

There is no murder, and the public are delighted by this, but the system is cruelly flawed. Murder is foreseen by the 'pre-cogs', mutants with pre-cognitive or psychic powers, twin boys and Agatha, played with great delicacy by Samantha Morton. They are practically slaves, shaved bald and kept prisoner in a kind of relaxation tank.

Although Samantha loved making the film, she hated having to act in a tank of water, something she said she'd never get used to, and her plight, as an actress and a character, is painful to watch.

Cruise, as Captain John Anderton, is an unhappy man, uneasy about pre-crime control, as he gradually realises that murder has become a thought crime and he soon finds himself framed for a potential murder and believes Detective Danny Witwer, who is snooping about for the government, has arranged this plot, as they want to close the experiment down. The government doesn't come across as benevolent, though, and certainly not caring, and Colin's character is confusing.

He seems to be a very arrogant tyro, someone that the cooler, more knowing Cruise could easily knock down to size. 'An arsehole', as Colin would put it.

'But he's not a bad guy,' says Colin. 'Not all right either... he's annoying... annoying and kind of self-centred and all of that. Very sleazy, too, but on the side of good, I suppose. Yeah. He thinks that all the things he is doing are for the good; he does everything for the right reasons.'

What many people will enjoy most about the film are its special effects. Cruise is armed with small storage media, clear plastic versions of Iomega's PocketZip discs, and a tiny in-ear cell phone, as he fights against terrifying powers, including policemen wearing jetpacks and electronic surveillance spiders which can't help being just a little bit cute.

They may have no murder, but this futuristic Washington is not a happy society. It is a world where video cameras have taken over, and you practically need ID to get into your own bed and, if you look under the bed, insects are listening to you by short-wave radio. Even adverts on TV screens in shopping malls know who you are.

The film also uses an amazingly prophetic idea by Dick, who died in 1982, of identification based on recognition of the human iris, now a routine process for identity cards. Taken to extremes, looking into eyes for reasons of security is an intrusive and unpleasant system and, in this film, there are a lot of eyeballs on show.

The film opens with an extreme close-up shot of an open eye, exactly the same opening as *Blade Runner*, and the eye motif is repeated throughout. People are identified by their irises, so in one *grand guignol* scene, Anderton has both his eyes removed by a back-street surgeon and replaced by someone else's, in order to evade arrest and carry on his pursuit of the man he thinks really committed a murder. In *Blade Runner*, Rutger Hauer's character also has artificial eyes, put in by a 'genetic engineer'.

Like certain jokes, certain hi-tech film tricks never fail to grab an audience. Anderton needs at least one of his own orbs to get back into his own building, so he has to keep the bloody eyeballs in a plastic bag and there is a scene of black comedy where he drops the eyes and has to chase them down a corridor as they roll away like ping-pong balls.

There is a lot of story, a lot of clues to follow, but all this is made clear and understandable and, at the same time, it is a very human story, about real characters.

Spielberg loves sci-fi, but he also loves film noir with its emphasis on twisted human motives. He doesn't judge too much, he likes people and relished putting in a whole host of minor characters, sometimes quite comic and all brilliantly acted.

Perhaps the most outstanding is Lois Smith as the sinister Dr Iris Hineman, the person who invented the whole terrible system, a role originally offered to Meryl Streep. An elderly lady in a straw hat, she drifts about her greenhouse full of terrifying plants, full of regret, but also sneaks a kiss with Tom Cruise full on the lips, which he politely pretends not to notice.

In bringing together all these disparate roles, and telling a very complex story in a lightly humorous way, Spielberg was at the top of his game and everyone who worked with him benefited and adored him, and they even got on with each other.

Colin plays well against Cruise. In the past, they could have worked as partners in a cop show or even brothers in a Western, there is that frisson of difference between them, dark and fair, one cute and feckless, one handsome and more introspective.

'Working with Tom was always extremely positive,' says Colin. 'He was always fucking great on set to all the actors and the crew. Forget that bullshit about extras not being allowed to look at him, that's a load of fucking wank. He was very generous. Obviously ambitious, very strong and very, very competitive, but really, a very generous fellow.

'Having said that, we didn't exactly pal around. That wouldn't have happened in a million years. I really had a good time with him, I've seen him around but I don't really know him. I mean, he's Tom Cruise. He's got so much going in his life. I never got to have a drink with him after work, but why the fuck would he?'

In fact, although Cruise probably doesn't know it, there are also some surprising similarities between them. They had both been educated by Franciscan monks, and both came from troubled childhoods with broken homes. Cruise was mainly brought up by his mother and he was 12 when his father left his family. Colin's parents broke up when he was slightly older. His father had been overbearing in the first part of his life, but absent emotionally.

In their lives, it seems that Cruise and Colin have a burning need to prove they can succeed on their own, as if they are both telling their absent fathers that they really don't need them. Both are workaholics, which Colin thinks is a good thing; up early, never late, practically word perfect by the time they first appear on set, both are really determined to deserve their million-plus.

They also share the successful actors' problem of utter single-mindedness. They are successful in part because work rather than relationships is at the centre of their lives. But, because of the stress and the tensions built up by acting for a living, they both suffer from excessive energy which has to find an outlet; in Cruise's case, in his adherence to Scientology, in Colin's, carousing and lechery.

In their careers, they have repeatedly been involved in films exploring the father–son relationship, which occurs again in *Minority Report*. Despite the originality of the film, in time-honoured tradition, Colin's character has a powerful dead father, also a federal agent, whom he has to live up to.

The patriarch in the film, a role which seems almost obligatory in US films, is provided by a brooding Max Von Sydow as Lamar Burgess, the man in charge of the pre-crime project.

'He is our father figure in the story,' says Spielberg, as if he accepts this as an integral element of any story, 'a surrogate father to Anderton.'

Burgess is a flawed, duplicitous father and Anderton has to bring him down in order to survive. But *Minority Report* was not just another of those syrupy films about sons and dads, a film made for teenagers presumed by studios to need cheap thrills, reassurance and easy resolutions. It was about interesting problems, including the concept of free will, and it touched on issues of basic liberty, which are increasingly to the fore in the public mind, whether it is about protecting society against possible terrorists, or dealing with mental-health patients, who might or might not be dangerous.

For a sci-fi film, this was very grown-up stuff. Cruise called it 'a summer film for grown-ups'. But it was far more grounded in psychology and realism than most summer films. He and Spielberg loved making it so much that, in 2005, they got together again to make *War of the Worlds*, based on the HG Wells sci-fi novel.

The public loved *Minority Report* and, by Cruise's 40th birthday on 3 July 2002, it was number one at the US box office and a worldwide hit. Critics hailed it the first great film of 2002.

Hart's War made $32 million at the box office but *Minority Report* grossed $353 million, almost on a par with the phenomenal success of *Spider-Man* and clearly beating *Star Wars: Episode 2* which took $250 million.

Colin took a more personal view of the film, calling it his 'most successful film', because it was 'seen by a lot of people'. Aside from the money, he really wanted to be known, to be recognised up there on the silver screen; that had always been his secret ambition, his passion, above all others.

It had been a challenge, but it had paid off. In six years, he'd gone from the Ardmore Studios 12 miles from Dublin, and going home to his mother every night after work, to 20th Century Fox and living in a luxury hotel. Still only 27, he'd appeared in 11 films. His mentors now included the likes of Steven Spielberg and Tom Cruise. He had arrived and this was success with a capital 'S', and professionally beyond anything he could have envisaged when he first booked that hotel room in Santa Monica.

But 2003 was to be his wonder year when he appeared in no fewer than six films. He was the new darling of Hollywood, and they dearly love an Irish bad boy, especially if he is not so wild in real life, secretly quite even-tempered, pleasing to work with and, of course, 'gorgeous', which is a word women of a certain age always seem to use for him.

After *Minority Report*, he told reporters he planned to go hiking round the world for six months, grow a beard and 'find himself'. He got as far as Vietnam, for eight days. 'Pipe dreams,' he says, exasperated with himself. 'And I never did get the beard going. It's like I'll go into a bookshop and buy some books with the romantic notion that I'm going to get through them – and then I never read them. I'm a complete idiot in that way. Once I've said something, it's like it's fucking done. Ridiculous.'

He was now much too hot a property to go off and investigate personal growth. He was the darling of Hollywood. Marcia Ross, the large and imposing casting director at Disney, wasted no time in snapping him up to play opposite Al Pacino in *The Recruit*. 'I loved him in *Tigerland*,' she purrs. 'When I saw that, I thought, We wanna go with this guy and we gotta go with it now before everyone else gets to him. When you spot it in someone, it is very precious.'

Again, it was his confidence and charisma that attracted her, not to mention those peaty dark eyes and Peter Pan nose.

So, after Cruise, he was lined up next to Pacino, the actor he and Glenda had watched as kids in the local cinema. Colin was suitably awed. 'He's a legend, a craftsman and a genius,' he says. 'I was over the moon when I found out I was working with him. When you grow up on films such as *Dog Day Afternoon*, it was like a dream come true. It was scary. I was nervous to start with. I nearly shit myself the first time I was on set with him, but he was brilliant and I loved it.

'I'd find myself watching Pacino rehearse his lines, and it was always amazing to feel I was part of his team. It never felt normal, but I got used to it.'

He was helped a little by having his mother with him on the set. 'I am totally a mummy's boy,' he told reporters at the time. 'I'm so close to her that I even managed to get her a walk-on part in the film, then I couldn't get her off the set afterwards.'

The Recruit is a result of the outpouring of emotion following 9/11 that takes us back to films of the 1950s praising the work of the 'G-Men' and the FBI. Colin did it because it meant playing opposite Pacino, but why Pacino chose to do it is another question.

Pacino plays Walter Burke, the tough instructor at a school for would-be CIA operatives. He seems dedicated to his pupils but, sadly, he has a goatee beard so, according to US screen codes, we know that he must be up to no good.

James Douglas Clayton, played by Colin, is apparently an

intellectual genius, getting straight 'A's in college for subjects most people have never heard of. He has also 'lived overseas' and so knows about how potentially dangerous 'foreigners' think. He is recruited by Pacino, although it is done in an unorthodox way, speaking in riddles in a bar.

We are told that James is a fatherless boy, as so many heroes are in US films. His father Edward Clayton, a hero of the CIA, died mysteriously in a plane crash in Peru.

In this film, the CIA is an unquestioned force for good; names like Hammas and Abu Nidal are thrown about against a background of intense music, which pounds out relentlessly, even when nothing is happening.

Burke's recruits are taken down to 'the farm', where they are trained to 'save the world', a real quote from Pacino's character. 'We are here because we believe in good and evil and we choose good,' he intones paranoiacally, 'our cause is just and our enemies are everywhere all around us. There is some scary stuff out there.'

On the farm 'where everything is a test', they are trained to be covert operatives, 'with or without diplomatic immunity'. In other words, it's so scary out there, no rules apply any longer. He says his class will be taught to undertake reconnaissance and detective work, learn tactical high-speed driving and use lie detectors. They are also given a lot of James Bond-type gadgets to play with.

Of course, there is a slight erotic charge from seeing Colin and the other beautiful young actors around him all sitting in class. His male colleagues are all reminiscent of Superman and the girls appear to have been snatched from modelling schools. Of this cream of American youth, only Colin is allowed to look a bit unconventional – dark, slightly dishevelled, wearing a black leather jacket and black vest, a bit like Marlon Brando in *On the Waterfront*.

At the same time, he is all round chin and pouty mouth, a

boy-man who is just a little bit rebellious, but really loves his teacher, the stern older mentor.

During a lie-detector test, he discovers that Layla Moore, a girl in his class played by Bridget Moynahan, loves him, but she is annoyed that he has used the test to find this out and it is the start of a very on-off romance.

After some rough treatment during training, in which we get a flash of some of his intimate tattoos, Colin apparently fails the course and is booted out.

Not surprisingly, Burke turns up again in the dead of night to tell him that he was really the best student they've ever had. It was all a ruse, and there is a mole among them. He says Layla is really working for secret forces in the Middle East.

Colin finds her and befriends her again in front of the Iwo Jima Memorial in Washington, which is dedicated to 6,821 US Marines who died defending two small islands south of Tokyo in World War II. This is one of the most emotive symbols of US heroism and, in a film like this, a rather cheap use of an expensive debt.

To keep things going, there is a brief shot of a very slender Layla in the shower, a bit like an advert for shampoo. They have a steamy lovemaking session, which manages to be totally un-erotic, after which he gets up and hacks into her computer, a new slant on post-coital etiquette. She is naturally annoyed but they get back together. She is seen later preparing a hearty breakfast, although she has obviously never eaten anything more than melon in her life, and so the duel between them goes on.

On set, following Richard Burton's dictum again, he was strongly attracted to Moynahan. Born in New York in 1970, she was a child athlete who became a fashion model for *Glamour* and *Vogue*. She once came 86th out of 102 in a 'Sexiest Woman in the World' contest held by *Stuff* magazine.

'What an amazing fucking woman,' said Colin in his inimitable way.

Along the way, he'd formulated a kind of ideal woman, whom he once described as 'humorous but tough, someone who can do her thing, hold her own and not be too affected by other people'. Moynahan was almost the image of this fantasy, and proved her sense of humour by appearing in seven episodes of *Sex in the City*, playing Natasha, a character dubbed 'the idiot stick figure with no soul'. One episode in June 2000 was called 'Attack of the Five-Foot Ten-Inch Woman'.

'I loved working with Bridget,' says Colin. 'I had a great time. She's a stunning chick. Beautiful but strong as an ox. Fucking tough, knows who she is and she's bold as brass but she's got that underlying softness as well, and sweet as they come and so cool.

'I'm not talking about chemistry, nothing happened between us, but our sex scene on set was fine. They are not always easy, there is nothing you can fucking do. You either like the person you're with and you have a laugh and you take it with a pinch of salt, or it doesn't work out at all. Bridget and I were such good pals.

'We had already been out on the piss together so our love scene was just another good day on the set.'

Sadly for him, or perhaps he was subconsciously relieved, she was unobtainable, another of his atomised female icons, of the type he once loved in magazines. When they met on set, she was in love with National Football League player Tom Brady, so he didn't make any headway off set.

There is a sudden twist at the end of the film, and nothing is as it seems, just as in *Hart's War* the trusting younger man realises he has been duped by his father figure. 'The CIA are just a fat bunch of white guys who were asleep when we needed them most,' he says, referring to the intelligence blunders that led to 9/11.

'Don't you understand the complexity of things?' says Pacino, who understands so much complexity that he doesn't know which side he is on, or so we are led to believe.

At the end of the film, Pacino desperately reprises his role as Richard III on his last legs at the Battle of Bosworth, and dies in a hail of bullets. Colin's character weeps for the lost older male, just as he did in *Hart's War*.

The film has the artistic merit of an explosion in a cheese factory, but Colin genuinely loved working with Pacino. The older actor was equally generous but perhaps more guarded about the work they were sharing when he said, 'I think Colin was magnificent in this picture. You really see why the studios have been touting him. My advice to him would be not to run after the money, but to keep his mind on what he likes to do and what he relates to.' In other words, in future do something a lot better than this.

But back in Ireland, his old friends such as Glenda were thrilled and astonished to see how far their friend had got in his film career. 'It was so funny to see Colin up there next to Al Pacino, my favourite actor,' she says. 'But fair play to him, I always knew he had it in him to be a big success.'

Conal Kearney, one of his drama teachers from the Gaiety, was also ecstatic. 'He's a genius,' he enthused, 'a rare talent. I have no doubt he will get an Oscar, or even two or three.'

There was no Oscar nomination but the film was a big commercial hit, blowing away *Spy Games*, an espionage drama starring Brad Pitt, and it pushed Colin up into the league of Hollywood big earners, requiring about $5 million at least to climb out of bed in the afternoon.

He went home for Christmas at the end of 2002 feeling happy with his career, and he was soon back at his old haunts, such as Reynard's. Inside, the walls pound with the music of U2, it's very dark and greasy menus offer cocktails called 'Lust' and 'Between the Sheets'.

'Colin still goes there because, no matter how famous you are, Robbie will see to it that you can really chill out,' says a friend. 'If he really likes you, you get to go to the VIP section upstairs with a private bar and snooker table.'

Because of Fox's attentiveness, the club has become a haunt of the glitterati. Robbie Williams was once seen there romancing Andrea Corr on the sticky dance floor and, although they left separately, rumours quickly made it into the international press. But guests who get publicity entering or leaving the club only do so because they want to, because Fox protects his guests inside and out. He has good contacts with the Dublin paparazzi. 'He has them in his pocket,' whispers a journalist from the Irish *Sun*. 'It's all tightly controlled. Colin can amble in, slip upstairs and he knows he won't be disturbed.'

Late guests often amble on to Lilly's Bordello, another club up an alleyway off Grafton Street, which was once chic but is now rather seedy. Guests can stay at Lilly's until 5.00am with the maximum of discretion.

Colin also still haunts O'Donoghue's Bar on Merrion Row, which is much more picturesque and offers no discretion at all. 'I do have the ability to be over the moon at the smallest thing – a few pints and a craic in the pub and I'm in heaven,' he explains. This is the place where he finds it. There are estimated to be exactly 1,000 bars in Dublin, and he most frequently chooses this one.

The bar is long and narrow with a low ceiling. It's dark and gloomy, with a black stone floor and peeling, sludge-brown Anaglypta paper on the walls, evidence of the days when people were allowed to smoke in public. Not giving up without a fight, all the spaces behind the bar are stuffed with cigarettes for sale.

Built in 1146 as a hostelry on the site of a vacant nunnery, it first became a recognisable pub in 1789, the year of the

French Revolution, and has hardly been changed or given a lick of paint since. It became a truly fashionable watering hole in the early 1960s when it was home to the much moustachioed musician Ronnie Drew, who founded The Dubliners. The band would regularly play there before they hit the big time and began appearing on *Top of the Pops*. It was also visited by writers such as Brendan Behan, although he usually got round the other 999 bars, too, often in the same night, and by the poet Patrick Kavanagh, also an alcoholic.

The walls are lined with hazy black-and-white photos from those glory days, and the place is still so popular that the barman often has to stand on a crate behind the bar and pass the drinks over the heads of waiting punters, out to the people queuing up in the doorway and on the pavement.

Even a shining Hollywood star can really get lost in there. There is still live music – the bar has its own festival-going banjo band – but it is chiefly a place to go to drink, talk and listen.

'Colin has a good lip for the Guinness,' says the barman. 'I've many times seen him mix it with whiskey. Sure, he'd lick the drink off a scabby leg, that one.'

No matter how near he gets to achieving his 'passion' for film fame, he still likes his old haunts, and the fundamentals in his life haven't changed. Just as in the old days before he became famous, when he didn't have anyone in bed waiting for him to come home to, he still goes home alone and fantasises about famous, unobtainable film stars.

He called the feminist actress Susan Sarandon 'a great actress and absolutely gorgeous'. She was another ideal, happily established with her long-time partner actor and screenwriter Tim Robbins, so Colin made do instead by taking her young daughter out.

Over Christmas 2002, he was spotted in the Spy Bar in Dublin with Eva Amurri, 17, the daughter of Sarandon and

Italian film director Franco Amurri. A strangely beautiful girl, five foot nine, with elfin features and large, round dark eyes, she looks like a rangy cross between Lisa Minnelli and Amelia Warner.

Sarandon and Robbins were in Dublin at the time performing their own tribute to the victims of 9/11 at the Peacock Theatre. They were staying at the exclusive Clarence Hotel in Temple Bar, which was bought and restored in 1992 by Bono of U2, whose aim was to turn it into a comfortable but grand private home for visiting celebrities.

While her mother was busy, Colin was entrusted with Eva, offering to take her out and show her the night spots of Dublin that he knows so well.

Eva is no pushover; she has been acting since she was seven and knows all about actors. She appeared as a child in *Bob Roberts*, Tim Robbins's political satire, and with her mother in *Anywhere but Here* and *Dead Man Walking*, where she played her mother's character aged nine. She and Sarandon also appeared as mother and daughter in the comedy film *The Banger Sisters*.

By the age of 16, she was attending New York showbiz parties and her mother once said that, when she helped her daughter with the business side of Hollywood, 'it was the only time I knew anything that she didn't know already'.

Colin was moving and shaking with US acting royalty now and, as his profile continued to shoot through the roof, he could reasonably regard himself as a bona fide Hollywood star.

CHAPTER SEVEN

STAR TREATMENT

Having kept his feet very firmly on the ground, despite the massive, ego-boosting success and acclaim he'd experienced with his last two films, Colin, like many before him, perhaps inevitably succumbed to the fantasy bubble he was now inhabiting.

Maybe he already felt things were spinning out of his control, or fate was about to bowl him a googly, because, leaving Dublin for LA on 3 January 2003, he was guilty of his first ever recorded 'diva' incident when he allegedly held up the whole plane for an hour by refusing to get on board until he had finished his champagne.

'The passengers were getting very agitated and the last thing the crew wanted to do was upset them for the sake of some movie star,' said a local reporter. Ireland is the opposite of LA in this way. 'They knew it would take about two hours to offload all his bags if they refused to take him. Luckily for them, he suddenly remembered why he was at the airport

143

and strolled on to the plane. He looked a bit drunk and was not in the least bit apologetic.'

He got on the plane the worse for drink and touched by self-loathing, probably depressed, leaving home again after a warm family holiday... and he also has a fear of flying. He has never got used to it and drinks on board to calm his nerves. This was yet another very long flight, from one familiar, comfortable world into his other life in LA which brings so many rewards and difficulties.

Once back in LA, away from the circle of mother, brother and friends, he went out on the town looking for company. Somewhere between Château Marmont, the Finn McCool Bar in Santa Monica and the Troubador Club in downtown LA, he met model Kim Bordenave, a five-foot seven-inch, dark-skinned beauty who slightly resembles Halle Berry.

It was a blind date. 'Kim met Colin through a mutual friend,' says an acquaintance friend of hers. 'He was in town, wanted a date and a friend hooked them up.'

They spent the night at a suite in the Château Marmont, or perhaps he took her by limousine to his temporary home, a bungalow at the Ritz Carlton Hotel complex in Pasadena. They were fascinated by each other. She came from the kind of poor urban background that he had never known. Originally from New York, when her father had disappeared back south to Louisiana, Kim, her sister Lisa and mother Renet moved to LA in the hope of finding a better life in the Sunshine State.

Moving south-west, they were among the ever-increasing number of new Californians, often desperately poor, but endlessly optimistic, who feel that just being in the town built on celluloid dreams is a kind of success in itself, always offering the chance of fame and fortune, the restless, ambitious people written about brilliantly by John Fante in his bleak novel *Ask the Dust*.

As a teenager, Kim had been very strong and athletic, a type that Colin likes, with a particular passion for surfing. According to a close friend, she loved to hang out with surfers and liked life on the beach. She lapped up the sand and surf culture, although she was no beach bum. By the time she met Colin, she was a successful, hard-working model contracted to M International Models and Talent. She'd been a successful catwalk model, and won good modelling contracts with the American mobile-phone giant Verizon, Movado watches and Pepsi.

He was equally fascinating to her. From a land she knew nothing about, he was totally foreign, with his wide brown gaze and strange, softly seductive accent.

They had sex, then she slept, and he lay awake thinking about work and the wide range of movie deals he was suddenly being offered. Now dubbed 'the sexiest, baddest guy in Hollywood', he was lined up for *Daredevil* in February 2003 and *S.W.A.T.* at the end of the year, both comic-book adaptations.

He got up, moved to another room, ordered a steak sandwich and a beer, and began browsing through scripts before returning to bed at 5.00am for two hours of fitful sleep.

In the morning, she had a breakfast of cranberry juice and a multivitamin, while he smoked. Then he called his driver to take her back to the wooden guesthouse that she was renting from a friend.

It was nothing unusual and he thought no more of it for the time being; after all, they had very little in common except ambition and the ability to be in the right place at the right time. She was gradually making her own way towards the success and fame she craved, and so was he.

Later in the day, when he went for a drink in Ye Olde King's Head, a mock-English pub in downtown LA, with Mark Steven Johnson, *Daredevil*'s writer and director, he hit three bull's-eyes in a row at darts. He and Johnson stared at the centre of the board in amazement and it was obvious to both of them that this boy couldn't fail at anything he tried. The gods were still smiling on him.

Daredevil, costing $100 million to make, was based on a 1985 issue of the cult *Marvel* comics. Colin plays Bullseye, a dementedly evil character who sports a dartboard tattooed on to his bald cranium.

Most darts players in the UK are fat, ugly men's men, in love with darts and warm beer. Colin manages to be grotesque, but he can rarely do ugly. 'It was just something they painted on,' he says, describing the thing on his head. 'They put glue on my forehead and stuck it on. When I sweated, it would start to bubble and I'd look like a leper, so they'd have to do it two or three times a night.'

This is the only American film where Colin is allowed his Irish accent, suggesting some connection in the American mind between Irishness and lawlessness, if not outright villainy.

Bullseye is intimidating but Johnson thought Colin would give him an extra ingredient. He seemed amazed at Colin's flexibility and facility as an actor. 'When he plays Bullseye, you can see the playfulness,' he says, 'it's scary but people start laughing.'

Like other directors, he also seemed surprised that Colin behaved like a normal human being. 'He was not a movie-star guy,' says Johnson. 'He just wanted to hang out with all the boys and people wanted to be around him. One night, we went to a club in LA and a doorman wouldn't let us in. Someone said to Colin, "Tell him who you are," but Colin wouldn't do that, which was very strange in a place like LA.'

In a town of fragile egos and show-offs, Colin was still noticeably down-to-earth and refused to commit the ultimate vulgarity of asking, 'Don't you know who I am?' His reasonable response seems to have been that, if they don't know, it didn't matter, although he would probably have said, 'Who gives a fuck?'

This devil-may-care attitude probably induced him to make *Daredevil*, which would give him more money, but little kudos. The film takes about ten minutes to start after endless credits and abstract shots of people in various stages of agony – always a bad sign. Delicate young boy Matt Murdock (Scott Terra) lives with his father Jack (David Keith), a failing boxer. Both tormented by their failures, they promise each other to 'never give up', they are just 'two fighters on the comeback trail'.

They live in a sepia-tinted science-fantasy version of Hell's Kitchen in New York, an area on the West Side between 14th and 52nd Streets, Eighth Avenue and the waterfront, which once glowed, simmered and frequently boiled over with crime and corruption.

Notorious gangs ruled the streets between the tenements, grog shops, slaughter houses, railroad yards and gas works. It was a place where characters like Bully Morrison pulled lamp-posts out of the pavements to use as weapons and, during Prohibition, it was the home of gangsters Owen Madden and 'Mad Dog' Coll who scared even the city's underworld.

The boy Matt is accidentally blinded, and Jack is murdered by the unseen forces of organised crime, but, despite coming from Hell's Kitchen, having his father killed and being blind, Matt somehow grows up to be a handsome lawyer, played by Ben Affleck.

A half-Irish poker player, Ben first came to fame in 1997, along with his childhood friend Matt Damon, when they wrote and appeared in the film *Good Will Hunting*, which went from their kitchen table to nine Academy Award nominations.

After his first film triumph, he'd gone on to appear in *Shakespeare in Love* and the sadly embarrassing *Pearl*

Harbor. He'd also had a well-publicised relationship with Hollywood's queen Gwyneth Paltrow.

As a boy, Affleck had been a keen fan of the *Daredevil* character, a masked avenging combination of Batman and Spider-Man, roving the city's rooftops, making computer-assisted leaps as he hunts down the men who killed his father.

Daredevil eventually comes up against the forces of Kingpin, or Wilson Fisk, a black man with all the charm of Idi Amin who heads the organised-crime outfits in the city. He murders not only his enemies but also their whole families. The plot centres on a vicious duel between Matt, supported by his black-leather-clad girlfriend Elektra, named after the Greek girl of legend who loved her father and gave her name to a Freudian complex, and Bullseye and Kingpin.

Elektra Natchios was played by Jennifer Garner, from Houston, Texas, star of *Alias*, a popular US TV spy thriller.

On the small screen and in *Daredevil*, her character was really just the same, a high-kicking, kick-boxing, wall-scaling girlfriend, who saves the world by storming public buildings, even the Vatican.

Bullseye also makes fantastic comic-book leaps over giant buildings to hunt down his victims. It is athletic stuff, and Colin had to be fit to do it. 'You breathe heavily in between takes,' he says, 'you suck it in and you do it again. It doesn't hurt the beer consumption at all... where would be the fun in that?'

He and Garner were trained in their elaborate fights by Hong Kong veteran Cheung-Yan Yuen, who also worked on *The Matrix* and *Charlie's Angels*. Unlike Colin or Ben Affleck, Garner, a former competitive swimmer, specialised in doing her own stunts and relished the rigorous training. 'If it's a stunt that seems like no fun, with no pay-off, like throwing myself to the floor again and again, then I'll let my stunt double do it,' she says. 'But all the fun stuff – being on a wire, being yanked about, fighting... I do all that.

'I trained pretty much night and day, ten hours at weekends and before and after going on the set. It was obnoxious how much I trained for that part. I was a disciplined machine. But Elektra's not a superhero, she's superhuman. She's like a freaky Ninja.

'Doing this film was just right for me, I wanted to keep training, to be able to train with some of the best, and I wanted to spend the summer fighting. I love the power that playing a powerful woman brings to you personally. And I loved finding my own physical power.'

In fact, Elektra isn't that powerful. Dressed in 'hooker chic', boots and bondage, one critic noted the 'repeated shots of her taut buttocks', and she is never allowed to rival the men.

The film is a comic-book series of clever visual stunts, 103 minutes of them, and, with his twinkling eyes and puckish grin, Colin managed to inject the only note approaching irony into the film. Not that his character is that amusing, as he constantly kills people by shooting minute darts, peanuts and paperclips into their throats. He will finish off anyone, including a man in a pub who calls him 'an Irish piece of trash' and a garrulous fat lady sitting next to him on a plane.

'It was much further from reality than anything I'd ever done,' he says. 'I just got to act over the top and hammy. It was a good time.'

Stephen Hunter in the *Washington Post* wrote, 'It is pretty entertaining as it adroitly manipulates cliché, archetype, trope and plenty of machine-guns over the streets of LA, all synchronised to heavy banging rock 'n' roll guaranteed to melt your IQ to a puddle in an hour.'

Mainly made for teenage boys and geeks of the type seriously addicted to violent computer games, yet again it concerns the relationship of father and son, and young men negotiating with flawed older males.

As a handsome young man, Colin, like Tom Cruise, seemed destined to be locked into films retelling this tale. It's a theme that has constantly recurred in US films and TV series, a factor which gives them all a certain sameness – and leads people to comment that they all resemble Westerns.

The early cinema Westerns not only showed that there was a ready market for films that put action and excitement over character and theme, but they also created a new kind of hero – honest, truthful, law-abiding and, above all, patriotic, a man's man, willing to lay down his life for his country, with a dad back home exactly the same. These men were often loners and, if they had any companions, they were invariably male. Women hardly existed.

The popular Westerns of the 1950s, 1960s and early 1970s, such as *Rawhide*, *Bonanza*, *The Virginian*, *The High Chaparral* and *Lancer* were all-male affairs, often with fathers and sons struggling together against a common enemy. They were all 'mom-free' zones, where there were no strong women helping to defend the frontier alongside the men, or even grey-haired ladies in gingham pinnies serving up hot cakes. Even in the cosy *Laramie* in 1959, Spring Byington only played the housekeeper, she didn't have the status of wife or mother. In 'family' Westerns, women were usually a distant relative, absent or expendable. Or, if John Wayne was in the film, they got slapped about.

Apart from the occasional fleeting love interest, it was a case of 'a man's gotta do what a man's gotta do,' and there was no place for weakness or femininity. For Western ranch it is easy enough to substitute army barracks, CIA training camp, US Naval Academy or futuristic police department.

Surprisingly, after all these years of feminism, the theme of men dealing with men in a dangerous, apparently all-male world seems more popular than ever – at least in the USA – but the relationship between father and sons shown in these films is perhaps not what we would immediately recognise in Europe any more. It is not about tenderness, closeness or understanding, but is more likely to be about duty, obedience and regard for conventional norms; young men learning to toe the line.

We see through characters like Tommy Hart and James Clayton in *The Recruit* that high-achieving, heroic young Americans are also supposed to be obsequious towards their leaders and highly conforming. Colin as a fragile-looking young man has often been given the part of the youngster with a lot to learn, relying on the older man, who turns out to be flawed. In *Hart's War* and *The Recruit*, his character has an idealised, noble father to refer back to, but, before he can be like the father, he has to wrestle for survival against a flawed leader.

It has been noted that Colin is often good in bad films. He always gives something more and stands out. This may be due to simple acting talent, but it might also be due to a special sensitivity he brings to the role of a young man in conflict with a father figure.

It has also been suggested that the father–son theme in US films is due to so many American directors and screenwriters having psychoanalysis, exploring Freud's idea of the Oedipus complex – the continuing struggle between father and son for the love of the mother. According to this theory, idealising dad is only one half of resenting him, compensation for childish, unresolved feelings of hatred towards him.

There is the natural disappointment, too, that he is not the hero that the boy once believed him to be. Perhaps this is particularly apt for Colin as, in his own life, he became estranged from the father whom he hero-worshipped as a boy. Even today, his father speaks as if he is somewhat distanced from his family.

And, despite the gung-ho attitude of studio bosses and some film producers, there are many people in the USA who feel they have been failed by the patriarchy of strong older males, the leaders in the government and the military that they once relied on. Pacino despairs of the CIA and its impotence in *The Recruit*; he has gone bad through disillusion, joining with the 9/11 generation who now feel the same kind of enraged bitterness towards their rulers as their parents did during the Vietnam War. Being the 'policeman of the world' is no easy thing, and *The Recruit* highlights a fundamental uneasiness in the USA about the whole concept of authority.

Daredevil was a moderate hit and quickly got a cult following. Showing his 'it' factor again, Colin won a nomination for Best Villain at the MTV Movie Awards.

As Joel Schumacher put it, 'Farrell's got that thing with a camera that I'll never understand. Some people have it, some people don't – it's a magic potion.'

Jennifer Garner as Elektra came out best. In 2004, she had a whole spin-off sequel made around her, in which she returns to her life as a hired assassin, bringing new meaning to the term 'drop-dead gorgeous', but with a kind heart, of course. She's not too callous, hesitating to kill a man with children.

For Colin, the Burton factor had kicked in again and he was seriously attracted to Jennifer, who, at 30, was one of his ideals – older, strong, yet 'in touch' with her feminine side, a woman who said she could 'take care of herself', she ticked all the boxes on his wish list. Perhaps he loved Elektra even more. Garner said her character was 'physically adept, beautiful but not vain, and a little dark', meaning a little dangerous, walking on the wild side. Colin has stated that he likes women with 'a little danger'.

In the flesh, Garner is as threatening as a High School cheerleader. One London journalist found her 'more schoolgirl than movie star, with cheerleader-like enthusiasm'.

Others have compared her toothy American wholesomeness to Geena Davis.

Real or just an idealised fantasy, Colin fell for her. Already divorced from actor Scott Foley, her husband of four years, during the filming she'd also broken up with her subsequent boyfriend, the handsome French actor Michael Vartan, her co-star in *Alias*.

She began to confide in Colin, attracted by his soft Irish ways, and he was available to listen. During the filming, though, she had fallen in love with Affleck, who'd been voted *People* magazine's Sexiest Man Alive the year before. But he was already engaged to another Jennifer, one more famous than Garner. He'd met her while they were working on a film together when she was still married to actor Chris Judd. But, in November 2002, he'd bought Jennifer Lopez an engagement ring costing $3.5 million. They were so famous as a couple that the press took to calling them 'Bennifer'.

The twists and turns of this unfulfilled love triangle were worthy of a film, but Colin didn't have too much time to sit about pining. He was now in an enviable position of being very well-known, but without a set image like Tom Cruise. He was considered to have 'range' and untapped potential.

The great US film director Oliver Stone, a bronze star medal winner in Vietnam, who'd gone from winning Oscars in the 1980s with *Platoon* and *Born on the Fourth of July*, to unpopularity in Hollywood with controversial work such as *JFK*, *Natural Born Killers* and *Nixon*, was hunting fervently for someone to play *Alexander the Great*, the young Macedonian warrior king, in his next great project.

The success of Ridley Scott's *Gladiator* had revived Hollywood's interest in sword-and-sandal epics, but this was a personal quest by Stone who had spent the previous 15 years mulling over the story, hoping to one day emulate the work of David Lean and Stanley Kubrick by producing some kind of vast spectacle on screen.

Stone had considered various actors – Tom Cruise seemed slightly too established; the hunky Australian Heath Ledger, star of the unsuccessful *Ned Kelly*, was too untried; Leonardo Di Caprio was seen as too soft-looking. He began auditioning actors from Britain who are reckoned to be rather rugged. At least, they don't have dazzlingly white teeth.

Then his trusted agent Bryan Lourde recommended 'an exciting young Irish actor, who was cast in *Daredevil*'. Stone was vaguely aware of him. 'I saw him in *Minority Report* and I responded to that,' he says, 'so I decided to meet him.'

Colin was invited for dinner at Michael's in Santa Monica, one of LA's top places for power lunching and celebrity dinning. He turned up dressed, as he put it, 'informally', which meant in a pair of Diesel jeans. He also had a closely shaved head for his part as Bullseye. He might have looked casual, but he was on tenterhooks; this was an invitation from one of the top film directors in the world, a man with not much time to waste, so obviously he had something to offer.

Even 18 months later, Colin remembered the cocktails Stone ordered for him – first, an appropriately named 'Bald Head', consisting of gin, French and Italian vermouth, a dash of Absinthe, shaken in cracked ice and served in a Martini glass with a twist of lemon and an olive. Then a 'Goldie', a mixture of Galliano, dark rum, refined sugar, orange juice, milk and cream, all gently heated and served with orange peel.

He also remembers that at dinner – poached Maine lobster and shoestring fries – he was 'very loud' because he was nervous. 'I had so much respect for Oliver Stone, that is probably why I overplayed it at dinner,' he says.

Stone remembers glasses being dropped and broken, other guests looking startled… and again the magic worked. Stone had always seen his film of Alexander as elemental, outrageous and barely tamed. After meeting Colin and seeing a display of unrefined table manners, he left thinking he'd found an actor who was 'young, raw and untamed'. Someone as exotic to him as the original Macedonian.

'The outsider has great allure, especially one who inspires strong feelings in others,' warns Father Mac in *Ballykissangel*. Stone, who had never seen the series, was thrilled with Colin, who could not have overplayed his glass-breaking or loudness if he'd tried.

Dinner was followed by breakfast the next day at the exclusive Shutters on the Beach Hotel, overlooking Santa Monica Pier and the Pacific. Stone brought along German film producer Moritz Borman, who was also surprised by Colin's rough appearance and bald head, but he was impressed by his energy and forthright manner. 'You've found your Alexander,' he told Stone.

Stone, known to be 'one tough sonofabitch' at the best of times, with a multi-million-dollar budget on his mind, decided to keep his options open, but he offered what he saw as a wild young Irishman a screen test.

It was the first audition Colin had been forced to take for three years. He wasn't usually happy at auditions as he is so highly strung, but this time he was delighted. 'I just wanted the chance to work with Oliver... that was the best thing about it.' He was also excited by Stone's manner, which some people find difficult. Unlike most educated Americans, he has dispensed with prim manners.

'He suffers from something that is almost dead in the world now,' says Colin, 'complete and absolute honesty. So, when you're horribly bad, he'll tell you and, when you're fantastic, he'll tell you. I just think he's brutally honest.'

As two individuals who didn't give a hoot about what people thought of them, they hit it off.

Most people found the auditions a nightmare. Actors were frog-marched in and out of the audition room for sessions that lasted only two or three minutes each. Irish actor Garrett Lombard tested for the part of Leonnatus. 'It was very intimidating,' he says. 'Well, you are going to meet Oliver Stone for a start, and he stands at the back shouting out, "OK, OK, go on... read this, read that, read this..." it's like a whirlwind. There is so much stuff going on in his head and he operates on a very fast level. It's difficult, but you have your stuff prepared and you just go in, do it and hope it comes off.'

Lombard was given 20 minutes to show what he could do, but Colin got eight hours, with some props thrown in. He arrived at the downtown warehouse for his audition accompanied by his sister Claudine. She had already encouraged him to watch the 1956 version of *Alexander* played by Richard Burton and heard him say his lines.

He decided to audition with Mark Anthony's famous speech, 'Friends, Romans, countrymen...' from Shakespeare's *Julius Caesar*, performed on a wooden stage, with a white sheet backcloth, in front of Stone, Borman and one or two of Stone's assistants. To get him in the mood, he was fitted with shiny black armour, a wig of blond curls – which, for some reason, Stone always associated with Alexander, whose hair was, in fact, tawny red – and some lace-up boots.

Colin declaimed in a Standard English accent, then Stone gave him pages from his script in progress, rousing lines addressed to his loyal army, and some impassioned reproaches towards some mutineers. From the back of the room, Stone would shout out supporting lines to help him along.

Claudine sat listening to her brother speaking in a polished, well-educated accent that she hadn't heard him use for years. 'Amazing,' she said, 'like a new Colin.'

This went on and on, with Colin put through constant changes of mood, with Stone pushing him to see what he could draw out. He left exhausted, but thrilled. 'One of the great days of my life,' he said. 'If I didn't get the part, it didn't matter; I had a great time and could enjoy the possibility of what might happen.'

A week later, CAA Casting called him round to watch a film of his test, with Stone, Bryan and Colin's agent. The result was a come-down, 'me in a bad wig', he said, rather prophetic words as it turned out. But he was offered the part. Stone liked the blond wig and he liked Colin's appearance, which accorded with his own private image of how Alexander should look.

'I wanted a combination of masculinity and, at the same time, beauty and femininity,' he says, 'a beautiful balance if you can pull it off.'

Colin was attracted to Alexander, a youth who had conquered 90 per cent of the known world, a two million square-mile territory by the age of 25. He understood him as well as anyone. 'What he did wasn't based on greed,' says Colin. 'All his life, he was looking for love. There was a hole inside him that couldn't be filled and his search for answers took him into great adventures. He'd grown up seeing his parents tear each other apart, and not that he would have dreamed of a reconciliation between them, but it hurt him to his very core.'

Knowing that he had the biggest project and probably the biggest money of his life ahead of him, he settled back to the more mundane work on offer on *S.W.A.T.*, a film based on a 1970s TV series about the Los Angeles police division, Special Weapons and Tactics, 'the most honoured professional police division in the world'.

While many Americans hate the image of aggressive policing, millions of others love it. Colin called this film a 'big wham-bam-thank-you-ma'am, action-popcorn kind of deal'. Like *Daredevil*, it was really designed for an audience of mainly testosterone-fuelled boys between the ages of 16 and 25 and, like most boys' toys, it was strangely expensive. Colin added to the budget by demanding and getting $5 million.

He played Jim Street, the right-hand man of SWAT leader, played by Samuel L Jackson, looking tough but very camp, like a French bulldog.

Jackson was slightly awed by Colin. A recovering alcoholic, he refused to join him on any of his late-night binges, and he was constantly amazed by his young co-star's ability to ignore a hangover. 'There were days when a car pulled up and we dragged Colin out and carried him into the trailer. But by the time the director said, "Places, please," he was up and ready to go. He's great.'

'It must be my Irish background,' says Colin. 'I can drink all night, sleep a few hours then be up early and back on set next day. I can play hard and work hard... it is no problem to me.'

Jackson, who is quite refined, found a way to curb Colin's swearing by keeping him stocked up with cigarettes. 'The one thing you have to do is make sure he's had his nicotine quota,' he says. 'If you keep him from a cigarette for more than three minutes, he's cussing.'

Together, they face trouble when a drug baron they're taking to prison escapes and offers a $100 million reward to anyone who can help him. The enemy has the look of Bin Laden about him and wears the orange prison outfit familiar to us from news stories about Guantanamo Bay Prison. Colin looks thinner than usual, very Hollywood, but also rather Italianate, like Al Pacino. There is a difficult older male boss who unjustly withholds his approval and has to be mollified with death-defying acts of heroism. There is also a lot of pressure from terrorists, lots of fighting and more hardware and special effects than ever.

For research, Colin went out with real police officers to the worst parts of LA, and went to SWAT 'school' to learn how to handle firearms. 'Here I am, getting paid a lot of money to act out the kind of games I did when I was a kid,' he said. 'I've been out on the range, shooting handguns, 9mms, shotguns, and I've learned how to hit targets while on the run. It's great fun.'

Some of the filming was done in Canada, and one day, while he was working, he was told that there was a 'special package' waiting for him in his trailer and he should collect it as soon as possible. It turned out to be Britney Spears, along with her brother and 'Big Rob', her bodyguard.

For Colin, hell-bent on popular celebrity, Britney was just the diamond-edged ticket, probably the most famous young lady in the USA, the last teenage pop superstar of the 20th century.

Britney is one of the most curious creatures created by Tinsel Town. Her mega hits 'Oops! I Did It Again' and 'Baby, One More Time' sold millions and she'd somehow stepped into Madonna's spike-heeled boots, and ousted the wannabe warbler Tiffany as the top girl pop singer in the land.

She started her career aged nine, with Disney's Mickey Mouse Club on TV, where she performed as a 'mousketeer', wearing large, black, floppy ears. In those days, she was more Snow White than Mickey Mouse, a lovely, wholesome teenage virgin, a possible prom-queen, the sort of girl any American mom would be proud of.

Then, as her records became huge, she rather foolishly tried to maintain this image while producing erotic videos, chain-smoking and making public appearances showing off her tattoos in the briefest underwear. She might well have remained a virgin as she claimed, as patient as Sleeping Beauty waiting for her prince to come, but she was quite obviously no sweet Sandra Dee, and was quickly seen as an awful tease.

In March 2000, she told Frank Skinner on his ITV chat

show in London that she'd been in a relationship via mobile phone, with a real prince – William – the heir to the British throne. She claimed they'd had a dinner date arranged, only he'd mysteriously not shown up. 'Gone fox hunting,' suggested the *Sun* newspaper. She also let it be known before the World Cup that she had quite an interest in David Beckham.

Her excuse for turning up on the set to see Colin was that she was a friend of the producer. Canada was quite a long way from her home in Santa Monica for an afternoon visit, but Colin was flattered and pleased.

The plot of *S.W.A.T.* held no such surprises and was less interesting than his current lifestyle. It consists of one side good, the other bad, with nothing in between. There is a shoot-out, the good side wins, survivors have a brief laugh together and, although tired out, dutifully return to work saving civilisation.

Although he found the work 'fun', *S.W.A.T.* is an extremely vulgar film in every way. Throughout, the word 'ass' is on everyone's lips. It is either 'in a sling', 'being chewed out', or someone is kicking it, but, sadly for those who might actually enjoy seeing one, there are none on show. It is a film for men's men. The ideal male, represented by Colin, is fit, fierce and ruthless, but totally loyal to his colleagues, while the older Samuel L Jackson is hard but trustworthy. Both are God-fearing killers on the side of good.

It is unsaid and unexplored in the film, but a sub-text of homosexuality keeps creeping through as the men make constant dark hints about male rape as if that is the ultimate form of humiliation and punishment one can suffer or inflict on someone else.

'It was just four months of, you know, too much testosterone,' says Colin, 'pushing each other about in the fucking locker rooms, with lots of guns and explosions and things.'

'Mad, fucking mad,' quipped Colin, referring to his fee, for doing a film which probably lives on only through its theme tune, which was later turned into a particularly irritating mobile phone ring tone.

On 21 January, he was back in LA for the late-night Golden Globe awards held at the Château Marmont, and was reacquainted with Demi Moore. He already knew her vaguely through her ex-husband Bruce Willis, but now there was a real attraction between them. She was still beautiful, if famished-looking, at 40, 14 years his senior, her famous triangular face looking pale and almost hidden under her thick dark hair, her beautifully shaped jaw nothing but delicate bone.

Anyone who meets her is surprised by how tiny and fragile she is, her five-foot four-inch frame usually raised up on six-inch heels and large platforms, which often look almost too heavy for her to lift.

On the night of the Golden Globes, in the thick of celluloid celebrity, her black hair was combed out simply as if she was a young girl again, and her partly exposed breasts looked enormous against her thin frame. Dark, experienced in life but very vulnerable, with a slight hint of danger about her, she captivated him.

Among the crowds of photographers, they sat together holding hands, not caring at all about the cameras flashing all round them. They had provided a scoop for every snapper present. She had, in fact, seen him at the beginning of the evening and asked to be introduced to him. She hadn't seen him since they'd met when Bruce had been present, 18 months before.

'Demi was dying to meet him again,' says a friend. 'They were introduced and, after a short while, they looked very intimate. By the end of the evening, they were kissing openly.' They were seen all over each other like teenagers when the lights go off.

A US magazine commented later on their 'prolonged lip-lock in the lobby' and later, in a friend's private room in the hotel, 'they continued to make out like crazy'.

Since her divorce from Willis in 1998, Demi had been a very vulnerable woman. After a ruinous and chaotic childhood, she has a permanent hunger for love and a need for male approval. Her stepfather Danny, whom she calls 'a charmer but self-destructive', committed suicide and her mother Virginia was a drunk living in a trailer, who had named her 'Demi' after a haircare product.

As a teenager, she used drink and took drugs to 'hide her feelings', as she puts it, and dropped out of school in west Los Angeles. People told her she was a lovely girl; she had great ambitions; she wanted to improve her life, but she couldn't even take acting classes because she was, she says, 'too fearful. I had no sense of what I could do and I was afraid of being judged.' She had to recreate herself. 'I knew I could only make it if I could fake it,' she says.

Like Colin, by largely concealing her true feelings and creating a vivid persona for the public, her all-American dream had come true. In 1985, she climbed out of an oblivion of booze to take a small role in *St Elmo's Fire* and, from there, bit by bit, using her looks, she had become the star of international hits such as *Ghost*, *Indecent Proposal* and *Disclosure*.

Also like Colin, she was always slightly abashed at her own success. Feelings of unworthiness made her constantly astonished at being one of the best-paid screen sirens of Hollywood. Her life was like a trailer-park dream as she was followed everywhere by security men, at least seven servants, a PR woman resembling a prison warden to protect her from the world's press, and a whole fawning retinue, creating a hullabaloo worthy of royalty.

By 2003, when she met Colin, her career was on the slide after flops in *The Scarlet Letter*, *GI Jane*, and then, worst of

Above: Colin getting friendly with the Beckhams at a party in 2003.   © *Getty Images.*

Below: Colin in his first professional performance, with the cast of the play *Kelly's Reign* in Sydney, Australia, October 1995.   © *Newspix.*

Above: Oliver Stone with Colin on the set of the 2004 epic *Alexander*.   © *Rex Features.*

Below: At the *Alexander* première in Germany.   © *Rex Features.*

Above left: Proving that spiky hair runs in the family, Colin shows off his mum Rita and brother Eamon at the LA première of *Daredevil*.   © *Rex Features.*

Above right: All dressed up with sister Claudia and his girlfriend Kim Bodernave at the 2003 Academy Awards.   © *Getty Images.*

Below: At a *Phone Booth* screening in New York, Colin relaxes with Eamon and sister Catherine.   © *Rex Features.*

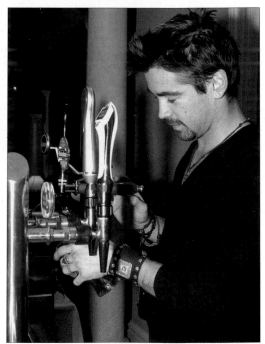

Top left: On the German TV show *Wetten dass..?* Colin is prepared to do anything to impress a woman.

© *Rex Features.*

Top right: Struggling to get around on crutches while shopping in LA after breaking his foot.

© *Rex Features.*

Bottom left: Colin in a moody pose from 2003.

© *Getty Images.*

Bottom right: Despite his fame and fortune, Colin hasn't forgotten how to pull a pint.

© *Getty Images.*

Above: At a *The Recruit* film première, Colin's Irish charisma doesn't seem to have worked on Britney Spears.   © *Rex Features.*

Below: Myo's in Castleknock, the venue for much of Colin's teenage revelling.

© *Author's collection.*

Above: Colin's cottage in the Ringsend area of Dublin. He paid for it with one of his first *Ballykissangel* paychecks.

© *Author's collection.*

Below: The beachfront home in Malibu, California, that Colin calls home when he's in the States.

© *Rex Features.*

Colin in 2004's *A Home at the End of the World*. © *Rex Features*.

Colin gets back into uniform for *The New World*.

all, *Striptease*, for which she had learned to strip professionally in the deep, dark dungeon of Scores in New York.

Her presence anywhere still created a tremendous stir. People working in hotels will plead to work on a Sunday if she is going to show up at an event on that day. But by the late 1990s, the woman whose body on film posters had once been slapped on bus stops all across the western world was no longer on Hollywood's A-list and slipping fast. For years, her only appearance in the gossip columns had been as a slightly lumpy housewife to Willis, devoting time to her three oddly named daughters, Rumer, Scout and Tallulah.

After the marriage ended and the girls grew up, she had decided to reinvent herself, partly with the aid of the Kabbalah, the Jewish religious cult, of which Madonna is a prominent exponent, but mostly with £300,000 worth of plastic surgery. With a new face, thighs and bottom, she set about challenging the younger women who had taken her place at the box office and she began dating a string of much younger actors – Leonardo Di Caprio, then 30; Tobey Maguire, 29; and then Colin, the youngest at 27.

They started going out as a couple and she told a friend it was 'the start of a hot relationship', and they were 'always on the phone to each other'.

'Demi is absolutely charmed by Colin,' said a friend. 'She knows he's a rogue, but that's what she loves about him.'

These flings never developed into 'hot relationships', but they did attract a lot of attention from studio moguls and she was eventually cast her in the new *Charlie's Angels*.

Being seen out with Colin generated a lot of publicity, on 31 January at the New York première of *The Recruit*, she was left at home while he went to the party hand in hand with Britney.

The former mouseketeer's efforts in Canada had paid off. Colin had invited her to a major Hollywood event, and she had managed to cop off with the most interesting young man available, and in front of the world's press. What more could any girl ask for?

As Britney, the US teen queen in skimpy, shell-pink satin chemise, and Colin, the wild Irish boy decked in leather bracelets and cuffs, strolled hand in hand along the red carpet, the watching audience and paparazzi went wild at what they thought was a magic Hollywood coupling – a Leigh–Olivier, Taylor–Burton partnership for the multiplex generation.

'I didn't know us turning up together would create such a stir,' says Colin unconvincingly. 'I was just sitting in my hotel room with 25 or 30 of my family and friends over from Dublin and she was talking to someone in the corner with her friends. I'm going, "Isn't this dandy?" Here we are all having drinks together at the première; we then go to the première, the limo door opens, we all get out and we are in the middle of a media frenzy. I honestly didn't think that would happen. But as soon as I stepped out of the car, I realised. I'm not that dumb. I just don't think sometimes.' He didn't need to think; instinctively, he'd done exactly the right thing.

Photos show how the Britney effect had bitten him. He is standing beside her with his wet tongue stuck out, leering, for once managing to do ugly. He looks as if he's turned into Robbie Williams, or is just some drunk who has walked up to her on the street.

But that chav/bling moment turned Colin from a mere film star into a pop celebrity. After this short walk with Britney, he didn't appear just in multi-million-dollar films and videos, but also on posters, screen savers and desktop wallpaper – the modern mark of someone who has really arrived. At last, not through any great piece of acting, but by going to the right party with the right girl, he achieved huge celebrity.

Later, he complained that 'everything had changed', because of his association with Britney. There were people outside his home in Dublin, reporters hanging around his local pub, all trying to dig up any dirt they could on him, but he and Britney were self-invented people; she was even more of a mass-market commodity than Demi Moore, they both needed publicity to live, and they understood each other's immediate needs.

At that party, the night Colin and Britney deliberately bamboozled the public together, the audience watching them went ecstatic with vicarious happiness. And, when the crowds had gone away, they still behaved like kids at a school disco. Although they were with four of her friends and 25 of his, they seemed to ignore everyone and just flirted outrageously with each other, posing for everyone as an item.

'They kept disappearing out on to the balcony and snogging,' said one reporter. 'Then they went into the adjoining bedroom and disappeared for over an hour.'

Later in the week, they were in LA together, spotted kissing in the VIP room of the Troubador Club, during a show by Irish musician Damian Rice. 'After a few minutes of looking over at one another, she ditched her friends and went over to him,' said an onlooker. 'Pretty soon they were all over each other, putting on quite a show. It looked like more than a one-night thing.'

'Was I kissing her?' Colin mused innocently to a reporter later that week. 'We're just friends, but a man can't have too many friends like her, gorgeous, a real sweetheart and not exactly hard on the eyes.'

He was the third young man she'd been linked with that month. He could hold his own; just as he'd always liked mixing with bad boys, he liked bad women. They obviously liked each other, and looked good together.

Although losing any last shred of privacy irked him, he had to admit that having Britney on his arm appealed to the show-off in him. It was miles better than entertaining his loved ones with karaoke impressions of Simon Le Bon. He was thrilled to be able to show her off, not just to the watching world, but also to his close family and friends.

He had flown 25 of them out to be with him at the première of *The Recruit* in LA, putting them all up at the five-star Château Marmont. A showman at the centre of his family, he loved to mix celebrities with his relations so that they could rub up against people they'd never dreamed of meeting. 'Everyone was stunned to see the big-name stars in the room,' says Glenda Gilson. 'Sheryl Crow, Britney Spears... All the lads were saying, "Look who's over there," they were all really excited, but so was Colin.'

Sheryl Crow had possibly got her invitation because she had recently described Colin as 'completely edible', and said she'd got a 'little crush' on him. Glenda, who had watched his whole progress from Assets Agency to Sunset Strip, was understanding. 'His partying with his family is typical Irish behaviour,' she says.

'Premières can be tiresome,' he explained, 'so that is when I bring all my family over. At the première – red carpet, flashbulbs and all that shit – there are usually 20 of them, relatives and old friends mulling around. It brings an air of reality to it all. It's all very real because they are there, but it makes a mockery of all the other shit. It's great because they are enjoying it for what it is, one night, one screening, one free bar. But to have too much love or familiarity around when you're working would be distracting.'

He must have the family there when he wants them. He likes Hollywood with them, watching his mother enjoying it, spending his dollars in the beauty parlour, sending his sisters shopping in Beverly Hills. The rest of his time is taken up by all those anonymous people who want a piece of him.

'What other lad who got famous at the click of his fingers isn't going to go out and enjoy the Hollywood parties and every girl that throws herself at him?' says Glenda. 'He's enjoying it and it's all new to him... so why not?'

Getting everyone he cared for, plus Britney, together inside the hallowed portals of the Château Marmont was showing them everything he wanted them to see about his extraordinary new life as a film star. The place is a perfect backdrop to his story – beautiful, but not quite what it seems.

A small, solitary white castle at 8221 Sunset Boulevard, overlooking the Sunset Strip, the hotel is pure movie set, a pastiche of old Europe, based on an exact copy of the Château Amboise in the French Loire, with gothic ceilings and spooky dark-wood panelling thrown in, a real Hollywood haunted house.

Built in 1929 at almost the beginning of the Hollywood film industry, the whole place is drenched in American cinema history, a living link to the past for someone like Colin who grew up infatuated with film.

Anyone who's anyone in Hollywood has stayed there – his first idealised love, Marilyn Monroe, Errol Flynn, Clark Gable, Paul Newman, Boris Karloff, Humphrey Bogart, Greta Garbo. In 1956, when Montgomery Clift was almost killed in a car accident, Elizabeth Taylor took him to the Château, where she rented the penthouse, the most expensive part of the hotel, as a place for him to recuperate. Robert De Niro secludes himself away there in the penthouse for extended periods. James Dean and Natalie Wood first met there at a script rehearsal for *Rebel Without a Cause*.

It has an atmosphere described by some as 'artsy', often veering towards the darker side of the artistic temperament. In 1982, comedian John Belushi, famous for the cult film *The Blues Brothers*, died there 'free-basing', injecting a 'speedball' of heroin and cocaine. Jim Morrison, the lead singer of the 1960s group The Doors, hurt his back trying to swing from the roof into the window of his hotel room while stoned. This was a scene later recreated in Oliver Stone's film *The Doors*. In January 2004, photographer Helmut Newton died from a heart-attack as he drove his Cadillac out of the front driveway and into a wall.

It is a place reeking of tragic stories and silly gossip. The most recent person to get into difficulties there was probably Scarlett Johannson who got caught making love in a lift with Benicio Del Toro, the Puerto Rican actor known as 'the Spanish Brad Pitt'. People go there to be both private and exposed, a hugely titillating conundrum only enjoyed by the very famous.

There are many reasons why Colin loves the place. There is the Bar Marmont, one of the hottest nightspots in LA, where he has held court for magazines such as *Playboy* and *Vanity Fair*.

It's his fantasy bubble. Just as the rich like to stick together, so the stars and guests at the Marmont can sip their cocktails within easy eye contact of Drew Barrymore, Johnny Depp and Leonardo Di Caprio, who stays in Suite 54. There is also a balcony where former prom queens and 'video artistes', who long to be movie stars, hang out waiting to spot potential casting directors.

It also remains an idiosyncratic place where the beautiful staff will serve you a drink at any time of the day or night, and, a very rare thing in today's USA, you can smoke in its public rooms, a sanctuary for anyone like Colin who smokes 40–50 Camel Lights a day. He has also been amused that sometimes when he returns to his room at 4.00am a Filipino night porter is often found sitting in a corner softly playing 'Hey, Jude' on an electric organ. Harry Cohn, who founded Columbia Pictures, might have been speaking directly to Colin when he said, 'If you must get into trouble, do it in the Château Marmont.'

CHAPTER EIGHT

THE HIGH LIFE PLAYING LOWLIFE

After the exciting antics of New Year with the Britney factor disrupting his life, and Kim Bordenave still in the background, it was back to the business of work, this time something creative.

Early in 2000, Colin and his first mentor, Joel Schumacher, were at the Toronto Film Festival, when the director said, 'I want you to be in a film that's all about a guy trapped in a phone booth. It's going to be all shot inside the booth and we are probably going to do the whole thing in ten days flat.'

'Nice one. When do we start?' Colin replied, thinking it was a possible wind-up. But he was on the track of one of his grimmest, strangest and most successful film roles. *Phone Booth* is the story of Stu Sheppard, a 'wild-side-walkin', potty-mouth-talkin' lad', strutting down New York's 8th Avenue, wearing shades and making dodgy deals into his mobile. It is a modern American morality tale. Stu is 'an asshole', as Colin puts it, until the day he finds himself held prisoner in a phone box by a sniper aiming at him from a nearby building, and is forced at gunpoint to reassess his life.

It was an idea that had been around for a long time. The 'Master of Suspense' Alfred Hitchcock had even been working on it with his writer Larry Cohen, just before his death in 1980.

Schumacher mentioned Colin playing the lead part to studio bosses at 20th Century Fox, but they had not yet seen *Tigerland*. After it was shown at Toronto and they were impressed by his performance, they agreed to cast him, but they had little choice of actors.

Well-known stars such as Jim Carrey and Will Smith had been approached about the role but they weren't interested. It was too tough, too off the wall for their established images; they had the expectations of their fans to consider, which Colin didn't. He was still gaining a reputation and was anything but typecast.

Sucking up the parts that other people didn't want once again, he made one of his most impressive films, with the camera intensely focused on him for 78 minutes, revealing, with slow deliberation, the kind of acting he could achieve. It was the biggest dramatic challenge he'd ever had and everyone involved felt stressed.

'On the first day of filming, I had this cold feeling in the pit of my stomach,' says Schumacher, 'a cold, sick feeling that it wasn't going to work. I turned to my assistant and said, "Apart from putting a needle into my arm for five years in the 1960s, this is the most insane thing I've ever done in my life." But I tried to keep all those negative feelings away from Colin.'

Colin picked them up anyway. 'Every morning, it wasn't just the usual pressure of "Will I be any good?"' he says. 'It was: "Can I really do this, can we get through the day?"'

'The first day was the worst,' says Schumacher. 'After that, we were all on a roll.'

'The fight was on,' says Colin.

He was in the phone booth with the camera in his face for ten days, filming from 6.00am until 4.00pm when the light failed. Then there were two days in different locations.

'It wasn't a marathon,' says Colin, 'more a 100m sprint. I've never liked running long distances. I like short runs, so this was heaven for me, really. We also had two weeks of rehearsal first… you never usually get that, but we were able to sit around and hash it out together.'

But he faced technical challenges. Although he may have been reticent and felt himself overshadowed in his acting class at the Gaiety, this time he discovered that he had a facility for accents. As Stu, he sounded, at least to an outsider, like a real New Yorker.

To achieve this, he spent two hours a day practising a Bronx accent for a fortnight before filming started. His voice coach was Michael Buster who lives in New Orleans and often works over the phone, his own disembodied, but controlling, voice sounding almost as sinister as the voiceover in the film.

'I don't ever want to hear an actor "doing" an accent,' he says.

Colin almost passed this test, but not quite. 'He has a very good ear for accents, but in *Phone Booth* his voice was a kind of sketch-comedy American,' he says rather grudgingly.

Emotionally, the piece was very draining. 'I play a tough guy but I am a softie really,' says Colin. 'After three days of shooting, I wanted to go back to my trailer and cry. To have someone on the other end of the phone bullying me all the time, by the ninth day, man, I was so tired. I hadn't been sleeping at all well because I couldn't shut my brain off from it, and I had just met Millie who had moved in with me three days before filming started and I was madly in love with her.

'But we all just went at it as best we could. Forest Whitaker, who plays the police officer trying to talk me down, has such honest gentleness, and Katy, who played my wife, was such a peach, one of those beautiful women who when you meet them they are more beautiful because of the gentleness and the integrity that comes across. And I had to say lots of filthy things in front of her.'

Although it wasn't entirely improvised, he was allowed to develop the role of Stu, putting bits of his own life into it. 'I say "fuck" 150 times in the film,' he says proudly, 'and only two were scripted.'

There is a pleasing bit of the 'fiadhair', or wild boy, in there as he struts down the Avenue, throwing shapes, head down on shoulder like a sleeping bird, talking into his mobile but letting go with the expletives, making a joke about 'Irish chicken soup', and taking note of any passing skirt. His wife in the film is given an Irish name and he even mentions Britney Spears, a hint towards the international showbiz gossip now surrounding him in real life.

But there the fun ended. This is a bleak story about cruel punishment leading to redemption of some kind, after what looks like a mental breakdown. Stu is a user in a city of users, and his antagonist, played by Kiefer Sutherland, is no kindly therapist interested in his development. He has been driven mad in the Vietnam War, and is mercilessly cruel to his trapped victim.

There is no humour in the film after the initial creation of Stu, and Sutherland sounds rather like Vincent Price as Edward Lionheart in *Theatre of Blood*, the 1973 film about an aged actor who takes bloody revenge on all the critics who have ever slated him. His whole motive for revenge is that Stu apparently once snubbed him in public.

Although this part of the plot is a bit weak, the psychological build-up in the film is very powerful. In one brilliant moment, Stu sees himself trapped in his phone box, being tormented, his plight reproduced on the screens of all the TVs in the local shops around him.

Eventually, Stu's beautiful wife turns up with the police and a large crowd to witness his humiliation. He breaks down, tells her he's been a bad boy and she forgives him. This, his biggest scene, was done at 6.00am on morning eight of the shoot and, by the following day, he says he was 'broken and very tired'.

Rather rattled by the character of Stu, he brought up his own character, or at least the one he insists on showing to the press, for public analysis. 'I could come across as an asshole,' he mused, 'but I prefer to be hated for who I am rather than loved for who I am not. And I couldn't give a fuck if people write that I'm a filthy-mouthed bastard who drinks too much. That's better than opening my mouth about my family and my real problems. So I drink pints and I say "Cunt." Fantastic!'

When the film was over, the stress didn't stop. After all that sweat and tears, it seemed for a long time that the work might never reach an audience. Like *The Manchurian Candidate*, made in 1962, which was delayed for years after the death of President Kennedy, it seemed that the film had been overtaken by real events. It was originally supposed to be released in November 2002, but got pushed back when, in October, a woman was shot dead in Virginia, there was an outbreak of real sniper attacks in Washington DC which killed eight people, and a long, drawn-out crisis with a sniper began at a petrol station in Maryland, involving John Allen Muhammad and John Lee Malvo.

As headlines screamed, 'SNIPER'S TERRIBLE THREAT – YOUR CHILDREN ARE NOT SAFE ANYWHERE, ANY TIME', the executives at Fox became jittery about the whole project which began to reek of bad taste. Schumacher made desperate pleas for reason, stating that there was no relation between the real and the fictional shootings as the real-life cases were random attacks, not planned like his fictional one. Others pointed out that, as there are 250 million people in the USA and 250 million guns, there would always be snipers and hostage situations going on somewhere.

As the film was delayed, arguments broke out about how much influence film and TV has over violent behaviour. 'Colin was very good about it all,' says Schumacher. 'He was great in the film, it was totally him, then he accepted the delay, he totally understood. But no one ever knows the right time to bring a film out. It is always a gamble, a crap shoot.'

Trailers put out for the film in cinemas had a good response and the film won good reviews in Toronto, so Fox was in a quandary. When Muhammad and Malvo went on trial in November 2003, Schumacher felt able to announce that the film would be released early in the following year.

By its second week, early April 2003, word had got around that here was something special and it grossed $26,716, 634 in the USA, and topped the box office. Colin was named 'Transatlantic Breakthrough Performer' at the MTV Movie Awards. His imagination in taking the role and all the hard work had paid off.

In Manhattan for the première of *Phone Booth*, Colin discovered Scores, the New York strip club, and celebrated there with a couple of leggy dancers, and some old friends from Dublin. A day later, he was seen at the club doing some dirty dancing with a girl called Sade, before moving on to another lady, then having a snog on the dance floor with a third, and finally going home with Rita... his mum.

The press were fascinated, realising how important his nocturnal world was to him. 'Going out so much stops me thinking about what I am missing at home,' he told them. 'Especially in the last three weeks of the shoot, I was so ready to go home, really missing it. I don't want too many moments of stillness to myself, I am really struggling.' Presumably, that is why his mother was with him. If he couldn't go home to her, she had to visit him.

He may have been unhappy, longing for the normal life in Ireland he once had, but cheques for his previous work and their video spin-offs were pouring into his bank account. He was also offered the chance to become 'the face' of the Ralph Lauren fashion house, a contract worth $3.2 million. Lauren met him at the première of *Phone Booth* and was 'blown away' by his looks and thought he was 'the perfect vehicle for Lauren clothes'. The offer, more suited to a fading actress, was not taken up.

Among the other benefits he received at that time was a gold card from the Abrakebabra kebab house in Dublin, across from O'Donoghue's Bar, worth £4.90 to the lucky recipient, and only given away to seven selected citizens of Dublin a year. He still had no time to go there and make use of it. He was now a leading player in Hollywood and everything he did was news.

There were still constant rumours about his relationship with Demi, and *US Weekly* reported that Britney had dumped her newish boyfriend, Fred Durst, a musician from Limp Bizkit, for him. Durst was said to be in pieces.

With other urgent matters pressing, Britney claimed she hardly knew Durst. 'We worked together and he's a really cool guy,' she said, 'really sweet, but he's not my type.' He took revenge by posting an item on his website describing his erotic dreams about Angelina Jolie. While he raged, Britney and Colin still denied there was anything serious going on between them.

At last, Colin escaped from this tangled web and got a chance to return to Ireland. While he was there, on 4 March, he recorded a three-hour TV interview with Gerry Ryan, edited down to half-an-hour after the removal of all his expletives, which the station described generously as 'part of his speech pattern', as if he was from another country, and not from Ireland at all.

During the session, over pints of Guinness, glasses of red wine and some good cigars, he talked about how much he loved to spend his new fortune on his family. He was obviously blissfully unaware of how his family, his nerves and his finances were about to be stretched.

Two weeks later, back in LA, Kim Bordenave announced that she was four months pregnant and her agency M Models issued a curt statement that she 'would not be working for a while'.

She was certain it was Colin's child and began telling everyone, it was '100 per cent Colin Farrell's baby'.

At first, Colin was bewildered and let slip that, for once, Rita was upset with him, although she hadn't actually spelled it out. 'My mother, I'm sure, had a few tears behind my back because it's not what one would think is an ideal situation,' he told a GMTV interviewer.

Other people were dismayed, too. 'I had friends on the phone,' he says, 'lawyers, agents, going, "You met this girl five weeks ago – what are you doing?"' He decided it was really nothing to do with him. 'It was outside my control,' he said, 'greater than me.'

He began justifying the situation on that basis, but there was also a dash of good old Catholic guilt there, too. 'There is no rhyme nor reason to life,' he said, 'no definite right and no definite wrong, so do everything as best you can and do it out of love and that's all I'm gonna try and do.'

Perhaps for the child, but not for Kim. He just couldn't quite fit her gangly frame into the picture. Looking for a bit of a distraction, a few days later, he sauntered over to Gwyneth Paltrow where she was seated surrounded by rose bushes out on the brick patio at the fashionable Ivy Restaurant in Beverly Hills.

With all his powers of persuasion, he told her she was 'the greatest actress on the planet', adding, 'Give me your number and we can get together.'

This was a bird too far. Paltrow, perched at the top of Hollywood's A-list girls and the Queen of Green, did not need that kind of thing over her spinach linguine and green tea. She has not called her baby after a fruit for nothing, and tries to live an entirely organic lifestyle. The sight of Colin with his three-day chin stubble, his whiff of nicotine and his proclaimed love of curry with chips on the side, was too much for her. Apart from that, anyone who read the papers would know she was about to marry Coldplay's Chris Martin. When he asked for her phone number, she said she couldn't remember it and waved him away with the flap of a slender white hand.

He retreated from the patio, which is reserved for the very select, and laughed it off in the bar. A few days later, he was also off his stroke with supermodel Sophie Dahl, who told him she was perfectly happy with her current boyfriend, US actor Dan Baker.

You have to applaud him for trying. Like an obsessive mountaineer, despite Kim, or perhaps because of her, there would be no female body in Tinsel Town left unconquered – or, at least, unattempted.

On 17 March, he was seen in London with the astonishingly beautiful actress Kate Beckinsale, who'd just split up from her boyfriend, the gifted Welsh actor Michael Sheen, who is also the father of her daughter Lily. The two dark-haired beauties were spotted at the trendy Sanderson Hotel near Soho, canoodling and touching one another as if they were very intimate. That weekend, the *News of the World* reported that they were 'very fond of each other', adding, 'It's too early to tell if it will turn out to be a long-term relationship but they will definitely be seeing each other again.'

They both looked like young, free singles out on the town rather than people with heavy baggage and responsibilities. A week later, he was back in LA with Kim, finally facing up to the situation.

She had dropped out of the news, given up work, shut down her website, and left the small apartment she'd shared with a friend. She, at least, was not running away from the inevitable.

It was a time of great uncertainty, but they were snapped strolling together, eating ice creams on the seaside promenade in Santa Monica, looking very casual, he in a woollen hat, she in slacks and trainers, both looking affectionate and happy. One English paper described them as looking 'love-struck'. An onlooker was quoted as saying, 'Colin and Kim looked very close and things seemed much more serious than many people are thinking. It looks like he is serious about Kim.'

Colin was seen patting her midriff. It seemed that he had decided that, however he felt about Kim, he was serious about being a father, it was the child, his 'mini-me' she carried that interested him. 'I'm chuffed, over the moon. It's due in about six months,' he told a waiting reporter.

A few days later, he took Kim to the Oscars in LA, along with his sister Claudine. Kim looked sophisticated and happy in a black lace gown. Perhaps, like many pregnant women, she had sentimental hopes about the baby's father, that her slender arms could hold him, that he would 'come round' and they would be a family one day.

But two weeks later, on 20 April, he was back in New York at Scores. Although he was with sister Catherine and an uncle, in the bar he became locked into a passionate kiss lasting half-an-hour with a young Australian woman, who excitedly told the waiting press that she wanted to be an actress and was 'obsessed with Colin's eyes'.

People naturally asked about Kim and he replied happily

that she was 'doing great, strong as an ox'. In fact, she was suffering from severe morning sickness and fatigue.

The papers still flickered with rumours about Colin and Britney. According to *US Weekly*, they had renewed their passion and, any time she wasn't shooting her new video, they were tucked up inside the Beverly Hills Hotel together.

He told the press there had been nothing going on. 'She was just one guest out of 25. Nothing's going on, we're just mates.' She insisted they had 'snogged', that something had been going on, but it was now over and, besides, she added, she'd only ever slept with one man, her ex-boyfriend Justin Timberlake, and that was two years into their relationship.

Demi, too, had moved on. In June 2003, she stunned crowds at the film première of *Charlie's Angels: Full Throttle*, in which she starred alongside Drew Barrymore, Cameron Diaz and Lucy Liu. She arrived not only sporting a pair of newly resculpted knees, but also with a new lover, former model and actor Aston Kutcher, aged 25.

He was a rising star in his own right, but instantly became, according to the papers, 'a new toyboy to replace Colin'. As if this wasn't enough for his ego, his former girlfriend, starlet Brittany Murphy, quipped that their romance showed that age didn't matter to him, and size didn't matter to her. It was also reported that Bruce Willis had told him, 'Kiddo, if you don't behave towards her, you'll have me chasing you.'

For a time, Colin decided to heed Willis's advice, and behave. There were rumours that he was being forced to face certain issues with Kim. He started paying her an allowance of £3,000 a month, an average wage, but her mother and sister were upset, pointing out that she had once earned at least three times that much as a model, and that he was a millionaire. After all there had been reports in the papers that he was happy to blow £10,000 on keeping a lap-dancing club open for a few extra hours.

He decided to sweeten things by taking her on holiday to Hawaii for a week, then he bought her and the unborn baby a nice, if not particularly grand, home. He paid about $1 million for a house in Malibu, very close to the beach. It is a California-style, two-bedroom beach house, not amazing and not in a prime location, but not bad either, at least for a girl who hadn't previously owned her own home.

He began to talk a lot about the baby, deciding that it was definitely the work of fate that one was on the way. 'It wasn't a surprise. I knew from the moment he was conceived,' he told one reporter. 'I knew before I was told. Feelings washed over me. I remember the moment – it was a moment of the unconscious creation of the future, grasping my destiny. It wasn't a decision, it wasn't talked about, it was just meant to happen. He was ready to come, ready to arrive. It was a thing outside my power, greater than me.'

He told people he knew it would be a boy. His mother wanted a grandson, and, although Kim wanted to call the baby Atticus, he insisted on James after his maternal grandfather, and even started referring to him as 'Jimmy'. As the pregnancy continued, he became more and more euphoric at the prospect of becoming a father. He told newspapers he was 'the luckiest little bastard in the world' to be an expectant dad. 'When I found out, I had a smile from here to here,' he said. 'I'm having a baby, I want one, it'll be a little friend and I'll look after him. I'll be a friend to him and he'll be a friend to me. It'll be grand,' he said, rather as if he was about to buy a puppy. 'I don't know anything about bringing up a child. I don't even know where we will bring him or her up. I am just going to figure it out as I go along.'

He begged Kim to let him have joint custody of the child. She didn't agree, although she said he could see the child when he wanted. To prove his seriousness, they booked a five-month course in parenthood together at Hollywood's

Parenthood Clinic on Hollywood Boulevard, which teaches breathing techniques to use during labour, how to change a nappy and the techniques of breastfeeding.

'I want to be a real hands-on dad,' he declared, 'and really be there for my kid. I want to learn all about it and put in 100 per cent.'

He also wanted his mother to be there at the baby's birth, as he felt her advice would be essential. As one friend put it, 'He's very excited about becoming a daddy but he knows he still needs his mother's help as he is still fairly immature.'

He told the *Sun* newspaper that he wanted the birth to take place in Dublin, somewhere Kim had never been. Perhaps alarmed at his enthusiasm and his apparent desire to take over the whole pregnancy and birth, and possibly give their child to his mother as if it was her own, Kim drew back. She said she didn't want to give birth anywhere but in LA, as she wasn't sure about maternity care outside the USA. For all she knew, it didn't exist, and she no doubt wanted her own mother, not his, at the bedside during her final contractions.

He gave way about the place of its birth and his mother being there, and made protestations that he was going to change his ways when the baby arrived, live in a different way, as if he had not been totally happy with his lifestyle for some time, and that he saw the birth as an opportunity for making a real change in his life. But Kim was not convinced and made it clear that she didn't want him using her house as if it was his own.

'Kim's grateful to Colin for buying her the house,' said a friend, 'but it's her space and he will not be staying over. She's over Colin and just wants to get on with her life now. She wants to stay on good terms with him, of course, but, despite what he says, he doesn't exactly present himself as an ideal father. He's always out partying and makes no bones about his real loves in life – drinking and women.'

With all these emotions swirling round him, he tried hard to fathom things out. 'I don't know whether I'll ever be married again or in a normal environment,' he said wistfully. 'I've seen families who have married and had kids and it goes pear-shaped. So, just because I'm not necessarily with Kim, it doesn't mean I'm going to be a bad parent. But I still want to have a good time – I enjoy life. It's the only one I'm going to get.'

As usual, his only certainty lay in work. Schumacher was eager to use his young protégé again. He took little interest in the mounting adverse publicity about Colin's private life; he was still only interested in what the boy could actually do on screen.

'It's no secret that I find him one of the finest young actors alive,' he said slightly defensively. He found a tiny hooligan cameo for him in *Veronica Guerin*, a film about the very darkest side of Dublin. With a menacing soundtrack, including two songs by Sinead O'Connor, the film chronicles the last two years in the life of Veronica Guerin, a reporter on the *Sunday Independent* in Dublin, who waged a lone war against the city's top drug-dealers. She was murdered on 26 June 1996 by a gunman on a motorbike, who drew up alongside her red sports car and shot her in the head at point-blank range through the window.

She comes across Farrell's character, Spanky McSpank, a drunken soccer hooligan, in a bar, all studs and stubble and obsessed with watching the football game on the screen over the bar.

'I made him do a Texas accent in *Tigerland*,' says Schumacher, 'and a Bronx voice for *Phone Booth*, so there is no way I could shoot on the streets of Dublin and not use him. He just happened to be visiting Dublin and he really wanted to meet Cate. He held her in such awe.'

If the camera does not lie, she was obviously on his list of desirable women and he manages to imbue his few moments on screen with her with a great sexual charge. This was definitely another Paltrow moment, but delightfully on screen in full view this time, as he suggests a man who knows a fine bit of skirt when he sees one and, although he knows that she is socially way above him, he has the nerve to proposition her anyway, just for the hell of it.

'A big stretch for Colin,' said Schumacher, laughing. But, self-parody or not, he does it all with his eyes which suddenly shine with admiration, and a few suggestive but subtle movements of his mouth.

Pursuing truth, Guerin marches into people's bedrooms, knocks on windows and doors, confronting the men such as 'The Monk', 'The Viper' and 'The General', Martin Cahill again, and she gets horribly beaten and shot in the process.

Her worst enemy in the film is gangster John Gilligan, played brilliantly by Gerard McSorley, from the Abbey Players, Dublin's National Theatre Company. He gives a terrifying performance as the personification of evil and weakness, and looks verymuch the real.

She can't really have been that brave or reckless, and her mother, hovering in the background, hands clasped, played by Brenda Fricker, surely can't have been quite that understanding about her daughter, the mother of her grandchild, going on what was tantamount to a suicide mission.

'She wasn't a saint,' says Schumacher with surprising frankness. 'She was very attractive and very smart, so she was seductive and manipulative and that's how she got her stories. We filmed in 93 locations in 50 days, an enormous amount of movement for a movie. But that's because Veronica could fit in anywhere, in a pub with the lowest criminal, or in Parliament with MPs. She was very bold, perhaps too bold, and it cost her her life.'

But there is authenticity there, and the final scene where she is murdered and her frail little body is stretched across the front seats of her car resonates unpleasantly in the mind for a long time.

Moved by her story, Colin took the opportunity, albeit from the bar of Château Marmont, to attack the IRA himself, calling them 'a bunch of scumbags and terrorists'.

The film was well received in Europe but largely ignored in the USA. 'You forget how many violent deaths there are in the USA every week,' said Schumacher philosophically. 'One million kids took guns to school last year. We're still the wild, wild West.'

Over on a three-day visit to London, Colin squeezed in a visit to Stringfellow's Club accompanied by fellow 'bad boy' Calum Best, the son of George, the patron saint of all bad boys. That night, he was seen kissing a lap-dancer called Bella while she had one leg over his shoulder, and he was also reported to have been linked with lap-dancer Maria Rothman.

He met London party girl, Chrissy Haines, who had once nearly achieved fame by being seen standing beside Pierce Brosnan's son Chris, at the Wellington Club, a late-night hang-out in Knightsbridge for A- and B-list celebrities wanting to have fun. A friend of Haines said, 'He singled her out immediately from all the other women who were queuing up to get close to him. She is just Colin's type; she's got a great body, very curvaceous, and a lovely brown skin, which he adores. There was no question that, as soon as he set his eyes on her, he was going to have his wicked way with her. They're both single and there's no law against it… they just wanted to have a bit of fun together while he was over here.'

After a night of passion, she gushed to the press about his 'five times a night' prowess. He flew off without comment to Dublin for the première of *Veronica Guerin*, and presented his mother with a Mercedes convertible. Haines says he told her he would return to London to see her after the party in Ireland, but she never heard from him again. He then jetted back to LA to finish work on *SWAT*.

She was worldly wise and the friend added, 'She was 'far from heartbroken. She's a top-class girl and knows she can get any man who takes her fancy.'

Colin insisted that any girls who fell for him were probably deluding themselves; they couldn't know him. 'I kiss girls, they kiss me back,' he said, 'but it's not me they're falling for, it's an image – it's something else, an idea.'

It was almost as if he no longer believed he really existed as a person, or that anyone could want him for himself. As far as he was concerned, they only wanted him because he was a film star. In return, he gave them a night with a famous person. That was the game they were all playing.

After finishing *SWAT*, he got an opportunity to work in Dublin again. In 1999, John Crowley, author of the award-winning play *True Lies*, saw Mark O'Rowe's play *Howie the Rookie* at the tiny Bush Theatre which is over a pub in west London. The play about gangland feuds in the dirty dives of Dublin showed that O'Rowe could write tellingly and hilariously about hard men. It won five major awards, including the *Irish Times* New Play Award. Crowley asked him if he'd ever tried writing a screenplay. The answer was no but, six months later, O'Rowe called him to say he'd written a script but not to tell anyone about it. It was the screenplay for *Intermission*.

Colin also saw *Howie the Rookie*, and it appealed directly to his fascination with the seamy side of Dublin life, the filthy, matted underbelly of the Celtic Tiger. He became friends with O'Rowe, a small, earnest, bespectacled young man who grew up in Tallaght, the area of rough council estates to the south of Dublin. In 2003, with great imagination and generosity, he asked if he could be part of the film *Intermission*.

Colin's agent on Wilshire Boulevard was now used to getting him at least $5 million and upwards a picture; Colin did *Intermission* because he really wanted to, taking only a few hundred pounds. The whole budget for the film was only £2.8 million.

'Not enough to keep him in drink and fags for a week,' said Crowley, who is now an associate director at the Donmar Warehouse. 'He came on side and really helped me.'

If New York wasn't nightmarish enough in *Phone Booth*, *Intermission* makes Dublin, 'the little big city', out to be even worse, full of people who are mean, violent or mad, often all three. The difference is that this is a comedy, albeit a very black one.

The action takes place over two days and Colin plays Lehiff, a petty criminal with psychotic tendencies whose story becomes intertwined with that of John (Cillian Murphy), a plain-faced deadbeat who treats his girlfriend Deirdre (Kelly Macdonald) with contempt. She takes up with an older man, a bank manager, and, in revenge, John decides to attempt a bank robbery, with a little help from his friend Lehiff.

The film begins with a camera focused on Colin's angel face as he chats tenderly to a young girl serving in a café. He oozes twinkly Irish charm, then, in a flash, he smashes her in the face, breaking her nose and knocking her to the floor, before seizing the cash from her till. It is a moment when the full power of those eyes and that mouth are used. He is horribly hypnotic as he changes mood from seducer – seducing both the girl and us as the audience – to vile and terrifying creep. It is a fearless performance.

It was Crowley's first film, although he had directed a TV play, and he was naturally delighted to get Colin. 'He radiates energy on screen,' he says. 'From the second the cameras rolled, he was thrilling to watch, nailing everything in one take.'

In the second scene, we see Lehiff in the men's loo, getting a bit of his own medicine from ageing police officer Jerry Lynch, a man who is desperate to be seen as both truly hard and heroically Irish, played with mad accuracy by Colm Meaney, a gifted and quirky Irish actor who made his break into Hollywood in 1997 in *Con Air* up against Nicolas Cage, John Cusack and John Malkovich. Lynch shows how he feels about Lehiff by getting him in a neck hold and urinating over his tracksuit bottoms.

Everyone in the film – and there is a vast array of characters – is tormented by impossible dreams, except Lehiff who is a nihilist or perhaps just a moron. Lynch, 'a warrior soul', vainly pursues physical perfection in the gym although we can see by his blotchy red face that he is past it. He also yearns for the fulfilment of his 'Celtic soul', and victory over the evil little 'shites' on the local council estate. A TV director wants to make serious films but is restricted to recording local activities, such as a man rabbit-racing in his back garden.

Two youths working in a shop cannot find what it is they really want to do with their lives. Sally, played brilliantly by Shirley Henderson, is in a deep depression after a terrible romantic trauma when she was tied up, excreted over and abandoned by her lover in London. She has let herself go to the point that her mother tells her on the bus that she should at least get rid of her 'ronnie', or moustache. Sally is devastated as she didn't know she had one. Apparently, the 'ronnie' gets its name from either Ronnie Drew of The Dubliners, whose face is covered in hair, or possibly from Ronnie Whelan, a moustachioed captain of the Irish football team who also played for Liverpool. Sally cannot quite accept that she has a ronnie at all and asks the driver, who tells her consolingly that at least it is 'no Tom Selleck' and 'no Bert Reynolds' either.

Even the bus driver himself is tormented by inner

demons. His bus is wrecked when it swerves to avoid a nasty little boy on a bike. The boy, who is literally unstoppable, gives a terrifying impression of feral Irish children. The driver becomes obsessed by catching the boy and bringing him to justice.

This bleak escapade is topped off by the 'the king on wheels', a pathologically boring old bully in a wheelchair who uses his physical problems to trap people into listening to him.

This is a Dublin infested by no-hopers, chancers and 'eejits', a world that fascinates Colin, somewhere he'd been on the fringes of in his youth, but had never really been part of. It's nasty, funny and woven together by mysterious jokes about facial hair and brown sauce, the stuff of these Dubliners' daily lives.

As the film ends, Colin sings, or rather growls, on the soundtrack 'I Fought The Law', the old Sonny Curtis song, which was successfully revived by The Clash in the late 1970s. As well as any punk artist, he captures the voice of disaffected, hacked-off corner boys, men like Lehiff with nowhere to go but the bar and prison. As he sings, he creates a pastiche of a culture that isn't his, the fantasy working-class life he viewed from a distance as a youth in Castleknock. He sounds brilliant and shows that Louis Walsh should have thought twice when rejecting him for Boyzone. But perhaps he was right. He didn't have a suitable voice for a teeny-bop band, and might well have scared a lot of little girls away.

One critic called the film 'rough and ready'. It became a cult hit, and some of the actors involved have prospered since – Colm Meaney appeared in the British gangster thriller *Layer Cake*, with Daniel Craig and Michael Gambon, while, in 2005, Cillian Murphy landed the juicy role of the villain in the latest Batman film, *Batman Begins*, starring Christian Bale as the caped crusader.

With no great ambitions in mind for once, on a spree from Hollywood and impending fatherhood, Colin was looking out for interesting projects, outside the normal studio remit. 'After *SWAT*, I definitely wanted projects that would challenge me a bit more,' he said.

He came across a script for *A Home at the End of the World*, the story of an unusual love triangle, composed of two men, one fully gay, one bi-sexual, and a straight woman. The script was taken from a novel by Michael Cunningham, who won a Pulitzer Prize for *The Hours*, a film in which almost every character apart from the cat was a lesbian, starring Nicole Kidman, Julianne Moore, Meryl Streep and Eileen Atkins.

Highly contrived, the most memorable thing about *The Hours* was the artificial nose that Kidman was forced to wear as the brilliant but neurotic writer Virginia Woolf, which looked as if she'd borrowed it from Fagin in Lionel Bart's *Oliver!*.

But Cunningham was 'hot', fashionable at the upmarket end of Hollywood. Colin was enthusiastic, full of hope for the quality of the product, which he called 'flawless, really beautiful'. 'The story is about love. It's about companionship,' he said, 'love in its purest form, which doesn't live in the realms of sex and can be woman–man, woman–woman or man–man.'

The story seemed to open up the possibility of finding lasting love and companionship within unconventional groups, outside the family. It was being produced by actor Tom Hulce who once starred as Mozart in the hit film *Amadeus*, and was to be directed by Michael Mayer, who is best known for his theatre work in New York. Mayer, who doesn't give a hoot about Hollywood, had never even heard of Colin.

'I didn't know who he was,' he says. 'We got the call from

CAA saying, "Colin Farrell has read the screenplay and he really wants you to offer him the role of Bobby Morrow."

'I said he's going to have to read for me as I haven't seen any of his work and they said, "Well, he's done *Minority Report* for Spielberg and he didn't read for that so he's not going to read for you." So I said, "Well, he's not going to get this part then, sorry."'

Colin, never as starchy or precious as his publicity people, immediately agreed to read for the part. He and Mayer met in the lobby of the Château Marmont and talked.

'He talked a lot about his life,' says Mayer. 'A lot of it related to the story. I watched this hardened, sort of party boy change while we talked, he sort of relaxed and I saw all this other stuff melt away and, into those incredible coal-black eyes, I got a glimpse of a truly poetic soul.'

Colin got the part and, in the winter of 2003, he headed for Toronto to start work. The film was a total change of pace for him. After all his wise-guys, villains and bad boys, he was now playing Bobby, all droopy eyelashes and winsome smiles. The film starts in 1967, when Bobby, aged nine, against a soundtrack of Jefferson Airplane, sees his older brother having sex and his mother tripping out on drugs. In the 1960s scenes, everyone appears to be wearing fluorescent colours and is completely deranged.

His brother dies after accidentally cutting his throat and both his parents follow him to an early grave, so Bobby practically moves in with his friend Jonathan, and becomes close to Jonathan's unhappy mother, played by Sissy Spacek, introducing her to pot.

The boy's friendship turns to love. They meet again as adults when Jonathan, played by Dallas Roberts, is living with Clare, a 'kookie' former drug addict, played by Robin Wright Penn.

Colin appears as an adult looking very strange, rather like

an Indian scout or a howler monkey, his small face peering out from a very large hairpiece.

'It was like they poured glue on my head and put a blow dryer on it,' he says. 'I wanted to cut all my scenes until we got to the scene where it all got cut off. You have no idea how bad it was... it was like going to church when I was ten. It was horrible. Somebody asked me, "What was it like when you looked in the mirror wearing that wig?" I said, "Are you kidding. Why would I look in the mirror?"'

'There were some problems,' admits Michael Mayer, patiently. 'There were some days when Colin had to have long hair, short hair, long hair, short hair, because of our crazy schedule, so things got a little funky.'

Robin Wright Penn, a natural blonde, playing Clare, was forced to sport a synthetic red wig, rather like a clown's. In the film, she cuts off Bobby's long hair replacing it with a short spiky cut that makes him look amazingly camp. Not since he'd been a line dancer had he appeared so pretty and feminine-looking.

Not surprisingly, the *Gay People's Chronicle* in the USA gave it a 'Best Film Award'.

Despite the shaggy hair problems, Colin turns in a very good performance, the best of anyone in the film. He has the trick of being able to show in his face what he is really thinking while he might be doing or saying something quite different, not something all screen actors can manage.

Fluttering his eyelashes and looking sensitive, he seemed to relish playing someone who is sexually ambivalent. 'Bobby's not gay... it's hard to say what he is,' says Jonathan, who soothes his own loneliness with casual sex.

During the film, Bobby and Jonathan had to kiss passionately. 'It feels odd, I don't like the feel of the moustache, but you just do it,' says Colin, sounding a bit like chef Gordon Ramsey forcing some poor kitchen hand to perform an unpleasant task. 'You are telling a story. It's your job as an actor to do it. If you can say to someone, "Put your hands on your head," while threatening them with an M-16 in your hand, you should be able to kiss a dude.'

They form a *ménage à trois*, finding something essential in each other that they are unable to get in just one other person. Clare has a baby by Jonathan. 'Babies,' says Colin as Bobby, 'let's have a dozen.' Both men make perfect dads and they form a functioning family.

In his interaction with the baby on screen – changing her, holding her foot in his mouth – it is easy to see how relaxed Colin is with infants, perhaps due to his own happy early childhood when he was everyone's darling.

There are a lot of protracted shots of cute home-making and high emotion, heightened by a soundtrack including Dusty Springfield, Leonard Cohen, Bruce Springsteen, Bob Dylan, Laura Nyro and Paul Simon.

The music is always more impressive than the dialogue. 'The film is about people talking and relating,' says Dallas Roberts, who plays Jonathan. But what they say is rarely interesting or convincing and, as everyone is so nice to each other, there is absolutely no dramatic tension.

The message of the film is that you can now choose your family, and it aims to show that ordinary, decent Americans can have extraordinary lives if they choose an alternative to the usual family set-up; in fact, it is a plea for tolerance towards different family units, particularly encompassing gay relationships.

'It's really quite moving,' says Michael Mayer, who has apparently been a little more moved than the general viewing public. But what happened was really not his fault. There were grave problems with the production. It was released by Warner Independent Pictures. Some Hollywood studios have cottoned on to the buzz word 'independent', but it doesn't really mean much to them. Mayer was given a mere $8 million to play with.

'They weren't really interested in investing in the film,' he says. 'I could feel that every step of the way... frankly, the people releasing it took so much control over the editing and over how to market the film. It broke my heart because they weren't terribly intelligent people and I knew they didn't really care about it.'

It ended up leaden, pious and lecturing. But, despite this, the production began and ended with some red-hot gossip in the press – all generated by Colin. Tongues originally started wagging because the start of filming was delayed by an outbreak of the SARS (Severe Acute Respiratory Syndrome) virus in Canada, which killed 12 people. For a time, the crew and actors were quarantined together. Naturally, they got to know each other well and Colin started spending a lot of time in Robin's trailer on the set and travelled to work with her each day in a mini-van.

Then there was the arrival of the pregnant Kim on set. The future parents were spotted out together in Toronto, but the press were fixated on the idea that Colin was falling in love with his married co-star.

'Sex-crazed Colin Farrell has set his roving eye on his new co-star Sean Penn's sexy wife, Robin Wright Penn!' screamed *Star* magazine a few months into production. 'Sources predict the wild Irishman – dubbed the "lusty leprechaun" for his admitted fondness of casual sex – is headed for big trouble with bad boy Penn. Everyone believes he has the hots for Robin. "He can't stay away from her," says an insider, "but he better not forget who she's married to."'

Although Wright Penn is skeletal and wan-looking, with a sad expression, facially she and Colin do look rather alike and, at ten years older than him, a grounded mother of two, she is the kind of strong, older woman that often attracts him.

The press loved the idea of a fight between the two bad boys, Farrell and Penn. 'Farrell is headed for big trouble,' one paper opined. 'Penn is someone Farrell shouldn't mess with… he's very jealous and has a hair-trigger temper. He's not afraid to let his fists do the talking – and he has guns, too.'

Colin was unmoved. He lived for the day, just as when he was a boy kissing his mother goodbye at the school gate; he just wasn't bothered about consequences. He continued hanging round her trailer.

'He'll often pause at the door, as if trying to delay leaving,' said one observer. 'He also doesn't care who watches his displays of affection towards her. He gave Robin a bear hug and planted a big kiss on her lips after shooting a scene. On another day, they shot a sizzling scene in which he kissed her tenderly among the trees. And when they shouted "Cut", it was clear Colin didn't want to let go. As they stood around talking to the crew, he put his hand on her back, then put his arm around her shoulder and looked intently into her eyes.'

Body-language expert Carmen Harra, author of *Everyday Karma*, examined photos of Colin shooting a scene with Penn. 'It's clear sex is on his mind,' she said, 'but she's uncomfortable with his attention. Farrell placed his arm around Robin's shoulder and on her back to claim her as his own, but she kept her distance.'

According to Harra, the other photos show his participation in 'a male mating ritual' with Robin outside her trailer. 'His body says, "I'm a James Dean-type sex symbol. Get this jacket off me,"' said the expert. 'Robin's holding on to the door because she refuses to be seduced by his charm. Hanging in the doorway, he flashes his sexy abs, saying, "Look at my sexy body. Come and get me." But Robin doesn't respond to him. Her head is down and he looks disappointed. But he'll try again.'

And everyone enthusiastically agreed that trying anything would be dangerous. 'Colin is crazy if he thinks he can target Robin as his next conquest,' said a source. 'He'll have Sean Penn coming after him.'

Part of the filming was done in New York, and Colin was so undaunted by the prospect of Penn, or perhaps excited by the possible danger, that he whisked Robin off to Scores, his favourite haunt.

Other clubbers watched as he openly canoodled with her on the dance floor. Relishing the attention, he shouted out to his impromptu audience, 'We play lovers in the film and we're rehearsing,' before downing several strawberry Kamikaze cocktails.

He spent £2,000 on drinks that evening and tried to keep the club open after hours so that they could go straight from there to the film set at 8.00am, but Robin wasn't quite so energetic. She got him to leave at 4.00am.

When the filming was over, he still had plenty of excitement for his audience. Colin's cheeky charisma acted as a direct challenge to the scared people at Warner Independent. They had produced a film about sex with no sex in it, not a bare nipple in sight, but news of what the film might have been soon leaked out to a public who knew they'd been knowingly undersold.

There were originally some full-frontal nude scenes in the film, which is, after all, about unbridled homosexual love. The film ends up with no bare flesh except a tiny strip of Jonathan's groin where he shows Bobby a nasty-looking mark which we are left to suppose is the early onset of AIDS. All nudity was chopped by Warners for the usual reason of prudish caution. They were looking for a big audience, not a small independent one, or a gay one.

'I have no problem showing my cock,' said Colin in rather an understatement. 'During the test screenings, it was said that audiences found it too distracting. I see my cock every day and I am not distracted by it.'

He asked for the images to be put back into the DVD release but they never were, and audience curiosity and rumour went wild. 'All of a sudden, all the magazines were screaming, "Oh my God, let's write about that,"' he said rather piqued. 'I'm surprised they didn't do a separate story on whether I have an innie or an outie belly button.'

In fact, with his usual luck, the rumour factory gave him the benefit of the doubt. It was said that the full-frontal love scenes were chopped because his male member was too large to be seen, that it had caused audiences to 'hoot and cheer'. Women were said to have become 'overexcited'; 'all you could hear was gasps,' said one report, and men were left 'angry and upset'.

In an outburst of surprising bitchiness, Dallas Roberts tried to play down any idea that Colin had anything particularly exciting tucked away in his pants. 'Don't believe the hype about Farrell's full-frontal nude scene,' he declared. 'The kid has nothing to be ashamed of, but I was at screenings where women allegedly burst into tears and men hid their faces in shame and I never saw any of it. There may have been a few guffaws, but there wasn't any gasping or dropping to one's knees.'

After all this publicity, *A Home at the End of the World* was fairly successful in the USA, 'by some miracle', said Mayer, but never made it to Europe, except on DVD.

The film made Colin interesting to the more intellectual Hollywood producers, and he was now seen as an actor with a seriously good range. There were rumours that he might be hired to play alongside Jude Law in a lavish new version of *Brideshead Revisited*, and that he was signed up for a remake of the steamy Blake Edwards 1979 hit *10*, taking the role from Hugh Grant.

He said he wanted to play Roy of the Rovers in a film about British soccer. He was now effectively King of Hollywood; he'd been everywhere and done everything it had to offer, and all the time he knew that he had a really big one up his sleeve, a film that could make him the top star and highest earner in Hollywood above Di Caprio or Pitt... if it came off.

In early September 2003, Colin confided to a reporter from *Esquire* magazine that he was going to play Alexander the Great for Oliver Stone. 'It's going to be, like, an epic production,' he said. 'No doubt, it is going to do wonders for the size of my head and it's going to be a mad fucking job. It's going to be a fucking trip, and that's what I am on about. Trying to do stuff to keep it interesting.'

The gods must have been listening, and they can't have liked what they heard, because, for the first time in his career, they turned against him.

CHAPTER NINE

LOOKING GOOD, FEELING GREAT

It is a terrific story – a rough, exuberant lad from a provincial outpost has a dream that he will one day be someone, better than his father. He dreams of founding an empire, ruling the known world. He grows up and, instead of putting away his lead soldiers, he sets out in pursuit of this passion, this dream, and ends up leading an army through 22,000 miles of sieges and conquests to forge an empire unlike any ever seen before or since.

Along the way, he also takes to bed three wives, four mistresses, a eunuch and an Amazon warrior, but his abiding true love was known as 'the most beautiful man in the world'.

Oliver Stone tried to tell this story using star performers, special effects, live elephants, trained warhorses and 2,000 extras. But he really wanted the image of Colin Farrell as Alexander the Great to carry it.

Colin had first ridden into public notice bareback on a glum, grey Irish pony; now, eight years on, he rode across the cinema screen as another bareback horseman, this time on a huge, black Italian charger, bare-legged and waving a spear, in what was meant to be his greatest film.

'I was looking for a young god who could act,' says Stone, 'someone with the confidence of a warrior and a leader. An Alexander who could walk into the room and look in the eyes of any man, and could move them beyond themselves.'

This hardly sounds like a description of Colin, an easygoing fella who likes a drink and a laugh, but there was something of the ancient adventurer there – in the same amount of time that it took Alexander to dominate 90 per cent of the known world, Colin from Castleknock had, by sheer will, determination and what he calls his 'passion', turned himself into one of Hollywood's leading players, famous throughout the world.

It was his eyes, his skin, his voice, his flashing thighs, rather than those of Brad Pitt, Leonardo Di Caprio or Ben Affleck, that were meant to make the film work and pull in the dollars. In the years since *Ballykissangel*, his career had turned into big business. He was the kind of buck-making star that the millionaire bosses at CAA were glad to have on their books. The money men were banking on the young lead star to do his magic and make it work.

Stone's adventure was costing millions to make; he was cutting through a budget of $160m (£87 million) plus a marketing spend of $120m (£63 million) and the film needed to claw back $50m (£28 million) in its first weekend in the USA to be considered a success.

More than any other film actor of his generation, Colin was seen to be the one with enough originality, independence and stamina to do it. And he really wanted to do it; this was his chance to become leader of the Hollywood A-list.

Because of his recent successes, his agent could have put in for a bigger fee from Warner Bros. But because of the trouble Stone was having raising the money – he needed to turn his epic into Cecil B DeMille proportions – Colin actually took a cut in what was offered and settled for $10m, plus a probable 10 per cent of the gross profits.

Sounds good, but there was terrible pressure on him and, at the same time, he was, of course, also expecting his first child. With that kind of pressure, most people would at least break out in a few pimples, but he told reporters that he was 'feeling calm and unconcerned'.

'Fear is rot, a waste of time' had always been his motto since he set out from Dublin on his life's adventure. Stone was so impressed by this Farrellism that he put it into the mouth of Craterus, played by six-foot-six Scots actor Rory McCann, as he tries to calm his men when they first see war elephants on the rampage.

'I always knew *Alexander* was going to be demanding,' says Colin. 'The emotional stakes were very high and it was also physically draining, a lot of work. I had to put myself through a lot. I was always on a kind of edge and it was upsetting at times because I found the story very sad. I quickly got over seeing it as something glorious.'

In April 2003, five months before filming, he began to prepare himself for the role of his lifetime by studying Ancient Greek poetry in translation, Sophocles and Homer, the texts loved and carried everywhere by Alexander. He also had to get stuck into the fourth draft of the script. There were to be many, many more of those as the script kept changing over the next six months of work, the structure of the story altered in terms of time, with constant switches back and forth between past and present.

According to Robin Lane Fox, the historical adviser on the film, going through the first script took Colin three-and-a-half hours, 20 Camel cigarettes and four beers. Reading about Alexander's early death in 323BC, aged 33, and how his vast empire had just melted away after his death, he began to wonder if he himself would succeed in this massive project and if it was going to be worthwhile.

In May, he visited Dublin for a script rehearsal with Stone and other members of the fast-growing cast. Perhaps as an incentive to keep up his enthusiasm, Stone invited him on to London to meet Angelina Jolie.

Stone had been a fan of hers since seeing her in the 1998 TV film *Gia*, in which she played Gia Carangi, a 1970s New York fashion model and drug addict who died of AIDS aged 26. He believed she was just right to make audiences understand a powerful woman. 'She goes for it in a strong, determined way,' he said, 'and it's rare to see that in young actors.'

He cast her as Alexander's mother Olympias, although, at 28, she was only one year older than her screen son. He had no idea how well that would work for Colin, if no one else. As he introduced them over dinner, it was love at first sight, or perhaps first 'need', for Jolie and Stone could only sit back and watch somewhat amazed.

'Colin was all over her,' Stone says, 'he was just falling in love with her, he couldn't help himself. He was like a baby towards its mother. Angelina was laughing at him. I don't know if actors sometimes act out their desires, but he wanted to be the infant to her mother.'

The next day, they visited the British Museum together to look at artefacts from Alexander's world, and he was seen kissing her long neck. The papers were full of it, wanting a romance. One even commented that, as both stars were born under Gemini, they would make a lovely couple. Others found it hard to believe that the young actress, most famous for playing Lara Croft in *Tomb Raider*, whose plump lips look like two widgety grubs stuck together, was going to be playing a cruel eastern matriarch who'd really been through the mill, experiencing abduction, rape and forced marriage by the time she had had her son.

But Colin was adamant that his new-found leading lady was just right for the part. 'I think that, once you get over the initial hurdle of the age difference, you just have to accept that she's such a fucking brilliant actor, such a powerhouse, such a sexy woman,' he gushed, 'so regal, that I never found it a stretch to think of her as Olympias.'

He loved older women anyway, and Jolie was puzzled about all the fuss as she had apparently no idea what ages the characters were supposed to be. 'I play Alexander's mother when he's seven and I age through the movie,' she says, 'though he was quite young when he died, about 19, I think. So it's not like his mother was old; at the end she's mid-thirties.'

She did hint later that she knew the mismatch of age was going to be distracting for some people. 'I wasn't sure how it was going to work. I met with Oliver and we kind of said, "We're either going to be criticised and attacked for this, or it's right and a really big chance." But, seeing us separately, I fit Olympias and Colin fits Alexander, so there is no problem about us being mother and son.'

Colin had no time to linger over his co-star, or to consider whether things really looked promising for the film. He didn't see any of the bad omens; a director who'd been off the scene for five years, who had been arrested in 1999 on alcohol and drugs charges, a confusing script without any sign of even one good writer anywhere near it, odd casting so that children were the same age as their parents, and that blond hair which Stone loved on Colin but which he said made him look like 'fuckin' Doris Day'.

He wanted to work with Stone for better or worse, and he had lots of work to do for the role. It wasn't just going to be a matter of learning the lines; for Stone, the project was about a profound use of 'Method acting', forcing the actors to turn themselves into the characters almost to the point of breakdown and death.

Colin retreated to a valley of avocado trees 70 miles north of LA, bought an Airstream trailer, a luxurious mobile home made of aluminium and fibreglass, which cost $100,000, and settled down to work, well away from the distractions presented by Dublin, New York and LA.

Banana trees grew over the site, so he slung his hammock between them and set about learning his lines, accompanied only by the sound of cicadas and sprinkler systems.

'I got the part by osmosis,' he says. 'I'd lie there drifting off for 30 seconds, then returning with a clearer grasp of a line or two.'

It sounds like an ideal way to study, but this lush, tranquil time did not last; Stone had other plans. He didn't want anyone getting too comfortable. According to 'the Method', Colin was going to have to *be* Alexander.

Three terrifying people arrived at his door – Ricardo Cruz Moral, the film's horse master; Julia Dewey Rupkalvis, a female body coach, with a PhD in 'Hoplology', the study of human conflict; and the aptly named Captain Dale A Dye, the film's military director.

Julia calls Colin 'a dear, dear man', but Captain Dye, dressed in army fatigues, US army baseball cap and a vest emblazoned with the words 'Pain is Weakness Leaving the Body', has no time for actors at all. A former professional soldier, between 1965 and 1967 he'd served in 31 major combat operations in Vietnam. Like Stone, he'd won a Bronze Star in Vietnam, as well as three Purple Hearts for wounds suffered in combat. A former editor of *Soldier of Fortune* magazine, a glossy for men who fantasise about being mercenaries, in 1985 he'd set up his own company, 'Warriors Inc', whose motto is: 'We turn your cast into a crack platoon in three weeks or your money back'. He'd organised boot camps to train actors on 40 films, including *Platoon*, *Born on the Fourth of July* and *Natural Born*

Killers, when he'd taught Juliette Lewis and Woody Harrelson to use automatic weapons.

Not a great theatregoer, Dye had a thing about actors, particularly disliking the fact that they are not usually very much like soldiers. 'Soldiers fit in, they are like cogs in a machine,' he said, 'while actors question everything. Soldiers question nothing; they just obey orders without question. When I take an actor, he is no longer an actor. I don't care who he is, I will wear his ass out, physically and psychologically.'

To emphasise this during the making of *Saving Private Ryan*, he addressed Tom Hanks, who is an icon in America, as 'Turd One'. As for Colin, he said, 'I don't believe there is such a thing as a movie star. I won't have it. I am gonna unscrew his Irish head and all of that "me, me, me" that actors all have and I'm gonna pour that out and teach him that the sun does not rise and set on his ass.'

As a boy, Colin had been good at football, basketball and a bit of gentle riding, but he'd always hated gym and now there was to be no escape from it. 'That was a mother of a film,' as he put it. Instead of dozing over his script, he had to learn to use a Kopis, the kind of curved sword that Alexander would have used. He also had to ride all over again, first a quad bike, then the horse, trotting while holding a spear, then he had to make the horse rear up on its hind legs. He was even sent on an equestrian course in Spain to master the finer points. He was to be on horseback without a saddle, mounted on Othello, his Italian mount, or Balthazar, a Dutch Friesian steed, throughout most of the film, usually wearing a short tunic, with nothing between him and the horse except his shamrock underpants.

Most afternoons in the orchard were spent seated at a low table with maps, diagrams, twigs and bottle caps laid out as Dye and Stone described to him the techniques of battle used in the third century BC. In particular, they explored the use of the phalanx, a square of men, 16 by 16, marching each with a spear that they lowered in synch to make an all but impregnable 256-man 'hedgehog' marching as a single, prickly unit against the enemy.

There were also lessons on wider military strategy that Alexander employed in his world-conquering campaigns. This was hardly essential preparation for an actor who would probably have preferred to concentrate on learning his lines, but Colin listened attentively. 'In the afternoon, I had to sit and listen to talks on battle formations,' says Colin wearily. The Castleknock and college days of skiving off were long gone. Stone believed that all this information and warlike exercise would help him as an actor to 'get inside the man'.

After three months of this, just as *S.W.A.T.* was released in the USA, it was time to leave for Morocco, where most of the film would be shot. This was difficult as his first child was due to be born in LA in just over a month. Although he'd put it out of his mind easily enough in his garden and in training, he dreaded actually leaving the USA to start filming. Something major in his life was happening that he couldn't control and he couldn't even be there to see it.

'I'm going to be sitting on a fucking horse in Marrakech shouting, "I'm Alexander,"' he said, 'and I'm just going to be wanting to be with him instead. It is going to break my heart.'

But he had no option; it was a case of do or Dye and there was a boot camp in the desert with his name on it. Stone was obsessed with how Alexander had conquered the world and he wanted everyone to share something of that historical experience, whether they appreciated it or not.

'We are going to make Colin uncomfortable,' said Rupkalvis. 'We're gonna make the soldiers of the Macedonian army uncomfortable. Uncomfortable won't kill you.'

Colin now settled down to a life in the desert, described by the writer John Fante as 'always there, a patient, white animal, waiting for men to die, for civilisations to flicker and pass into darkness'.

Just as in Alexander's distant time, there were no beds in the camp, just a hole in the ground with a leaky bit of canvas as cover. 'We had 170 people in the Moroccan desert in tents, keeping warm with fires and living on rations,' says Colin. The men were woken up at 5.00am every day by Captain Dye's grating voice screaming, 'Love this shit! Wake up, turds!'

Dye put on the kind of pressure that Tony Jordan at the Castleknock football club must have dreamed of and, if Castleknock College had failed to make a saint of Colin, fate was having another go now. First thing in the morning it was callisthenics, then a five-mile jog and a physical routine of military drills, formations, horse-riding and press-ups in the dust. Despite Dye's efforts, actors are not soldiers and a film taken at the time shows many of the poor thespians just lying in the dust not even attempting to rise on their spindly arms.

Running and doing physical jerks together was supposed to bond the actors into a fighting unit and, in the interest of historical accuracy – Alexander and his Macedonian warriors lived on tight rations while they were on campaign – they were also allowed very little food. When they finally got breakfast, it was just a few nuts and some smelly cheese. Colin has been quoted as saying that he eats like a pigeon, hoovering up food where he can find it. 'There were only two meals a day,' he says with a shudder.

'Lunch was a little square of rotten cheese that had been left out in the sun for two days with dirty fingerprints on it,' recalls blue-eyed Jared Leto, who plays Alexander's great love, Hephaistion. 'We would have maybe a couple of pretzels, a tiny cup of nuts and maybe two or three oily anchovies out of a tin, probably past their sell-by date, if we were lucky. Dessert would be a couple of canned peaches.'

Stone ordered that the actors (his troops) got one meal a day because that's what Alexander's men received every day of their ten-year route march across the world, and Colin was on exactly the same rations as his men.

One day, Leto made the mistake of complaining to Dye about maggots in the food. 'It's character-building,' he growled back, sounding surprised, as if he ate them himself all the time. 'Hell, a professional soldier doesn't worry about maggots. Maggots are good. Maggots are protein.'

'Basically, we were starving all day long until dinner,' says Leto, 'which would be some form of lamb stew. We cooked all the food ourselves which is probably why everyone was sick. Our tent was right by the lavatory. I woke up each morning for 21 days to the sound of retching and crapping.'

During filming, Colin, who always liked his pals to have a touch of wildness about them, teamed up with Gary Stretch, who was playing Cleitus, his father's chief general. Stretch was once the glamour boy of British boxing, who, in 1991, challenged Chris Eubank for the World Middleweight Championship in London, and went a good five rounds with him. Later, he became even more famous as the boyfriend of Raquel Welch.

He'd gone a little bit soft since he'd retired from the ring. 'During the filming, we were so hungry,' he says, 'we were on peanuts, dried fruit and water for three months. I lost lots of fat. Really, I need to go back and do it again.'

Colin, Leto and Stretch appreciated the way the camp life licked them into manly shape. 'Some actors didn't like it,' says Stretch, 'but I thought it was an amazing experience.'

'I'm an artist,' says Leto sensitively, 'but I got to understand in a small way what it's like to be a soldier.'

Some, like Irish actor Ian Beattie who played Antigonus, found Oliver Stone and his vision a little hard to take. 'On the first afternoon, I was up to bat,' he says. 'We all had individual fight sequences, all choreographed, we'd been working on for an hour a day. And there's 100 vehicles over there. There's 30 chariots, 75 horsemen, 300 extras in front of me, 500 behind, and there's all the crew – electricians, caterers, cameramen, soundmen, eight stuntmen, and I'm thinking, This is all for me, for just this one shot!'

'I really loved playing soldiers,' says Colin, who, despite the lack of food, had to be ferociously full of energy for his role. He was involved in battle scenes lasting 40 minutes, going full-tilt bareback, with 70 head of horse around him, 600 men on the ground and sometimes herds of battle-dressed elephants. The whole scene would leave the desert sand awash with artificial blood. 'They were a tough bunch of motherfuckers in those days,' he commented.

Throwing himself into everything with full enthusiasm, he chose to do most of the stunts himself and, with the all-round emphasis on genuine toughness, Stone and Dye let him.

'It was great,' says Colin. 'Actors are so overprotected, it's like being goalkeeper in football. I can't believe they let me get away with the stuff I got away with, it was great fun to do. I got a chance to do so much shit that I don't do in normal everyday life. I mean, like being on a horse that is going up on two legs in fright as you've got 400 screaming Indians around hacking at you. It was often scary and I came off a couple of times.

'In a battle with elephants, I had to get my horse to rear up slightly, but I pulled the bridle too hard, I was very tired, and the horse reared up and fell over backwards. It crashed to the ground and just missed my leg. It nearly finished us.

'I also got stuck in the left thigh with a sword and a few other things went wrong but I came out alive, that's the main thing.'

Colin also had more to contend with than the others. It was

decided by the slightly crazed powers higher up, who seemed to think the film was a military campaign in 'Nam or Nicaragua, that he not only had to be trained as a soldier, but also had to learn to be a real leader of men. Everyone on set had to call him 'Regent', even off screen, with no exceptions.

Dye taught him a mnemonic – 'Jedd J Buklet, III – which he had to try to repeat to himself. Each letter stood for a leadership quality – 'Justice, Enthusiasm, Dependability, Decision, Judgement, Bearing, Understanding...' and so it went on... he never got to the end of it.

The worst thing was that they forced loneliness on him, something he finds genuinely difficult in real life. 'The really tough thing, though, was that they deliberately isolated me a bit from the rest of the lads,' says Colin. 'They did it to make me feel like Alexander, the leader.'

As Regent, he had to face the unglamorous, boring aspects of soldiering, where men learn to respect and fear their commander. What the Macedonians – all made to speak with Irish accents to suggest they were kinsmen – felt for Alexander, the troops of actors had to feel for Colin. He had to be the one standing out front yelling at them to do their press-ups faster. He could not demand anything from them that he could not do himself, and they had to obey him. It was Method acting par excellence.

But their commander wasn't always there. Just like Alexander, Colin liked a drink and sometimes beer was smuggled into the camp. 'One morning I slept in,' he says. 'We'd had quite a good night and they didn't wake me. The whole camp went off for a jog and they all came back after an hour out in the desert under the blazing sun and I was still lying there in bed. I was also in charge of taking them out for PT. I was supposed to be leading them as part of my preparation for my role as Alexander, but there I was still in bed. It was a small thing, but I will never forget it.

'Then I was forced to live with older men, the type who would have been Alexander's mentors. I was put in with the captains, me and two 50-year-olds in one tent. That did my head in a bit because I like being one of the lads, I like being in the fucking mix.'

He managed to remain 'in the mix', despite being slightly removed as leader. Robin Lane Fox was impressed by Colin. 'He never had a double take unless he was exhausted,' he says. 'He is a really open-hearted guy, that is unusual, a wonderful encourager of others. He is much more than just a lucky tearaway, you know. Everyone admired him. I never heard a catty word about him during 97 days' intensive hell of filming.'

Apart from Colin hectoring in as nice a way as he could, and Dye growling, there was also the director yelling for 12 hours a day. Whatever the fantasy about 'Regent', everyone was under Stone's control, who strode about wearing his favourite banded felt hat. He exercised total control, allowing the actors no space for their own ideas. 'Oliver will yell at you, laugh at you and laugh with you,' says Leto. 'If I suck in my role, it's his fault because he got what he wanted.'

Everyone had to deal with the 'honesty' that Colin so admired. Anthony Hopkins, who played Ptolemy, a puppet ruler of Egypt, said working on the film was 'the most frightening thing I've done since I worked on *Nixon*'. Stone introduced him to Colin with the words, 'Do you know Colin? He hasn't slept in six years.'

'He's a wicked man,' says Hopkins. 'He'd come on set and say to me, "Are you going to make it? Because, God, you look so old."'

Colin got on well with Stone, regarding him as 'the master', and rather enjoyed the older man's control. 'He could pinpoint how to pull you out of yourself,' he says, 'and he taught me how to dance to his tune. But he was honest with me from day one, very tough. He would look at me and say, "Colin, that was a shit take, a terrible mistake, just terrible! OK, now fuck it, let's get out of here for a minute and work it out." On other days, he'd smile and say, "We're here." There was no dancing around the truth.'

Garrett Lombard, who played Leonnatus, was amazed by what went on. 'He'll come straight up to you after doing a scene and go, "That was terrible, awful, what are you doing?" Then he'll just walk away and you're left there going, "Oh God!" and you either sink or swim for it.

'You say, "OK, I'm useless," and shrink into a corner, or you say, "Well, I'm going to prove this guy fucking wrong." That's what he does; he riles performances out of people.'

Colin, with large amounts of charm, could sometimes play Stone at his own game. In a scene filmed for video on the set of *Alexander*, he is apparently mouthing off at the fearsome Stone. Colin looks annoyed, tired and absurd in his blond wig. Stone waves his hands trying to pacify him, explains why they have to do things a certain way, and Colin suddenly smiles serenely. It was a joke all along, a bit of craic to break the tension, lighten up a difficult day. He wasn't angry, not really, he was just winding the director up, then, after deflecting any ruffled feelings with a joke, he goes happily back to work.

Boot camp did not last for ever. As the non-combatant cast members arrived, including Val Kilmer as Alexander's father King Philip and Angelina Jolie as his mother, everyone moved to the particularly pleasant hotels in Marrakech and one can only imagine the joy they must have felt. Colin moved into the Marrakech Hotel, in a suite costing £1,000 a night. His sister Claudine arrived and set up in her usual role as his secretary.

'She was with him all the time,' says Lane Fox. 'She sorts things out, arranges meetings, chats to him, keeps him calm. They both have good Irish instincts.'

But she also left him alone for a good deal of the time. 'There were a lot of pleasures to be had in Marrakech,' said a BBC producer who was filming some of the shoot for a documentary. 'I think Colin and Gary Stretch took full advantage of them. When they weren't working, they were playing.'

For a time, Colin took up with Rosario Dawson, a young black Puerto Rican actress from New York, who plays the wild and barbaric Roxane, Alexander's first wife. Her career had started in storybook fashion when she was discovered sitting on her front porch in New York City, and asked if she wanted to 'be in a movie'. That turned out to be *Kids*, a hit film of 1995. After that, she appeared in Spike Lee's emotional film *25th Hour* and in action adventures such as *Welcome to the Jungle*.

On set, they were lovers and, on screen, she and Colin had the only vibrant sex scene in the film. Provoked and jealous of his mother and his male lover, Roxane, naked with black snakes painted on her back and bottom, furiously punches and slaps Alexander.

'Colin was being very cocky about it,' she says. 'He was like, "Go ahead, smack me as hard as you want." After about 72 goes, there was this one that just really connected, I could feel it, and he looked at me and he was like, "That's the one that's going to give me a purple one later," and it did.'

She also set about him with a knife covered in snake skin, after telling Stone that she had 20 knives at home in her closet. There might have been some real feeling behind her blows, too, as it was rumoured that Colin had broken her heart.

According to an American source, the two were an item until Jolie arrived in Morocco. 'Rosario said that sex was great with Colin,' said a friend, 'but he blew her right off once Angelina got on the set. Of course, those two ended up getting together and Rosario was devastated. She thought

213

they were going to really fall in love or something, but I told her, "C'mon, it's Colin Farrell."'

Rumours emerging from the set described the two leads sitting up together kissing and flirting until 3.00am. There was also a story that, after drinking sessions, Colin had returned to his old habit of showing the ladies his tackle, lifting his short tunic and presumably opening his lucky underpants to expose himself.

There is a history of willy-waving on film sets, where it is sometimes put to creative purpose. In 1935, while he was making *The 39 Steps*, the appropriately named Alfred Hitchcock whipped his out and waved it at blonde beauty Madeleine Carroll to give her the right look of horror and astonishment when she came downstairs in a Scottish B & B and saw two thugs waiting for her. However, the late Oliver Reed was sacked from the film *Cutthroat Island* in 1995 for similar behaviour when he presented his credentials to Geena Davis... but then she was married to the director.

'It wasn't alcohol-related,' Colin's press secretary patiently explained, as if that would make it OK. 'The incident happened when he was with the whole cast; they were in costume and he lifted his up and everyone laughed.'

Jolie – seemed to take it in good part. 'Colin's crazy,' she said, laughing, 'but a great guy and a wonderful actor.'

Omar Benjellou, who works at the hotel, recalls his room was 'a bit messy, towels everywhere, it was a real bachelor apartment, hard work for the cleaners'. There were rumours that the hotel had complained about cigarette burns on the furniture.

But no wild nights with Jolie or parties in his room could disguise the fact that Colin was in some turmoil. 'The baby was happening when I was starting *Alexander*,' he says. 'It was fucking life-changing.'

In LA, without the baby's father but with her mother and sister on hand, Kim bought a white crib costing $799, which economically converts into a small bed, and a changing table, named the 'Royale Grande', with an antique finish, costing $1,200.

Far away, Colin fretted. 'I knew that in LA this very good thing was happening,' he says, 'but I couldn't feel the joy, so it was terrible.'

Kim gave birth on Friday, 12 September 2003 to a boy weighing a healthy 7 pounds 9 ounces. Colin's sister Claudine was in the delivery room for the birth. 'At least someone from the Farrell family was there,' said Colin.

Six days later, he announced that the boy would be called James after his maternal grandfather, who was dying in Dublin. 'My grandfather was on his way out,' says Colin, 'but this was another one on the way in, doors opening and closing all the time.' He joked that he would also be calling the child 'Fokker', as in 'little Fokker'.

He began keeping a diary to give to Jimmy when he was older and it was six weeks of toil in the desert on *Alexander* before he came within a sniff of his new son. Until then, all he had were emailed photos of little Jimmy, which he proudly showed off to everyone on set, a change from other things he'd been showing them.

'Isn't he a fucking marvel?' he asked everyone who came near. 'It was horrible that I wasn't there. I've got the pictures but I haven't met the little fella yet and that hurts.

'I know how fortunate I am, believe me, but the fact that I missed my son's birth was a nightmare. Then he was not there beside me for weeks of the shoot. I hadn't smelled him, hadn't touched him, hadn't looked into his eyes, that was bad.'

He also talked to the new mother a lot on the phone, but a source said 'they get on well but there is no chance of a serious relationship'.

In early October, Kim risked leaving the safety of LA and brought the baby out to Marrakech, so at last he was able to hold and cuddle his son. 'I can't describe what it feels like the first time you hold your baby in your arms,' he says softly, still full of emotion months later. 'I looked down at that bundle of helplessness, fast asleep, and I practically had a fucking breakdown. A strength of love washed over me that I never thought was possible. I am so fortunate that I can give him whatever he wants – a good education, decent home, a lot of love. Whatever he wants to do, I'll support him. I want to give him every chance. I just want to be there as much as I can. It's the most gorgeous, gorgeous thing. He's just my friend, someone to have a laugh with. A little human who can't quite speak and say what he wants yet and it's wonderful. I adore him. Please God there will be a shared custody, but I know whatever happens I will be in his life for ever – he'll always know who his dad is.'

He'd often hinted at loneliness, complaining that LA was a lonely place, that he could feel alone in a crowded room, that things had changed since he first invited people back to his room because then you knew that they liked you, but now you didn't know if they were there because of who you were. But to this baby, he would always be just 'Dad'. He was a person who had been unable to make close relationships outside his immediate family – his mother was still his main source of strength – and he was lonely. But now this infant lying in his arms offered him a ready-made relationship, unconditional love, with no sudden cooling, none of the switching off which had distressed him so much in his marriage.

'For me, fatherhood is the ultimate success,' he said, as someone on top of the world with $10 million in the bank. And he was speaking the truth. Becoming a father was somehow essential to his development as a person. In emotional strength, it was like nothing he'd known before – at 28, it was his own coming of age.

'I love him in a different way and a stronger way than I love my mother,' he told one reporter with astonishing frankness. 'I adore my mother. But this love for my son is very strange, a beautiful and pure love – unconditional in the extreme.'

Little James had been able to do what no woman had ever done, move him on from the deep but claustrophobic bond with his mother towards other strong emotional possibilities. Temporarily, at least, freed from loneliness, feeling good about himself as a man, he had found that the birth had had a very uplifting effect on him, dragging him out of his ever-present, lingering depression.

'There are things I may have done before my son was born that I won't do any more,' he said. 'He's given me a will to live that I never had before, a will, a purpose to stay around for a long time because I want to see him grow up.'

Colin was no longer courting nihilism. After leading a life that outwardly looked incredibly successful but which he felt was empty, he now had something to fill the void. Sweet Baby James had healed him, at least for a time.

But there were still problems. In the three weeks before Christmas, his work hit a rough patch. He had three major scenes to tackle: first, he had to murder his officer and friend Cleitus, Gary Stretch, in a drunken rage. As no one was acting but having to 'feel' everything according to the Method acting tradition, Colin felt upset and the act took a full day of retakes before finally finishing at 9.00pm.

The following day, he accidentally stabbed Stretch in the stomach, right through his protective padding. Stretch was stretchered off to hospital, but was allowed back to work the following day. The event was probably due to tiredness but there was an unfounded ugly rumour that there was a genuine tension between the two actors over Rosario Dawson.

His next big scene was to receive the news of his lover Hephaistion's death. Still emotional about the birth of his son

217

and the impending death of his grandfather, he refused to come out of character and, despite his sister Claudine's pleadings, insisted on sleeping the night on the floor of the unheated Indian palace set. In fact, he hardly slept at all, going over and over in his mind what Hephaistion meant to Alexander, and how his lover's death would change the warrior king for good.

Then he had to die himself, mysteriously, in bed, and try to make such a passive scene memorable. He felt under great strain, exacerbated by problems with Kim.

He wanted to take her and the baby home to Dublin for Christmas for a big get-together, a €50,000 party at Reynard's, with the Farrells, the Foxes, the Gilsons and everyone he loves. But Kim did not want to go and she said the baby was too young to travel.

He felt too unhappy and restless to go home alone as he had always done in the past. 'I didn't want to go home because I didn't feel I was myself,' he says. 'I didn't feel like Alexander either, but I was immersed in the role and teetering on the edge of something.' Instead, he went with Jolie and her adopted Cambodian son Maddox to Egypt.

To the delight of the world's press, they were seen canoodling by the pyramids. They rode across the Giza sands on camels, Colin throwing his arms out to show what a keenly balanced rider he'd become, while Jolie kept a firm grip on Maddox.

'I love to see her with Maddox. She is gorgeous with her son,' he said. 'She's been giving me tips on being a good parent.' Of course, being a successful parent is partly down to just being there, but he spent most of that winter filming at Pinewood Studios in England.

He and Jolie were spotted dancing raunchily at the Café Royal in Piccadilly, and the clubs Elysium and Annabel's, before he accompanied her to her suite at the Langham Hotel.

As they shared a passionate kiss in the foyer in front of the mainly rich American tourists that stay there, a photographer from the *Sun* took a picture. Colin snapped, too. It was a rare occasion in which he lost his temper in public. Screaming obscenities, he tried to grab the camera and there was a struggle. Then, just as suddenly, he stopped, laughed and walked away. Too sensible, well bred or just too cynical, he was not going to get into a public brawl.

He and Jolie were strongly attracted to each other. They were both single; she'd had a series of disastrous marriages and seemed oddly disassociated, while he had been without a regular partner for five years. They gave each other sex and good company but wisely recognised that they were 'too alike' for a real romance and, apart from sex, were really just colleagues.

Jolie moved on to Jared Leto, although she later denied this was anything significant, and, when the company moved to Thailand to film the major battles with elephants, Colin met 21-year-old Thai soap star Orravin Ngernyuang. A college student from Bangkok, she was hired as an interpreter for the cast.

'She's really beautiful, everyone on set was coming on to her,' said a contact. 'It started between her and Colin one night when they all went out for drinks. Sparks flew between them. She has told people about kissing Colin, and her friends are all very jealous.'

On the final location, up country in dense jungle as the end of the whole project was in sight, the cast began to relax. Two days before the end, Val Kilmer held a wild party for the cast and crew and, at some point, Colin fell down a stairway and passed out. He lay there all night and awoke the next morning in agony with a badly broken ankle.

'He woke up on the ground outside the hotel,' says Kilmer. 'Someone had put a tent around him and he had a box of

Pringles in his right hand and a bottle of ketchup in the other. With a broken ankle and a bloody leg and he didn't even know his wrist was broken, too.'

For the first time, Stone was furious with him. 'He came very close,' he says ominously, 'he gambled, but we got some fill-in shots and we made it.'

Everyone feared that he'd have to take about eight weeks' rest and the whole crew would have to return in two months to finish off. But he was flown to Bangkok where Thai doctors put on a soft cast and, three days later, he was back on the set, leading his army, with two casts and a realistic limp.

But, after all he'd been through, 94 days of filming, usually half-naked in the desert heat, he wasn't going to let it all end quietly. During the last two weeks of the shoot, back in Morocco, he stayed in the beautiful Le Meridien Hotel, overlooking a road junction crowded with camels and horses, in a suite costing $600 a night. While he was there, he managed to clock up a $64,000 bill, much of it spent on drink, to be paid for by the film company. 'The company are furious,' said one insider, 'but they will let it go because they know he is a huge star and will more than make up for it by pulling in audiences when the film comes out.'

But they didn't get their money back... no one did. *Alexander* was, to quote Stone's own words to Colin, 'a terrible mistake, just terrible!'

At least it wasn't a small, mean mistake; it was bad judgement on a massive scale. *Alexander*, a project that had cost so much to so many, took just $10 million in its first crucial weekend, and made $30 million in the USA in total, about one fifth of the cost of making it, and some critics declared that it was the worst film ever made.

It did better in Eastern Europe and the Far East. 'It just depends where you live whether you can appreciate it,' says Lane Fox testily.

Although Stone claimed to be making 'an intelligent epic', he had produced something with such a poor script that it disappointed anyone who spoke English as a first language. Anyone watching the film hoping to find out anything about Alexander's heroic exploits would have left the cinema none the wiser, and it was so simplistic and unreflective that anyone hoping for a meaningful, multi-layered script, or some erudition, would also have been left wanting.

In a very old-fashioned way, Stone believed that big was going to be better, but, if he'd just taken a few good actors into a small studio with a well-written script and spent no more than a week on it, it might have been a more successful endeavour.

The main flaw was in the writing. Perhaps there was some talent involved in the script when the project began, in the previous century. Colin told a reporter from the *Radio Times* that the director had spent 'ten years' writing the script, but it seems that everything just ended up overcooked, steamed to mush in Stone's desert cauldron. Obviously, he never had a 'Eureka' moment where he saw the whole thing as an edited whole. Instead, there is a mish-mash of undigested material, an unwieldy tenth draft, not a finely honed, finished piece. Just as Alexander himself tried and failed to unify an empire without a centre, Stone struggled to unify this rambling mess, which had no heart, and in which even Alexander is inexplicable with no recognisable character or motives. Because of a basic lack of any controlling idea, the film falls apart.

Stone also thought he could rely on the old Hollywood preference of casting actors for their looks and image rather than their suitability. Orson Welles once said that it was difficult to find an actor who looked as if he had ever read a book – in this epic, no one looked as if they had any knowledge of the period at all. Angelina Jolie as the female lead, rather like Michael Caine in *Quills*, looked as if she hadn't a clue about what happened the day before yesterday.

The leading characters don't look comfortable; they are obviously too young, too distractingly pretty and, in Jolie's case, very obviously acting, as she utters gnomic phrases in an accent belonging to Raisa Gorbachov. Her poor husband Philip, played by Val Kilmer, who was surely a heartthrob not so long ago, looked very odd, too, more like an extra from *Lord of the Rings* or *Monty Python and the Holy Grail*.

The faces of famous but not particularly well-liked older actors popping up from the past, with all their baggage, only added to this rag-bag feeling of fragmentation and confusion. But one of the worst aspects of the film is the way it deals with sex.

Alexander was homosexual. No one compelled him to sleep with men; he was the ruler of the world, after all. He ran the whole gamut, from boys whom he loved and kept beside him to eunuchs who took his fancy, and women he needed for marriage and children. But reports from the time, the ethos of his court, and its artefacts – the statuary, in particular – later copied by the Romans, show that his aesthetic preference was for boys.

Stone, who is supposed to be so brave and uncompromising, fudges this entirely, either to try to please the money men back in LA or because he just couldn't face up to those issues himself, and decided to opt for a policy of old-fashioned repression. The subject is glossed over in a moment by Alexander, armed with that very ancient cliché, 'there are many different ways to love'. No, there aren't – there are two, usually one or the other, unless eunuchs are involved.

In one fumbling scene, Colin has to kiss a eunuch, Bagoas, but it is an unhappy episode. 'He froze,' says Colin, 'I had to tell him, "It's just lip on lip, it doesn't matter, just act it."' It was yet another occasion where the Method just didn't work. And, according to insider gossip, the men at Warner Brothers also froze inside their sharp suits. 'They are not happy about it,' said a source, 'they don't think that audiences are ready to see that.'

What little sex there is is toned down again for the DVD. Twenty minutes, most of the scenes between Alexander and Haephestion, are cut altogether. 'It's not a gay film, it's not a straight film – it's just a fucking story,' said Colin in confused exasperation.

Worthy, pious and dull, the film has Colin at its centre, looking like a *Cosmopolitan* centrefold, with no place to go. No human relations survive to seem credible. There is also the strange relationship with his mother, which makes no sense, although Manohla Dargis in the *New York Times* saw a sub-text coming through when she wrote that the film was really all about Alexander 'running away from his mother, portrayed by Angelina Jolie as a monstrous *kvetch*,' using the Yiddish word to describe his mother's constant griping. *Empire* magazine's reviewer called the film 'a fleshy sprawl of personal issues'.

The straightforward heterosexual sex is also gutless, so that even the scene where he wrestles with the naked Rosario has all the erotic charge of peeking at a Victorian lady in a particularly dull school book.

There is a nice moment when Alexander climbs naked into bed, with his back to the camera. 'Did you see my ass?' Colin later asked a reporter hopefully, because you certainly had to be sharp-eyed. 'Didn't it look good? I'd spent ages training and it was the most toned part of my body.'

More of that would have been memorable but it was not a film intended to give anyone pleasure, and it is a moment so brief and furtive that the audience is encouraged to play the role of keyhole-spying Peeping Toms.

The film could have been a fine exploration of closely

observed character against a stunning, spectacular backdrop, like *Gladiator* and *Ben-Hur*, which develop tight and entertaining stories and characters you get to know and understand, and then feel strongly about. Or perhaps it could have been a tightly plotted spectacle, like the last *Lord of the Rings* film. In the end, it was less interesting in its characters than Elizabeth Taylor's *Cleopatra*, and less effective as a spectacle than the simplistic *Troy*, which did much better at the box office. Perhaps the film simply slipped away from its original genre and really belonged to Bollywood.

Alexander, which should have been his best, was his worst, but Colin walked away from it richer and greatly more experienced than he had been a few months before, at least in riding and swordsmanship, and largely unharmed. He once said that 'most of his films' had 'tanked', but he was still a star.

This was Stone's tragedy; he had fought an epic battle with his ego, and lost. So had the marketing men at Warner Bros. The film joined the list of all-time box-office bombs, keeping company with *Cleopatra* in 1963, Warren Beatty's *Ishtar*, *Heaven's Gate* by Michael Cimino, *Cutthroat Island*, and *Howard the Duck* by George Lucas.

With the long months of filming over, Colin returned to America with a feeling of futility. He told an Irish journalist that he felt 'devastated' by the film's failure. 'It was tough,' he said. 'I mean, I've had some mixed reviews in the past, but this was like, "Wow, you really think it was that bad?"'

His sister Claudine was distressed and disappointed and the two went on holiday for a while to get away from it all. While they were away from the madness, Colin must have wondered what it had all been about. Had it been the story of a young adventurer from the ancient world, or a young adventurer from the 21st century? It had told the audience nothing about history but it had run strangely parallel to his own life.

'Often during the film, I felt lonely and sad,' he said. 'Alexander himself never reached a place of comfort, a place of joy, a place where he ever felt like he was achieving something, and that reflected on the way I ended up feeling.'

He knew that, to Alexander, the great hero, love had proved more elusive than finding the end of the world, and every girl he had tried to love had turned out to be just a pale reflection of his mother.

After five months of shooting across three continents, he returned to LA, the place he'd once called 'a hard town', with very little to show for his experiences in the desert and working with one of the world's greatest living directors, but at least he now had his child there and he was a father, a set role that would not change or end for years.

'I am going to be the best father the world has ever known,' he told the press jubilantly, 'Colin the great dad. I can manage to change a nappy... it's just about working the Velcro.'

In August 2003, he began making concrete plans for the baby's future. Kim filed a paternity suit against him, but this was a formality to establish a paternal relationship and set an amount for child support. They settled on $5,000 a month, but he will be liable for much more as the child grows up. He could be up for massive child support, perhaps $35,000 a month, for clothing, housing, bodyguards, private schools, and a plethora of recreational activities, all of which are normal, everyday requirements for the offspring of Hollywood stars.

But he also established a trust fund for his son with 33 million at the outset, which James cannot touch until he is 18, when it is to be hoped he doesn't follow in his father's footsteps as a teenager.

Things were not easy between the new parents. Although always complimentary about Kim as a mother, he was distant about his own feelings for her. At best, he saw her simply as a means of access to his son. 'I don't care how many lawyers get involved, how many tears I have over the phone, I would never say I rued the day I met that woman,' he told a *Sunday Times* journalist. 'I could be lashed by the cat-o'-nine-tails to the edge of death and I would never say anything about that woman, because she gave me him.'

He loved to describe to the press in detail how he had become a real hands-on dad, how he slept with his son, woke up in the early hours and played and read to him, spending as much time with him as he could, also teasingly suggesting that he was changing his wild ways. 'Now there's Jimmy around, I'm seeing life a bit differently,' he told a journalist in a TV interview. 'I want to be around.' Did he mean in close proximity to the child, or was it a hint about an early death? His comments were tinged with darkness.

He was going to cut down on the Camel Lights. 'I've set up a smoke-free zone around him,' he told one reporter. 'I make a choice to smoke but I am not going to let that affect him. I am not having smoke getting into his lungs; he's much too young for that. I make sure that everyone knows there is no smoking within 50 yards of him or I'll knock them out – no exceptions.'

Part of this was down to pleasing Kim. 'She's a wonderful mother,' he said, 'she loves her son and, if she thinks my way of living is unhealthy for him, then that's a problem.'

He was even going to cut down on his beloved Carlsberg and Amstel Light – or slightly, at least. 'It's not like I've taken the pledge and started singing in the choir. There are things I can't be arsed doing now anyway. I've had my fill of them. I am 28 now and all I need these days is a few drinks.

'Jimmy is not going to grow up to be one of those rich latch-key children with a mother out working and a father in rehab. I don't want him thinking his father is some obscene drunken actor and, as I spend a fair bit of time looking after him, I have to be far more responsible and help Kim.

'Having a son has changed things a lot and it has given me the greatest source of love I have ever known. In the past, when I was bored, I'd dabble in stuff but not now. I feel a sense of responsibility to be more level-headed and a better man. James is the love of my life now – not partying. But that doesn't mean that I don't want to go out and misbehave and have a good fucking laugh sometimes.

'I'm just figuring it all out, living through it, seeing what happens. I like the idea of going off to work and him there at home, always knowing where his dad is.'

He'd always had a fear of flying; now he thought even that would be helped, because, as he put it, 'it will be about going to see my son'.

At Christmas, he managed to get his son to Ireland for the first time. 'It was brilliant,' he says. But Kim was not there. Relations between them were souring at a rate of knots. 'I don't know where the hell she went,' he growled to a reporter. As he promised, he won't ever say anything bad about her, but, when a reporter asked how they got on, he made a face as if he'd eaten something nasty, and didn't smile while he was doing it.

But it wasn't long before he was separated from his son again by a period of intensive work. Colin the dad would again have to make way for Colin the actor; there was now even more reason to keep the Hollywood movers and shakers happy, and the money rolling in.

CHAPTER TEN

THE WORLD AT HIS FEET

At the start of 2004, Colin set off to make two new films, *The New World*, filmed in the American South, and *Ask the Dust*, filmed in LA and Cape Town, South Africa. They took up the rest of the year, and spilled over into the following spring of 2005.

The New World is another epic, but this time backed by a relatively low budget of only $30 million. The director was the publicity-shy Terrence Malick, a reclusive, former philosophy teacher, a maker of strong films who, not that prolific as a movie-maker, has been known to leave 20 years between his films.

Most schoolchildren, at least in the USA, know the story of John Smith, the English explorer whose life was saved when a young girl threw herself at him. Surely no part was more appropriate for Colin? But, in this case, the girl wasn't Britney or Lindsay, but a 17th-century Red Indian princess.

In *The New World*, with a release date of November 2005, Colin plays the English explorer Captain John Smith, who, in 1607, was saved by the 11-year-old Princess Pocahontas who threw herself over him just as an axe was about to fall on his neck.

This historic episode, the coming together of wily English explorer and native princess, has always had the quality of a fairytale. It is not surprising that Disney made a successful animated film about it in 1995. But from the music and the pre-publicity images alone, this version by Terrence Malick looks as if it will be as disturbing and uncompromising as his other work.

He is best known for work such as *Badlands*, released a year before Colin was born. Set in the 'badlands' of the Midwest, a vast desert area, it was based on a spate of vicious, motiveless murders carried out by two teenagers in the 1950s. Searingly violent and disturbing, it launched one of his central themes, the relationships forged between outsiders, in this case a feral youth, played by Martin Sheen, and a bored, magazine-reading girl, played by the youthful Sissy Spacek.

His next film, *Days of Heaven*, starring Richard Gere and Sam Shepard, again focused on two bored, amoral people, Bill and Abby, who listlessly travel south and end up committing murder. Twenty years later, *The Thin Red Line*, starring Sean Penn, Nick Nolte and Jared Leto, was set in a desolate stretch of land where a man who has stepped outside society becomes entirely responsible for his own moral acts, and has to create a whole new world order.

In *The New World*, Colin, as Smith, with long wild, dirty-looking hair, struggles for survival, both physical and moral, out in the swamps and steamy jungle of 17th-century America, a land of seemingly endless primeval wilderness, populated by an intricate network of native tribes, each with their own culture and language. All of Malick's films are allegories of the development of modern America. In this one, we have settlers who try to create a whole new society and answer to themselves alone.

The story of Smith and Pocahontas is usually seen as chiefly romantic, but it is only a pretty story if you ignore the context, the arrival of the white colonists and the subsequent catastrophic effect on the native Indians and the American wilderness.

Pocahontas stopped her relations killing John Smith, and she eased tensions between the Indians and the Europeans by marrying widower John Rolfe, played in the film by Christian Bale, but he then founded the English tobacco-growing industry in Virginia, a labour-intensive crop which, along with sugar and cotton, became the genesis for the movement towards slavery. She and her husband were the harbingers of US imperialism, with all the social dislocations that entails and, to prosper, she had to abandon her own people.

Clever at English, a true 'wannabe', Pocahontas converted to Christianity, and travelled with Rolfe and a group of Indians to England where she met King James I and his court, becoming the first ever American celebrity.

When the poet and dramatist Ben Jonson, a friend of Shakespeare, met her, he stared at her without speaking for 45 minutes until, Gwyneth-like, she waved him impatiently away and, when he wouldn't go, she got up and flounced off.

A great hit wherever she went, her picture was in demand. There is a portrait of her on copper plate in the National Portrait Gallery, wearing the hat of a fashionable Jacobean lady of 1618, and a lace ruff. Prints of it sold like hot cakes to the curious, eager to see their first ever exotic princess from the New World, who had so bravely assisted the colonists.

Her story also had a sad ending, suited to those times. She died of tuberculosis aged 22, and is buried in Gravesend. After her funeral, Rolfe decided to return to his new life in Jamesville but, having been told that their baby son Thomas would not survive the journey, he left him with his uncle and sailed back to the colony, never to return.

Sadly, but perhaps appropriately, Q'orianka Kilcher, aged 15, who plays Pocahontas in this new version of the story, doesn't have a drop of indigenous North American blood. She is descended from the Huachipaeri and Quechua tribes of South America. Q'orianka means 'golden eagle' in Quechua, the ancient language of the Incas of Peru. Once a street performer on LA's Third Street, singing and performing Tahitian dances, in 2000 she appeared in *How the Grinch Stole Christmas* as Little Choir Member.

The New World has a surprising variety of performers. Snowy-haired Christopher Plummer, recovering from his appearance as Aristotle in *Alexander*, is back as Captain Christopher Newport, an English officer, who was among the initial settlers in the New World and became the first President of the Jamestown Colony.

Among the settlers gradually drawn into conflict with the Native American overlord Powhatan, the father of Pocahontas, are the gangling English actor David Thewlis, who is now also well known as the boyfriend of popular actress Anna Friel, and Yorick van Wageningen, who resurfaces at last.

Although it was months before any of his new work would appear, Colin's name is always hot stuff for the gossip columnists. He no longer needs to have work on release to be front-page news. On 3 May 2005, Dame Eileen Atkins, best known for her stage and radio performances as Virginia Woolf and a legion of yearning spinsters and frustrated housemaids, revealed that, while she was making the film *Ask The Dust*, an actor 42 years younger than herself had spent over two hours begging her to sleep with him.

'Three weeks before my seventieth birthday, a simply stunning, gorgeous, big film star aged 28 years old came into my hotel room in Cape Town,' she told an ITV chat-show hostess, 'looking for sex without strings. I spent two-and-a-half hours saying no. But it was pure bliss, cheered me up fantastically and it made me sail through my seventieth birthday without a care in the world,' she explained winsomely. 'Of course, I was tempted but I followed the advice of my friend, the actress Siân Phillips, and kept saying, "This is deeply inappropriate." I said no in the end because he said, "The reason you won't do it is because your body isn't as good as it was when you were young, isn't it? But I don't care about that. "

'But I'm too proud of how I looked when I was younger. My body is still the same weight, but it's all distributed in a different way.'

It was a strange and outlandish situation for her to recall, perhaps flattering but potentially embarrassing for both her and her mystery admirer, unless she enjoys discussions about her age, weight and level of attractiveness.

The information was dropped too early to make good publicity for the film which wasn't due for release by Paramount until winter 2005 at the earliest. She said she had initially intended to spare her unsuccessful suitor's blushes by keeping his identity secret. In an interview with the *Daily Mail*'s *Weekend* magazine, she said he was 'not American or English'. No one put two and two together and came up with Irish, but, despite that, the truth just came slipping out anyway and her agent confirmed that 'it was Colin Farrell who made the advance'.

As if there had been a grisly murder or a natural disaster, her revelation unleashed a torrent of newsprint and every pub and office in the land abounded with theories to explain what had happened; she was making a joke... perhaps it was wishful thinking on her part... let's face it, he'd sleep with anything... he was going for an 'any three in under three hours' bet... he is 'pan-sexual', addicted to random sexual conquest... a necrophiliac... or, at best, he was probably just enthralled by her talent.

Women the world over didn't care why it had happened, only that it had. They were delirious, feeling a little bit more hopeful about the future, and perhaps got out of bed the following morning to face the day with a slightly springier step.

Colin, who never 'went out with just anyone', had fancied someone eight years older than his beloved mother, put her on his list and almost notched her into the remaining fragments of wood left in his bedpost. And not only was she well past her prime, but also she had never been a great beauty in the first place, even in the bloom of her youth. Dame Eileen comes from a generation of strong, plain-looking, feminist actresses. Glenda Jackson was once said to have 'the face that launched a thousand dredgers', and one critic had described Eileen as 'a cross between a Grimm hag and Medea'.

She herself liked to say that her prominent eyes gave her a resemblance to the thyroidal comedian Marty Feldman, and she was fond of recounting how, in the 1970s, in the heyday of the feminist movement, some workmen in the street had commented that she didn't need to burn her bra, as her breasts were too small to need one. But now she was being resolutely propositioned by an international movie star, one of the most desired men in the world.

In addition to feeling a little past her sell-by date, people speculated that she might have refused because she is a married woman. What should a married woman do when propositioned by Colin Farrell? Married or not, at 70, offers like Colin's aren't that thick on the ground; it could have been one last, mad, glorious way to wave goodbye to sex. It would also have been an opportunity for her to do her duty by revealing the truth about one of the world's most discussed members. He's been self-deprecating in that department; after *Tigerland*, he compared it to 'a cashew nut' and, after the publicity following *A Home at the End of the World*, he'd declared 'it ain't nothing to write home about'.

But other voices from film sets have proclaimed it to be vast. Garden hose pipes and donkeys have been mentioned. But, thanks to Eileen's noble negligence, we will probably never know the truth.

Men, on the other hand, were simply unsettled by the news. A lot of male reporters on tabloids were desperate to explain why a young 'Hollywood stud', as they referred to him, would suddenly desire a significantly older lady. This was breaking one taboo too many.

But, in their shock that he fancied a 70-year-old, most reporters missed the fact that, during filming, he was also a victim of the Burton syndrome again and had made a determined play for Salma Hayek, the beautiful Mexican actress from Coatzacoalcos, who brought the artist Frida Kahlo brilliantly to life on screen in 2002.

Although she is ten years older than Colin, approaching 40 when they met, he called her 'the sexiest woman alive'. An insider revealed that they had a lot of late-night phone calls and dinner dates and started meeting in LA during film breaks. 'He loves talking to her. He thinks she is a marvellous person to confide in,' said a friend.

Of course, he has always liked older women. He famously claims to have lost his virginity as a teenager to a 36-year-old, and he'd often fallen for his older co-stars, from Eva Birthistle to Robin Wright Penn and Angelina Jolie. But the incident with Dame Eileen may well have happened because of the part he was playing in *Ask the Dust*, which is taken from the disturbing Depression-era novel by John Fante. The book is hard to read and must have been even harder to cope with over several months, and it touched him deeply.

In a rare case of appropriate Hollywood casting, Colin and Eileen are ideally suited for the roles they play. Colin looks exactly right for the part of Arturo Bandini, 'not tall but solid, proud of his muscles', while another character comments on his particularly black hair and dark eyes. And, although the book was written in 1939, Fante might have been writing with Dame Eileen standing in front of him. 'She was not beautiful, but she seemed attractive and mature,' writes Bandini, as the novel's narrator. 'And she had nervous black eyes. They were brilliant, the sort of eyes a woman gets from too much bourbon, very bright and glassy and extremely insolent. She was dressed intelligently – black coat, black shoes, black skirt, a white blouse and small purse. But what got me were her eyes, their brilliance, their animalism and their recklessness.'

What happened in Dame Eileen's bedroom could reasonably be interpreted as Colin's response to a story of terrible anguish. He was not so much attracted to Dame Eileen, as to the woman she was playing, Vera Rivken, an elderly Jewish housekeeper.

At the start of the story, Bandini, a penniless short-story writer, seems to be a character a bit like the hapless Stu in *Phone Booth*, a tiresomely unrealistic egotist who thinks of himself as 'absurdly fearless', while being clogged with anxiety.

He swaggers about the dusty streets of downtown LA, observing and despising other people who are as poor as he is, describing them as 'the uprooted ones, the empty, sad folks who hid in the alleys by day and slunk off to flop houses at night'.

But as his story develops, Bandini's voice sometimes boasting and pretentious, at other times destructively self-critical, he is revealed to be a hypersensitive youth who, obsessed with the idea of becoming a great writer, sacrifices everything, including security and decency, for his passion.

At the start, he has only had one story published in a magazine, but all his hope, his very survival, rests on his becoming a successful writer. He has nowhere else to go or, as he puts it, 'You were born poor, son of miseried peasants, driven because you were poor, fled from your Colorado town because you were poor, hoping to write a book to get rich, because those who hated you back in Colorado will not hate you if you write a book.'

Starving much of the time, nourished mainly on rotten oranges and cigarette butts found in the street, he lives in one of LA's squalid boarding houses in Bunker Hill, where his nearest neighbour is Mr Hellfrick, an obese, thieving alcoholic, who wanders round his filthy room with his dressing-gown open, played in the film by Donald Sutherland. He also visits Benny Cohen, who has a little door in his wooden leg where he hides his marijuana cigarettes.

Undaunted, driven by his dream, Bandini plugs away at the typewriter and every story he writes gets published. He is on the path to success but there is no break in his loneliness and misery, until, down to his last nickel, he goes into the Columbia Buffet, 'a saloon where old men gathered', for a bad coffee, and meets Camilla Lopez, a Mexican waitress serving cheap beers, played by Hayek. She turned the script down when she was shown it eight years earlier, because it seemed too harsh. But she says she's 'grown' to appreciate it.

More true to the usual Hollywood casting, Hayek is not like the fictional Camilla, who, in the book, is very dark-skinned, at a time when that was a gross handicap. Bandini is partly disgusted by her skin colour and describes her as 'a racial type', flat-nosed with large nostrils and 'a negress's lips'. But he becomes obsessed with her. Like Colin, the ambitious young writer's emotions quickly spin out of control and become confused. They start seeing each other, and he calls her his 'Mayan Princess', but, because of his plunging self-esteem and the stress he imposes on himself, he torments her about her race calling her a 'Spick', 'Wop', 'a filthy little greaser' and 'ragged shoes'. Bewildered by him, she sneers back, calling him a 'Dago sonofabitch'.

Both are ashamed and upset by the way they behave but, living in the City of Angels, surrounded by wealth and images of beauty, they yearn to be seen as Americans, but that is part of their dream of unobtainable success. A vicious insult-trading contest goes on between them and a lot of the time they hate each other. Then into his room and his life staggers Vera, the elderly Jewish housekeeper, who came from the east looking for a better life but never found it. Vera had spotted him in a restaurant, got drunk to get up some courage and followed him back to his boarding house because, she says, his eyes had 'pierced' her soul.

She is highly educated, slightly self-dramatising and a misplaced outsider like himself, and they become friends.

Bandini is fascinated by her intensity but also repelled by her age. 'I could smell liquor on her breath, and the very peculiar odour of decay, sweetish and cloying, the odour of oldness, the odour of this woman in the process of growing old. I got back to my room and her personality and that mysterious smell of old age still possessed it, and it was not my room at all, its wonderful solitude was spoiled.'

Vera quickly becomes sexually obsessed with the young writer, who is only supposed to be 20 in the novel, and she becomes violently out of control. He tries to push her away but she is full of desperate needs, growing old but longing to be, if not desired by a man, at least recognised as a worthwhile human being.

'I am lonely,' she tells him straight. He sees that something is terribly wrong with her and feels ashamed of being harsh. He plays it tough and often makes cruel remarks but he is agonisingly compassionate and cannot bear to see pain, in humans or animals.

In a drunken frenzy, she strips off and reveals that she has a small birthmark, a dry patch or scar in her groin. It is nothing much, but she is obsessed with it, she focuses on it all the loathing she feels for her own body.

'I know how I revolt you,' she screams, 'and you know about my wounds and the horror my clothes conceal. But you must try to forget my ugly body, because I'm really good at heart. I'm so good and I deserve more than your disgust. Tell me I am beautiful like other women,' she pleads.

One night, after failing to make love to Camilla on the beach, because he is so overwhelmed by his ambivalent feelings for her, and seeing how she despises him for it, he makes love to Vera, pretending all the time that she is Camilla. While they make love, he thinks about 'Camilla, complete and lovely, with no scars and no desiccated place', and Vera even refers to herself as 'Princess Camilla' to try to comfort him. She becomes both an expendable sex object and a mother figure to him. Afterwards, he is full of Catholic guilt and prays for forgiveness for his 'mortal sin' of using Vera, and he is still obsessed with the younger woman, who does not love him.

Together, they form a trio of self-persecuting people, all hopelessly trapped by their unfulfilled needs. This is the dark side of love that Colin has always feared, especially since his unsuccessful marriage when he became scared of the power of love to take over the mind.

Vera is desperate for the young man, needing his appreciation to make her feel valid as a woman again, to heal her scars, both physical and emotional. He is desperate for closeness with someone but can't make it work. Camilla loves a man who abuses her. None of them can help each other, and Fante's writing is so piercing that, although the book is compulsive, their terrible situation makes for a disturbing read.

Colin has often been deeply affected by his work, throwing himself into it, becoming utterly consumed by it. During *Alexander*, he told a reporter that he had cried a great deal during shooting; sometimes, such as after the death of his screen lover Hephaistion, he refused to come out of character and went through a kind of protracted grief, projecting his own pain on to the loss of a man he had never actually known.

Perhaps because *Ask the Dust* is so much more contemporary, and set in the very mean streets that Colin, too, was trying to make home, he was almost unbalanced by playing Bandini, and his dramatic response created world headlines.

Bandini doesn't like to see pain; he has to help. Dame Eileen is a fine actress, and perhaps her performance was just too convincing as Vera. Or perhaps the great actress was not quite as composed as she liked to think. After all, approaching 70, she was alone, far from home, working hard and living in a hotel room, which can be trying at the best of times. Did she display more of the lonely, terrified Vera than she intended? Whether it was the real or the fictional woman, Colin wanted to help.

'Colin has a special magic; he can sense what people need and gives it to them,' observed actress Sissy Spacek after working with him. But he also has unfulfilled needs. He and Bandini are both lonely young men without a permanent relationship, who used casual sex to try to escape loneliness.

Not a lot of sex is altruistic and, by putting other people right, people suffering from a pain similar to his own, Colin and Bandini thought they could somehow feel better themselves. Eileen, of course, stepped right out of character and did what Vera could never have done – turned him down. She had a husband waiting at home and all the love she needed.

Back in Hollywood, the film's director Robert Towne was, no doubt, bemused but pleased by all the emotional turmoil created by his film long before it even appeared before the public. He has been called a film director whose work has the power to change its audience; now it seems he could change the lives of his actors, too.

All this human turmoil is despite the fact that the main subject of the film is really the town of Los Angeles, a place of 'eejits' and chancers without the social infrastructure that cushions poor people in Ireland and the UK. The novel and the film are haunted by the idea that the city built on celluloid dreams is where people flock to die, eaten up by sunshine and dreams gone sour. It's a sunny film noir, if that is possible. Reflecting that restless, tormented culture, it also touches on mental instability and aggression in the form of racism and snobbery.

One critic seeing an early print of the work said the film reminded him of why *Chinatown*, written by Towne in 1974, was such a great film, because it understood Hollywood's rich history but managed to deliver it on a human scale, concentrating on little people and their ordinary lives. *Ask the Dust* also gains its power from this tension between the grand and the minuscule, the comfort of dreams and the terror of reality.

A local lad, Towne became well known in the early 1970s as a brilliant scriptwriter. In 1974, he wrote *Chinatown*, set in 1930s LA; it was directed by Roman Polanski not long after the brutal murder of his wife Sharon Tate, and starred Jack Nicholson and Faye Dunaway, the hottest stars of their generation. The following year, he wrote *Shampoo*, a hip comedy set in the LA of the late 1960s, starring Warren Beatty, Julie Christie and Goldie Hawn.

He also contributed scenes to the cult film *Bonny and Clyde* and wrote the famous garden scene between Marlon

Brando and Al Pacino at the end of the first *Godfather* film. He is really part of the old Hollywood elite, like Oliver Stone, a survivor from more turbulent times. Able to span the generations, he is close friends with Tom Cruise, who produced this film with Paula Wagner, his partner in C/W Productions.

Ask the Dust was truly interesting work and, despite the *Alexander* debacle, in Hollywood studio terms, Colin Farrell was a success with a capital 'S'. Still only 28, he'd made 11 films in three years, while avoiding being typecast.

The Recruit, *Minority Report* and *Daredevil* had notched up half-a-billion dollars for the studios. His films often seem to be just extensions of his personal charm, but *Minority Report*, *Phone Booth* and *Intermission* were outstanding. This is not a bad record, encompassing both commercial and serious film-making, something for everyone's taste.

Named as one of *People* magazine's 50 Most Beautiful People in 2003, fabulously wealthy, worth about $18.4 million and unfeasibly famous, he has a career beyond anything he could have envisaged when he booked that first hotel room in Santa Monica in 2000.

But, in his personal life, he has much less control. Neither money nor fame can buy you lasting love. All around him, people were moving on. Photographed regularly slumped on his local beach, there was something beginning to be rather beached about him.

Kim went back to modelling, this time for Innovative Artists in LA. Her agents there, Maria and Carol, are keen to say that she is taking bookings for jobs. Early in 2004, she started going out with Ryan Condor, who owns a Los Angeles clothing boutique, and in May it was announced that they were engaged. 'She wants a father in the baby's life every day,' said her sister, 'not just when Colin can visit.'

There was now a new man in his son's life, not an easy

situation for any father to cope with. Pictures showed Colin cuddling the ten-month-old, whom he liked to call 'his little friend'. He wanted the press to know he was a good father and began complaining about his bad-boy image.

Perhaps because of the new competition from Condor, in July 2004 it was leaked to the press that he bought his tiny son a new toy car – no wooden box on wheels pulled by a string, not even a pedal car for him. Costing €21,000, this was a roaring red Ferrari, two-seater, convertible sports car, able to do 30mph.

Ordered from the LA-based Cars for Children, it was very similar to the model David Beckham bought from Harrods for his one-year-old son Brooklyn in 1999.

He ordered all the bling extras – a stereo CD and DVD player, alloy trims, cream leather seats, tachometer, hydraulic shock absorbers, lights and double horn. It had its own driver keys, but could be controlled by an adult standing elsewhere holding a remote control. Obviously, he wanted a perfect toy for the son he adored, the ultimate toy, a gleaming chrome symbol of his fatherhood, rather than something small that the child might have been able to use.

But no matter how big or extravagant the toys, the reality was that he could never be a full part of his son's life and the boy had only been to Ireland once. 'I see him as much as I can,' he told a reporter from the *Irish Independent*. 'I will be able to see him more as he gets older and becomes more aware. I'd have full custody if I could, but that's not going to happen.' In that interview, he also indicated with a grimace that there was a deep gulf between him and Kim.

So his life is now completely split between two continents, his son in one, his beloved family and homeland in the other and there was little hope of somehow bringing them together in any lasting way.

Whatever his personal turmoil, Colin carried on as ever. In the summer of 2004, he was spotted out again with Jennifer Garner. They were seen in a corner of the Pig and Whistle in LA, both in baseball caps and jeans, holding hands, chatting intently, obviously not wanting to be disturbed. He waved away lap-dancers to concentrate on Jennifer, and they left the club together at 8.00am.

That same month, the press caught up with him again in London, when a 'stunning model', Stacey Watson, featured in a nude centrefold spread in the *News of the World*, after a steamy night with Colin. After meeting her in Stringfellow's, he'd tempted her into bed with compliments such as 'fucking lovely tits and arse'. He'd then whisked her back to his suite at the plush Mandarin Oriental Hotel, where, perhaps still dreaming of Angelina Jolie's tastes, he'd smacked her bottom and used the 'F' word constantly while they made love.

Stacey certainly had no complaints. 'When we made love, he was very attentive,' Stacey revealed. 'He was strong and powerful but he definitely paid as much attention to my needs as he did to his own.

'It was a night I will never forget, it was like a dream come true. Afterwards, we had champagne and ripe, juicy strawberries, he was so sweet. I just couldn't believe there was such a soft, caring side to him. He was one of the most considerate lovers I've ever had.'

Throughout the interview, looking rather like a squashed, plastic inflatable doll, she revealed how astonished she was that any man would treat her politely. Sad and undemanding, she was docile as a kitten. He was well mannered, but largely unmoved. 'In the morning, we kissed at the door and he told me it was a night he wouldn't forget either, and then I left,' she gushed. 'I didn't ask for his number as I knew nothing more could have come from it. He has his career to think of and I have mine.'

'The women I have sex with are in it for the same reasons I am,' Colin said, repeating a mantra he'd used many times. 'The cards are on the table. Everyone knows where they stand and it works out fine. Drinking, one night stands, drugs and the rest, that's the safe stuff... the rest you release at greater personal risk.'

His name was fleetingly associated with Kelli Young from Derby, a teenage member of the Brit Award-winning group LibertyX. Blonde American heiress Paris Hilton and rising US starlet Lindsay Lohan, the star of *Freaky Friday* and *Mean Girls*, were also apparently potential notches, but at 17, he said Lindsay was just too young. He didn't write her off, though. 'Maybe in a year or so,' he said.

Towards the end of the year, his reputation preceding him, he was tipped to be the new James Bond. Pierce Brosnan suggested his fellow Irishman to succeed him as 007 in the next film, earmarked for 2006. He spoke generously as he'd just been dropped from the role himself, despite wanting to carry on for another hi-tech adventure. At the Irish Film and TV Awards in Dublin in early November, he said, 'I'll give it to Colin Farrell. He'll eat the head off them all.'

But Colin didn't see himself in that role. One thing Bond has is unshakable self-confidence and a special English *savoir-faire*. He doesn't suffer from the self-loathing brought on by Catholic guilt, feelings of insecurity or depression.

Colin had no doubt about his response. 'The idea of me playing James Bond has got into the press,' he told Reuters, 'but it's not true. I would not like to do it. And Her Majesty's Secret Service wouldn't have me on the payroll.'

Since he said that, bookmakers have been tipping Australian actor Hugh Jackman, the star of *Swordfish*. Clive Owen and Ewan McGregor have also been mentioned.

Colin felt at home in something far more democratic than the upper-class English Bond fantasy. Rather than posing as an

English toff, in February 2005 he featured in a cameo in *Scrubs*, the offbeat US TV medical drama, shown in the UK the following May. He appeared as a heavy-drinking Irishman, whom the young doctors treat after a bar-room brawl.

Then he started work on a role that really suited him, as the smooth-talking, fashionable cop in *Miami Vice*, the role that once made ruggedly handsome, dirty-blond Don Johnson such a star. 'Yeah, it's true. I am playing Sonny Crockett,' he told a reporter for a gay Internet site.

On screen from 1984 to 1989, *Miami Vice* was like no other cop show before or since; each week's episode began with pounding music and a catalogue of Miami iconography – sun-baked beach houses, Cuban–American festivals, women in bikinis and pastel-coloured cityscapes. In this tropical environment, two vice detectives, Crockett and his black sidekick Tubbs, dressed up like Armani models, combated drug-traffickers, broke up prostitution and gambling rings, solved vice-related murders, and cruised the city's underground in expensive cars.

'We're going to do it again in an updated format,' says Colin. 'There will be none of those 1980s fucking pastels and loafers without socks. Nah, man, Michael Mann, who created the TV show in the 1980s, is a genius. Back then, pastels and loafers and shit like that were the style.

'This is going to be fully updated, a big, slam-bam-thank-you-ma'am movie, the big summer film of 2006. Wait and see, trust me. It's going to be much better than *S.W.A.T.*'

This new, big-screen version for Universal Pictures will transport him back to the world of the TV that provided his escape when he was a troubled child in Castleknock. 'I have always gone for American television,' he says. 'I grew up watching *TJ Hooker*, *The A-Team*, *Six Million Dollar Man*... I've fucking watched them all.'

To prepare for this fun role, for once he has thrown himself into gym work, intent on gaining 15 pounds of upper-body muscles for the part of the tough, sexy, fashion-victim cop. He claims to be in 'the best shape of my life'. Pictures issued to the press of him wearing a tight white suit show that this is probably true. They have already prompted drooling admiration from female commentators and afternoon chat-show hostesses.

He will also get the chance to sing in the film, once and for all silencing those critics from the past – Louis Walsh, for instance – who didn't believe that he could sing. 'It's a little joke, singing, so that anyone watching will realise that I can hold a tune,' he says, 'and everyone will know it was Boyzone's loss.'

One of the other reasons for his enthusiasm about the part is the chance to work with Jamie Foxx as sidekick Ricardo Tubbs. Foxx is also thrilled to be in the film. 'This film is going to redefine cool,' he says. 'You're going to see our Crockett and Tubbs suits and be like, "I want those!" You'll see our car and go, "I want those, too," and you're gonna see our women, and man, you're gonna be like, "Now that I *gotta* have."'

A remarkable character in real life, Foxx is a former football star, classical pianist and stand-up comedian, who won an Oscar in 2005 for his role as Ray Charles, in the hit biopic *Ray*. And he is just the kind of man that Colin might have a laugh with. His favourite songs are 'Do Me, Baby' by Prince and 'Sexual Healing' by Marvin Gaye, and he likes a good night out with the lads. In February 2004, he pleaded guilty to the charge of disturbing the peace in a plea bargain involving a previous charge of battery against a New Orleans policeman in a casino. He received two years' probation and a $1,500 fine.

'The chemistry between us is already there,' says Colin, 'so making this movie is going to be a total blast.'

Michael Mann, the film's director, has already anticipated what the two men's friendship might lead to. 'I need to budget for a bail bondsman for both of them,' he says.

Mann's whole career has been based on the entertainment value of bad boys and the humour that comes from their antics, particularly as partners. He started his career writing for *Starsky and Hutch*, followed by *Thief* in 1981, starring James Caan, which portrayed crooks as funny and loveable.

In *Miami Vice*, Crockett and Tubbs were never entirely good guys. They were inept police officers, sometimes arresting the wrong people and always teetering on the thin line between their actions and those of the drug lords and gangsters around them. One frequently posed question in the series was: were they pursuing wrongdoers for the love of law and order, or to exact personal revenge? One season ended with Crockett actually becoming a real gangster, after conveniently suffering a bout of amnesia.

Miami Vice was Mann's first real hit. It became a cult, running for 114 episodes and nominated for 15 Emmy Awards, attracting guest stars such as Julia Roberts, Helena Bonham-Carter, Bruce Willis, Frank Zappa, Liam Neeson and David Schramm. And it made all previous cop shows, such as *Dragnet* in the USA and *Dixon of Dock Green* and *Z-Cars* in the UK, look somewhat quaint.

It earned the nickname 'MTV cops' through its liberal use of popular rock songs and a pulsating, synthesised music track created by Jan Hammer. No one can say yet whether Hammer will also work on the new film. If he doesn't, something will certainly be lost for long-term fans.

Segments of the programme closely resembled early music videos – viewers enjoyed quickly edited images, without dialogue, often accompanied by contemporary hits such as Tina Turner's 'What's Love Got to Do With It?' and music from Phil Collins, Ted Nugent, Glenn Frey and Sheena Easton. It came from the same genre as music-oriented films such as *Flashdance* and *Footloose*, and probably could not have existed before MTV began to popularise the music video in 1981, now a standard component of youth-oriented television and cinema.

It also started the trend for cynical, nihilist cop shows on TV, a genre borrowed from film noir in cinema. It imbued every frame with an aura of moral decay, a fashion in TV that has never gone away and can still be seen in the ambiguity and moral relativism of *NYPD Blue* and *Homicide*.

Due for release in January 2006, there is no way of knowing at this time how the remake will fare. Remakes are often best left unmade. After all, who are they for? With the possible exception of *Dr Who*, the first audience wants only the original, while a younger generation can rarely see what all the fuss was about.

There is also the danger that a new *Miami Vice* will spawn a new generation of men wearing medallions, brightly patterned shirts and tight white flares.

The plot revealed so far involves a brotherhood of Nazi white supremacists and a group of US federal agents working undercover as Russian gangsters. One of Tubbs's informants is killed by the Nazi gang, and it's personal because Tubbs was once in love with the man's wife. The Feds' operation is threatened by a mole, and a Colombian drug network is also involved, which will provide an international dimension and keep the Latino audience hooked.

Whatever the plot, the casting looks attractive. Apart from the central partnership provided by Colin and Jamie Fox, Mann has lined up highly intelligent actors, who are always interesting to watch. Chinese film actress Gong Li, plays Isabella, Crockett's love interest. In real life, like Colin, she has been included in *People* magazine's 50 Most Beautiful

People list, but she is probably only really known to lovers of serious Chinese cinema.

She starred in a series of films which painstakingly revealed the inner life of Communist China to the outside world – *Red Sorghum* in 1987, *Raise the Red Lantern* in 1991 and *Farewell My Concubine* in 1993. She was also named Best Actress at the 49th Venice International Film Festival for her role in *The Story of Qiu Ju*.

Belfast actor Ciaran Hinds also appears. In the early 1990s, he created a brilliant Richard III for the Royal Shakespeare Company at the Donmar Warehouse, taking over at short notice from Simon Russell-Beale, who damaged his back while attempting too accurate a portrayal of the hunchbacked king.

Hinds also shone in classic TV drama playing Mr Rochester in *Jane Eyre* and Captain Wentworth in *Persuasion*, but became better known for his role in *Excalibur* alongside Liam Neeson, Gabriel Byrne and Patrick Stewart. Alfred Molina has also been mooted to play a bad guy.

As he began to work on *Miami Vice*, the darker side of West Coast culture touched Colin in reality. About to play an on-screen fearless hero, he found a real-life enemy in Dessarae Bradford. In a handwritten lawsuit filed in Santa Monica, the beautiful black girl, a former chat-line sex worker, said Colin had called her on her Internet chatline. Her dark, passionless, dead-eyed face above a semi-naked torso stares out from the screen as she offers submissive male callers 'SM/Fetish, Sexy, Nasty, Sweaty Talk'.

She says that, after Colin used the service, she gave him her cell-phone number and he spent £158 on calls, then made and cancelled a number of dinner dates with her. Then she says he started 'harassing' her, causing her mental anguish by phone and text message, and even started stalking her.

She claims that, while all she had wanted was sex, he only wanted to call her and talk about his childhood and his life. 'He may be a big movie star to most people,' she declared like a true dominatrix, 'but to me he is just a pest. For the past few long, agonisingly draining months, since September 2004, I have had the misfortune of Colin Farrell seeking my attention,' she told the press. She demanded the return of 'artwork', an erotic tape and the meagre sum of £2,632 in compensation.

She can't write well, but is surprisingly verbally articulate. 'Not only did this voided, lonely soul reach out to me amidst his vast fame, fortune and women – a broken vessel,' she writes, 'he also persistently used my empathy as only a misogynist would. Colin shared his innermost secrets and fantasies with me, and also told the tales of his tawdry affairs with such female leading actresses as Paris Hilton, Britney Spears, Angelina Jolie and Rosario Dawson, leaving no graphic detail out.

'He also dumped upon me his feelings about his fellow A-list actors, some he liked, most he hated. I have a story to tell, a great tale about a man-child who is dying amongst the lights in loneliness and tried to pull me down with him. But I showed him discipline.'

Various websites began calling her 'a smiling Hollywood creature' and a 'tattling temptress'. Colin's representatives dismissed her as 'crazy', and said he'd never met her. They also called her 'publicity-seeking', a bit of a case of the pot calling the kettle, as that statement also included a reminder to watch Colin on *Scrubs*. It was OK for Colin to discuss his early interest in telephone sex, and to ring Salma Hayek to confide in her, but the claims of Dessarae were rather less credible.

Her case was not helped because, the year before, she'd made claims about lurid S & M sessions with actor Alec Baldwin, and even wrote a book about it called *My S/M*

Romp with Alec Baldwin. In it, she insisted that she had been 'tappin dat ass' with a vibrator and a Hershey Bar. He declared that he'd never met her, but didn't sue.

Her attorney, Michael Henderson, served Colin with the papers when he stopped his car at traffic lights, after following him from the *Miami Vice* film set. The matter eventually came to court on 17 March. 'I will prevail,' Dessarae told her public on the way into the Santa Monica courthouse, but the judge threw the case out. She offered to go on TV and take a live lie-detector test, but no one took her up on her offer and she complained bitterly that Colin, his lawyer and his image consultants had deliberately undermined her claims. Like a character from *Ask the Dust*, she hadn't a prayer of ever being heard by the rich and powerful.

Undaunted, her second book is about Colin, rather poetically called *Colin Farrell: A Dark Twisted Puppy*.

Back in the world of the publicity that he could control, in the spring of 2005, Colin talked about a mystery lover who'd become 'the best friend I ever had', then his name was linked with another older lady, Australian supermodel and underwear designer Elle 'The Body' McPherson.

He was staying in the nine-room, luxury Rock House Hotel on Harbour Island in the Bahamas, and Elle met him there for late-night drinks. 'I am a 42-year-old mother-of-two, and he is 29,' she laughed, as if she didn't know that those were points in her favour.

The rumours probably had no substance; it was just a bit of toying with the press, to throw them off a scent, or to create the endless publicity he needs to fuel his career in Hollywood.

'I can't take any of this seriously,' he says. 'I just have to enjoy it for what it is... the unreality of it. It has been a mad ride, and I'm a lucky bastard. When you start out, you just dream of getting the next job. And, when I finish a film, I still dream about getting the next one. I don't have any plans, I don't have a map. I've made more money over the last few years than I thought I would ever make in my whole life and I've had such a good time doing it. But acting is now where my happiness in life comes from. If it all went away tomorrow, I'll have so many stories for my kids, and I've got it all on film.'

At the same age, Alexander the Great, nearing the end of his adventure, wept because there were no more lands to conquer, no more work to do. That can never be true for a real actor; there is always more challenging work to tackle, and with such success he can pick and choose from any projects he wants.

'The work is great,' he says, 'except that it stops me seeing my son.'

Apart from work, he has his family, and likes to mention 'kids' not yet born to him. He plans a settled life at the centre of a family of his own, sometime in the future and, although he has no pattern for building a successful family, he is investing emotionally in the people around him.

'I'd be nowhere now without my family and friends,' he says. 'We are still all very close.' He once resented his father's authority but now the old wounds have healed. 'My father and mother are like mates now,' he says. 'They've been separated for a long time, and now they are mates. He's never said anything about the things I've said about him, and I haven't asked him what he thinks about it.' Like most close relatives, they've come to a respectful truce.

He rushed back to Dublin to be with his grandfather James just before he died on 12 May 2005. At the funeral, at his mother's parish church in Drimnagh, he showed his grief openly, as the family and friends, including Robbie Fox and Glenda Gilson, gathered round.

He has his Irish heritage, work, friends... but, like Alexander, he is still searching for someone or something special in his life.

He will be 30 in 2006, a very big age to grapple with for someone famed for their looks and vitality. An age which sends some married men racing off looking for pastures new, and unmarried men straight to the church or register office.

At 30, even top film stars, though they may not feel old, know that one day they will be. And, if they look like their father and are prone to put on weight, as Colin is, the future has an unpleasantly retributive feel about it. The wild years can take their toll, and time has a way of clipping all heels.

He may decide to settle down, but where? He loves Dublin but lives in LA. 'I am not seduced by Hollywood. I'll indulge in it, I'll be in Los Angeles for two weeks and have a laugh, get battered and have a buzz but, at the end of the day, I'll go home. It's just me earning a few more stories to tell everyone at home and all.'

His son is there, and the majority of his work. Settled in neither place, he spends his days on the beach with his son, chatting up local girls, but would rather spend his evenings in O'Donoghues or Reynard's.

The most tantalising chapter of Colin's life and career is as yet unwritten, and how will it all end? As a career of increasingly good, mature work, or will it be a long, drawn-out comedy of bad manners, a sweaty lowbrow entertainment with flashes of brilliance along the way? Or is this winding epic going to end in obscurity – after all, he often tells girls that he wants to retire to Dublin and open a pub?

The seeds of all these possible endings are within our hero right now. Drunk, often lonely in his distant kingdom of LA, home-loving but wildly ambitious, still with everything to play for, he alone knows where the next chapter will take him.

FILM AND TELEVISION APPEARANCES

What Love Is and What's It All About(2006)
Miami Vice (2006) – Detective James 'Sonny' Crockett
Ask the Dust (2005) – Arturo Bandini
The New World (2005) – John Smith
Alexander (2004) – Alexander the Great
A Home at the End of the World (2004) – Bobby Morrow
Intermission (2003) – Lehiff
SWAT (2003) – Jim Street
Veronica Guerin (2003) – Tattooed Youth
Daredevil (2003) – Bullseye
The Recruit (2003) – James Clayton
Phone Booth (2002) – Stu Shepard
Minority Report (2002) – FBI Detective Danny Witwer
Hart's War (2002) – Lt Thomas W Hart
American Outlaws (2001) – Jesse James
Tigerland (2000) – Private Roland Bozz
Ordinary Decent Criminal (2000) – Alec
… aka *Ein Ganz gewöhnlicher Dieb* (Germany)
David Copperfield (1999) (TV) (scenes deleted) – Milkman

Love in the 21st Century (1999) TV Series – Mattie *The War Zone* (1999) (as Colin J Farrell) – Nick

... aka *Tim Roth's The War Zone* (USA: poster title)

... aka *Zona di Guerra* (Italy)

Ballykissangel (1996) TV Series (as Col Farrell) – Danny Byrne (1998–99)

Falling for a Dancer (1998) (TV) – Daniel McCarthy

Drinking Crude (1997) – Click

The Disappearance of Finbar (1996) (uncredited) – Extra

... aka *När Finbar försvann* (Sweden)

2nd Irish Film and Television Awards (2004) (TV)

Charging for Alexander (2004) (TV) – Alexander

The Teen Choice Awards 2003 (2003) (TV)

2003 MTV Movie Awards (2003) (TV)

The 100 Greatest Movie Stars (2003) (TV)

The 75th Annual Academy Awards (2003) (TV) – Presenter, singing 'The Hands That Built America'

Beyond Hell's Kitchen: Making Daredevil (2003) (TV)

Daredevil: From the Comic to the Big Screen (2003) (TV)

101 Biggest Celebrity Oops (2004) (TV)